Social Science Research and
Women in the Arab World

Social Science Research and
Women in the
Arab World

Frances Pinter (Publishers)
London and Dover N.H.

Unesco, Paris

© Unesco 1984

First published 1984
by the United Nations Educational,
Scientific and Cultural Organization,
7 Place de Fontenoy, 75700 Paris, France
and
Frances Pinter (Publishers) Limited
5 Dryden Street, London WC2E 9NW and
51 Washington Street, Dover, New Hampshire

British Library Cataloguing in Publication Data
Social science research and women in the
Arab world
1. Women—Arab countries—Social
conditions
I. Unesco
305.4'2'09174927   HQ1784

Library of Congress Cataloging in Publication Data
Main entry under title:
Social science research and women in the Arab world.
    Bibliography: p.
      1. Women—Arab countries—Social conditions—
Congresses.   I. Unesco.
HQ1729.5S63   1984   305.4'0917'4927   84-8941
Hardbound ISBN 0-86187-387-4   (Frances Pinter)
Limpbound ISBN 92-3-102140-0 (Unesco)

Typeset by Joshua Associates, Oxford
Printed in Great Britain by SRP Ltd., Exeter

Contents

Preface

This book represents an important contribution to Unesco's programme in the Social and Human Sciences involving research on the position of women in different societies. For the first time, Arab women social scientists came together in the framework of an Experts' Meeting on 'Multidisciplinary Research on Women in the Arab World' (Tunis, 18–21 May 1982), organized by Unesco to examine the state of research on women in their region and how future research could be rendered more relevant to their concerns and to the needs of other women in the region. The meeting was attended by seventeen women social scientists from twelve Arab countries.

The book presents the seven studies prepared for this meeting by women specialists from Algeria, Egypt, Iraq, Libyan Arab Jamahiriya, Morocco, Saudi Arabia, Tunisia and Sudan, which describe the situation of women and research in their respective countries, address theoretical and methodological issues, and present their views on the objectives and priorities for future research to be undertaken. In addition, the book includes a survey of research trends on women in different social and human sciences disciplines and of themes dealt with, followed by a select bibliography of Arab, English and French language sources.

The recommendations in the studies and the report of the meeting call for research to be undertaken—no longer by outsiders in a descriptive, over-simplified and often biased manner—but by women specialists of the region themselves in a manner that reflects the complexities of social reality and the situation of women of different social categories. The basic assumptions and hypotheses underlying research need to be critically examined and the right questions raised, so that research on women in the region may be renewed and strengthened. Furthermore, the human rights dimension of research was stressed: research should serve to enhance knowledge of women's position and problems faced and should have as one of its principal objectives the improvement of the status of women.

This work permits us to gain further knowledge of the efforts and work of women social scientists in this region. It represents part of Unesco's on-going programme of co-operation with women social scientists in different regions and support to their research on women. Two other regional meetings of women specialists were organized within the framework of the Unesco Approved Programme and Budget for 1981-1983: a Regional Seminar on Women's Studies Programmes in Latin America and the Caribbean (Rio de Janeiro, 24-27 November 1981) and an Asian Regional Experts' Meeting on 'Women's Studies in the Social Sciences' (New Delhi, 4–8 October 1982).

It should be noted that the opinions expressed in the studies presented are those of the authors, and do not necessarily reflect the views of Unesco.

List of Contributors

Soha Abdel Kader, Egypt. Sociologist (Ph.D. in mass communication), working in social research centre, American University in Cairo. Works include 'Conservative and Modern Egyptian Family' (thesis, unpublished), 'Status of Egyptian Women 1900–1973', and 'Image of Women in Drama and Women's Programmes in Egyptian Television'.

Farida Allaghi, Libyan Arab Jamahiriya. Sociologist (Ph.D), presently employed with Unicef. Member of Research Committee on Sex Roles and Society of the International Sociological Association. Her works include: 'Libyan Women in Transition' (unpublished MA thesis); 'Programs to Improve the Position of Women in a Traditional Culture: An Evaluation of a Rural Women's Development Centre in Libya' (paper presented to IXth World Congress of Sociology in Uppsala, Sweden); 'Rural Women in the Kufra Settlement Project in Libya' (Ph.D dissertation).

Aisha Almana, Saudi Arabia. Sociologist (Ph.D), Director of the Women's Social Bureau in the Eastern Province of Saudi Arabia. Her fieldwork has included the following areas: women's work conditions and the differential in wages in an American oil company in Saudia Arabia, and women working in oil industries in the USA (1978). She has also prepared studies on 'Women's Education in Saudi Arabia (in the Primary and Secondary Schools)', 'The Impact of Foreign Labour on Saudian Arabian Society' and a study prepared for Unesco on 'Economic Development and its Impact on the Status of Women in Saudi Arabia' (1981).

Alya Baffoun, Tunisia. Psychologist, researcher and academician. Currently, she is professor in the Faculty of Letters and Humane Sciences at the University of Tunis. She is also a research associate at the Center for Economic and Social Studies and Research (CERES) at the same university.

Aicha Belarbi, Morocco. Social Psychologist, Professor at the Ecole Normale Supérieure, Department of the Sciences of Education, Rabat.

Fatiha Hakiki, Algeria. Economist and researcher on Algerian women, and one of the organizers of the *Journées d'études et de réflexion sur la femme algérienne* organized in Oran in May 1980. Assistant lecturer, Institute of Economic Science at the University of Oran.

Hegge Kashif-Badri, Sudan. Secretary of Friendship Committee of National Council for Friendship, Solidarity and Peace (Sudanese Socialist Union).

Formerly Minister of Social Affairs in her country, also Chairman, National Council for Social Welfare and Development. Founder member of the Ba Bakr Badri Scientific Society for Women's Studies, established in 1975. Her research has included studies on the national women's movement in her country.

Fatma Oussedik, Algiera. Sociologist, Professor at University of Algiers and researcher at the Centre of Applied Economics (CREA) in Algiers.

Amal Rassam, Iraq. Anthropologist (Ph.D), Professor of Anthropology at the Graduate Center and Queens College of the City University of New York. She has had extensive fieldwork experience in Morocco, Iraq, Northern Yemen and Egypt. Her areas of interest include: sexual ideology and women's status, ethnicity and ethnic group relations and social change. Co-author of *Peoples and Cultures of the Middle East* (with Daniel Bates), Prentice-Hall, 1983.

Claude Talahite, Algeria. Researcher in Research Group on Algerian Women at the Human Sciences Documentation Centre and one of the organizers of the *Journées d'étude et réflexion sur la femme algérienne*, Oran, May 1980. Assistant lecturer, Spanish literature and semiotics at the Institute of Living Foreign Languages, University of Oran, Es-Seria, Algeria.

Introduction: Arab Women: the Status of Research in the Social Sciences and the Status of Women

AMAL RASSAM

In this Introduction we shall seek answers to the questions: how do social scientists assess and explain the secondary status of women in Arab society? How has economic development affected the role of women? How do Arab women researchers interpret the current position of Arab women, and what do they prescribe for improving the status of women and for achieving a more just and sexually equitable social order?

As it is impossible to deal fairly and systematically with the vast social science literature on women in the Arab world, I will be highly selective. My aims are first, to delineate the major approaches utilized to interpret the position of women; second, to assess the contributions made; and third, to identify serious gaps that remain. In this, I will rely heavily on the general surveys and critical evaluations provided by my colleagues who participated in the Conference on Research in the Social Sciences on Women in the Arab World. The conference was sponsored by the United Nations Educational, Scientific and Cultural Organization and was held in Tunis from 18 to 21 May 1982.[1]

Western received images of the Arab woman most often assume one of two extremes. On the one hand, there is the image of the exotic and mysterious odalisque, the creature of the harem whose existence is dedicated to a life of luxury and sensuous pleasure in the service of the man, her lord and master. On the other hand there is the image of the silent and invisible 'beast of burden', born and nurtured to suffer the twin burdens of childbearing and heavy household chores. Orientalists of different backgrounds and conviction did much to spread the image of the Arab woman as odalisque, while missionaries and sundry explorers emphasized the physical and mental exploitation and degradation of women, especially those of the poorer classes. Being mostly men, and foreigners at that, these orientalists, explorers and missionaries had little opportunity to observe the wide variations that exist in women's conditions in Arab society, let alone to talk to and know these women in any meaningful fashion. This situation did not improve much with the advent of the social scientists (most of whom were also men) who began to conduct fieldwork in the Arab world, beginning in the early 1950s. Ignorance of the real condition of women is, of course, not limited to the Arab region, but tends to be true worldwide. It stems partly from the general attitude which, until very recently, regarded the roles that women assume as being unimportant, or at best marginal, to an understanding of the working of the social order under study.

The serious study of sex roles and women's status has advanced rapidly in the past two decades. For the Arab world, a series of articles, books and monographs has now been published, all exploring various dimensions of the question of women.[2] What is slowly emerging from all of this activity is a vastly complex and far from clear picture of the lives of men and women in the context of a rapidly changing environment. These studies, which differ in theoretical approach and ideological commitments, all seem to share an explicit or implicit recognition that women in Arab society occupy a secondary and inferior position to that of men. This inequality, which is found in the legal, social and political domains, assumes various expressions and has various impacts on the lives of women of different classes, ethnic or educational backgrounds. Much of the current research, in fact, is devoted to the study of these permutations— which is as it should be, if we are to begin to generalize with confidence about the status of Arab women.

In attempting to understand and explain the status of women in the Arab world, social scientists adopt one of a number of theoretical approaches. These same approaches have been utilized to shed light on the status of women world-wide and on the related issue of the role of women in development. For there is little doubt that the status of women everywhere is inferior to that of men; otherwise women would not become the specific target of development pro- grammes and the focus of international conferences such as that of the World Conference of the International Women's Year, held in Mexico City in 1975. The stated goal of that conference was 'the integration of women in the develop- ment process as equal partners with men'. As far as I know, no one has yet declared an International Men's Year!

Research on women's status has generally been formulated in terms of one of the following two broad approaches: the Nature/Culture Dualism, which hinges on a specific view of female sexuality, and the Social Evolutionary Approach, which includes theories of modernism and developmentalism.[3] I shall briefly discuss each approach in turn and illustrate how it has been used to analyse the status of Arab women.

In their effort to understand the universality of women's inequality and subordinate status, some scholars have sought the explanation in pan-cultural factors or 'givens' of the human condition, notably the duality between the male and female sex. This basic physiological differentiation is believed to be at the core of the perceived duality of the 'natural' and 'cultural' spheres, women being identified with the natural order and men with the cultural. In her book, *The Second Sex*, Simone de Beauvoir attributes women's universal subordination to her identification with the domain of 'nature' and to that domain's relation- ship to the domain of 'culture'. Briefly, de Beauvoir argues that all societies sharply oppose 'nature' and 'culture'; nature is always identified with the passive element, while culture is viewed as being active. She adds that human beings are distinguished from the animals by their efforts to transcend the limitations of nature through culture, i.e., by their success in transforming nature and controlling it. But since women are constrained by the biological facts of reproduction and lactation, they are less free than men to pursue sublimation, i.e., to be culturally creative. At the same time, man cannot live and reproduce himself without women, who represent nature to him specifically in terms of their sexuality. This need for women, argues de Beauvoir, is at the root of the ambivalence displayed by men towards women, or, as she puts it, the second sex. The result is that men simultaneously exalt and denigrate women, but in any case they always end up wanting to control them, just as they want to control nature.

The French anthropologist, Claude Levi-Strauss, has interpreted the Nature/ Culture Duality in different ways, suggesting some answers to the universality of male domination. Levi-Strauss reconstructs a mythical past where humans existed in a state of 'nature', one of whose characteristics was the promiscuous mating of males and females within the group, much as many animal species mate. At some point in this past, men saw fit to posit the rule of exogamy, which forbade them sexual access to their own women and forced them to seek mates outside their group. This act, the first 'cultural' act in the opinion of Levi-Strauss, was at the base of all social organization and cultural evolution. Exogamy helped to limit conflict among the male kin within the group and established ties of affinity and alliance between different groups—in both cases contributing to survival and social elaboration. In time, elaborate systems for the exchange of women were developed and maintained. It must be noted here that in this scheme, men play the active role; women, the passive ones, are reduced to objects of trade. The systems of domination and control of women would presumably have developed to ensure the passivity and obedience of women, and facilitate their exchange as objects by the dominant men.

There is no doubt that some of the similarities in the status of women cross-culturally are the result of a basic and continuing sexual division of labour which is related to the universal facts of childbearing. But the confinement of women to the private/domestic sphere and the near monopoly by men of the public domains of politics, religion and the market do not necessarily follow. Furthermore, such universal and timeless explanations cannot account for the wide variations that exist in women's status, nor for its historical change. None the less, arguments based on perceived innate differences between men and women, and on the presumed role of women in ensuring the cohesion and survival of the male kin groups, are at the heart of Islamic and tribal ideologies which are still very powerful in the Arab world.

According to Islamic ideology: 'Men are the protectors and maintainers of women, because Allah has given the one more [strength] than the other and because they support them from their means. Therefore the righteous women are devoutly obedient . . .' (The Koran, sura 4:34). The thirteenth-century Islamic scholar-jurist, al-Baydhawi, identified ways in which men are superior to women. He wrote that

> Allah preferred one over the other in matters of mental ability, and good council, and their power of duty and for carrying out divine commands. Hence to men has been confined prophecy, religious leadership, pilgrimage rites, the giving of evidence in law courts, duties of the holy war, worship in the mosque on Fridays, etc. They also have the privilege of electing chiefs, have larger share of inheritance and discretion in matters of divorce.[4]

Arab social scientists, most notably the Tunisian, A. Bouhdiba, and the Moroccan sociologist, Fatima Mernissi, have examined this ideology and related it to key institutional features of Arab society, namely, the veiling and segregation of women.[5] The Islamic ethos (which in different variations exists throughout the Mediterranean, including the northern Christian part), reflects a widely shared male view of female sexuality. In this view, sexual instincts are believed to have no connotation of good or evil apart from how they come to serve a specific social order. Women's sexuality, however, is believed to be specially powerful and potent. Unless controlled and socially channelled, female sexuality is capable of causing havoc and social disruption. But women are also believed to lack great powers of reason and self-discipline. Men are, therefore, charged with the duty to protect women (and society) from the consequences of unbridled female sexuality. 'Protection' of women translates into their control through an elaborate code of sexual modesty which revolves around the cult of virginity and strict marital fidelity. It is significant that a beautiful woman is often referred to in Arabic as *fitna*, a term that can also mean 'social chaos'. This concept is similar to that of the *femme fatale*.

The perception of women as both passive and yet having the capacity to disrupt the moral and social order is used to rationalize the institution of veiling and segregation of women, seen as necessary to the preservation of society. Despite local variations in ways of life in the Arab world, attitudes towards sex roles seem to be shaped by this fundamental psychosexual belief system. The code of sexual modesty as expressed in the powerful notions of Honour and Shame (*sharaf, 'ard, 'ayb, hshuma*), is to a large extent predicated on these notions. One may also add the link between women and the idea of the sacred or *haram. Haram*, meaning 'sacred' or 'taboo', can refer to the religious sanctuary of the *ka'aba* in Mecca, but is also used to describe the women of the household, who collectively are referred to as the harem of the male head. The different women have different claims to this status; the patriarch's daughters and daughters-in-law are part of the harem, as they are sexually taboo to him. His own wife, on the other hand, is part of his harem in that she dwells in the sanctuary of his household. It is ironic that the word harem has come to acquire a popular meaning which is virtually opposite to its original, as it now refers to concubines and dancing slave girls!

While there has been some exploration of the status of women in Arab society in terms of these cultural notions of female sexuality and the 'protective' role of men, this has been mostly done by writers and journalists, rather than social scientists. One exception already mentioned is Fatima Mernissi. In the first part of her book *Beyond the Veil: Male-Female Dynamics in a Modern Muslim Society*, she writes,

> There is a fundamental contradiction between Islam as interpreted in official policy and equality of the sexes. Sexual equality violates Islam's premise, actualized in its laws, that heterosexual love is dangerous to Allah's order . . . The desegregation of the sexes violates Islam's ideology on the woman's position in the social order; the woman should be under the authority of fathers, brothers or husbands. Since she is considered by Allah to be a destructive element, she is to be spatially confined and excluded from matters other than those of the family. The woman's access to non-domestic space is put under the control of the males. (Mernissi, p. xv.)

In the rest of the book, Mernissi explores the contradictions which result from this ideology and the imperative need to mobilize all human resources (including women) in the Arab world in order to achieve full economic and political development.

The lag between a 'traditional Islamic ideology' and the demands of full development seems to be a common theme in much of the work done by social scientists in the area. In their excellent survey of research on women in the Arab Gulf region (an area that includes Kuwait, Bahrein, Saudi Arabia, the United Arab Emirates, Qatar and Oman), Farida Allaghi and Aisha Almana write that customs, values and male attitudes which are important variables in explaining women's inequality tend to be religiously legitimized.[6] They add, however, that the available studies do not trace the genesis or perpetuation of these beliefs and attitudes. In fact, as they point out, much of the research in this area is descriptive in nature, with little analysis of how these attitudes actually affect women's status. We also know very little about women's own beliefs regarding their sexuality or about their attitudes towards the dominant male ideology. How do women view themselves? And how do they interpret their own status? Do women of different class backgrounds react differently? Is the same religious ideology evoked equally by women?

The work of C. Makhlouf on middle-class Yemeni women, and that of S. Messiri on poor women in a Cairo neighbourhood seem to suggest that women do not necessarily share the hegemonic male view of themselves, but that they have an alternative view both of themselves and of their menfolk.[7] If this is the general case, it would be important to find out how these different male and female views are negotiated in everyday life. It would also be interesting to know if the current rapid change in women's roles is affecting these traditional views. For example, as women participate more and more in the wage labour sector of the economy, is there a corresponding change in their image on the part of the men? And if so, is this change of any real significance when it comes to structural changes in their position both within and outside the household?

Recognizing that most research on the Arab woman deals with such issues as their legal status, rates of employment, family planning, etc., the Algerian Fatma Oussedik cautions that such studies, which seek to find the means for integrating women into the process of development, will not be very meaningful if they are not accompanied by investigation into the prevailing ideology with regards to women and their sexuality. She urges her fellow women researchers to work 'to demystify the prevailing view on women and the Arab-Islamic tradition whose ultimate premise is to reject women as producers and to recognize them only as bodies (reproducers)'.[8]

A similar point of view is expressed by Aicha Belarbi, who has surveyed research on women in Morocco. Belarbi points out that, much like the case of Algeria, research on Moroccan women has tended to concentrate on such issues as women and the family, women and law, and women and employment. What is also needed, she writes, is to look into the equally important areas of images of women in society, virginity and sexual repression, prostitution and the various forms of sexual violence against women.[9] This need is also echoed by Alya Baffoun, who writes 'it would be worthwhile to direct some of the research effort towards the North African woman's self-image and experience of the world in which she lives. By this means certain hypotheses can be invalidated or confirmed.' Further on, she adds that among the priorities for future research is 'the role of the superstructure and ideology in perpetuating the "innatist" image of women, conducive to their subordinate status and the various forms of violence against women in North Africa'.[10]

There seems to be, then, a consensus among social scientists, especially the women, that the dominant sexual ideology, as interpreted and maintained by Islamic and tribal traditions, is an important element affecting the status of women. There is also the realization that much research has yet to be done concerning the genesis and perpetuation of this ideology and to find out the precise ways in which it contributes to the prevailing sexual hierarchy.

The problem of women's status has also been approached by social scientists from a number of theoretical perspectives which for convenience I shall group under the general heading of social evolutionary theories. These include, among others, theories of modernization and those of developmentalism and dependency.

Social evolutionists seek to understand the dynamics of social change and its direction. They generally tend to perceive society as being propelled forward by changes in the population/resource balance, the organization of production and labour and the competition among the constituent groups. They argue that human societies proceed from a simple division of labour (one based primarily on age and sex) and little differentiation of institutions to increasing division of labour and more specialization of institutions. The result is an ever-increasing social and economic complexity and interdependence, as witnessed in the modern industrial societies of the West. Within this overall scheme of evolution, women's inferior position is usually seen as the result of their performance of a less specialized and, therefore, less productive role in society. In other words, since their labour is in the more 'backward' sector of the economy, namely the domestic, women are not rewarded or esteemed as well as the men who work in the more modern and productive sector of the economy, namely, the wage labour market. Simultaneously, the increasing gap between the domestic and public sectors (itself a product of evolutionary differentiation) and the development in the latter sector of the state and the professional army, from which women are excluded, contribute further to their subordination.

The classic Marxist explanation of women's subordination is a variant of social evolutionary theory since it holds that women's inequality is the result of their being relegated to the domestic economy and thus deprived of the opportunity to participate in the more prestigious production of goods for exchange in the market. Some Marxist revisionists and critics of general evolutionary theory and modernization have, however, contributed to the formulation of two theoretical approaches relevant to the study of women and development, namely, developmentalism and dependency theory.

Developmentalism is less of a unified framework than a number of interrelated concepts and ideas, all of which seek to understand better the complex and often contradictory nature of economic development. Unlike the naive optimism of the students of modernization in the 1950s who predicted a rapid, even and equal progress for the nations of the Third World, developmentalists are more cautious in their assessments. They do not perceive society as one organic unit where changes in one sector will invariably lead to compatible changes throughout; they also underline the contradictions generated by the process of change. For example, programmes introduced to increase women's employment in the public sector may actually contribute to the further exploitation of women if these same programmes do not see to it that wages and working conditions such as child care centres and maternity leave are also provided. A woman who has no control over the wages she earns by working in the fields or on a construction site becomes doubly exploited, both inside and outside the house. But perhaps the most important issues which developmentalists have emphasized is the key role played by government leaders and policy makers in development and change. Ideological commitments of political leaders are rightly viewed as critical to the nature and direction of national development which directly or indirectly have great impact on the status of women.[11]

The stubborn persistence of poverty and backwardness in Third World countries has led scholars to consider the constraints placed on development by international factors, specifically the capitalistic world system which directly or indirectly controls the world's markets and affects the development of both nations as a whole, as well as regions within a nation. For just as the capitalist world system is believed to lead to underdevelopment in Latin America, Africa and parts of the Middle East, the urban élite within these nations 'cause' and perpetuate the backwardness of their own rural regions by their uneven investment in export crops, heavy industry and the urban centres.

Concerning the status of women, some scholars working within the framework of the dependency theory argue that the world capitalistic system is, to a large extent, responsible for the 'backwardness' of the household. H. Saffiotti, a Brazilian sociologist, writes that the household functions to maintain women as a reserve labour force available to join capitalistic production only when required, and withdrawing them from the labour market when necessary.[12] In wartime England, for example, women were encouraged to leave their houses and work in factories and offices to replace the absent men. But as soon as the war was over and the men got back, a strong effort was made to entice women back into the household. National and religious leaders began to extol the virtues of women as wives and mothers, and psychologists emphasized the crucial need of the child for a full-time mother.

Saffiotti points out that the function of the household in maintaining women as reserve labour (by putting them on the market and withdrawing them as needed), contributes to ease the economic stress and social tensions that accompany the chronic presence of unemployment, enabling capitalism to survive its recurring cycles of inflation and depression. From this perspective, women are seen as the victims of capitalism, confined to the less valued sector of domestic economy and held within the household as passive labour reserves to be released or withdrawn from the market in response to the cyclical nature of free-enterprise economy. If this is true for the core capitalist nations of the world, adds Saffiotti, women's conditions in the dependent countries are even worse.

In these countries, the demands of world capitalism have dislocated the peasant economy. Commercialization of land, heavy investment in cash crops at the expense of subsistence, uneven mechanization of agriculture, etc., have resulted in dislodging the peasant from agriculture faster than he or she can be absorbed into the weak industrial sector. The result has been massive rural–urban migration and the sudden availability of unemployed (and unemployable), unskilled ex-peasants concentrated in shanty-towns and urban slums. In this kind of population, women tend to find and hold jobs more easily than the men. But these jobs are all in the low status, low pay sector of the economy (one not usually counted in the GNP), referred to as the informal labour market: these women work as domestic servants, street vendors and prostitutes. There is a need for detailed studies of this trend and its long-range implications for the Arab-Islamic countries where it can be observed, notably in Egypt and Morocco.

In a series of published and unpublished articles and reports, F. Mernissi has examined the impact of modern capitalism on Moroccan women, especially rural women and the urban poor.[13] In one such study she discusses the deterioration in the status of female carpet-weavers and their loss of personal autonomy. The young ones do not have the cash/capital necessary for them to buy the imported wool and loom to set themselves up in business, and are forced to join the factories where, lacking any state or labour union protection, they are underpaid and exploited.

Similarly, the older master craftswoman (or *m'allma*) is unable successfully to compete with the factory and is forced out of business. The plight of these women is most poignantly expressed by one of the carpet-weavers from Rabat in an interview with F. Mernissi.

Mernissi: And how do you get the wool now?

Craftswoman: In the past we used to buy natural, local wool and send it to the local shop to be dyed. Now the wool is machine made. It used to be part of the woman's job to cord and spin the wool. But today, we buy it ready made from the *suq* (market). You have no idea how high the price of wool is now; we pay 36 dirhams ($9) for one kilo, where we used to buy it for 17 dirhams ($4). I buy wool from the retailers since I can only afford to buy it in small quantities. The factories can buy it cheaper since they buy in large amounts and directly from the wool factories. I now barely make enough money to pay my helpers and feed myself. One of the big problems I have is that my helpers leave me to go to the factories because the factories can pay them more money. They come here totally unskilled. We, the old *m'allmat*, train them; this is part of our job. Factories have no school to train workers. As soon as the girl is a *m'allma* herself (i.e., trained to the level of a craftsmistress), she leaves for the factory. It is unfair . . . and the ministry is doing nothing about it. The factory takes the women in whom we have invested six or seven years. Allah does not punish the factories, either; they are doing well. This has been going on for years.[14]

The dilemma expressed by the Moroccan woman in this interview seems to be commonly experienced by women of her background in the region. Studies indicate that the capital transformation of the economy and mode of production has had an uneven impact on the lives of women. Upper and middle class women have generally benefited from the increased opportunities made available in the areas of education and employment. Those of rural and urban poor backgrounds, on the other hand, suffer a decline in their status as they lose the productive role they traditionally played in the pre-industrial economy as the goods they produce are replaced by imported or locally produced factory ones.

The impact of socio-economic changes and the overall process of modernization on the status of Arab women is still problematic and not fully understood. The concept of 'modernization' itself has come under much criticism from scholars, both Arab and non-Arab. Apart from the fact that it tends to be both vague and descriptive, modernization is often applied from a Eurocentric perspective, when it is equated with 'Westernization'. Modernization is thus contrasted with its presumed polar opposite: traditionalism, the two being viewed as being mutually exclusive economic and cultural systems. Women are then urged to strive for 'modernity', which is taken to represent an ideal. Aware of the various forms of inequality which persist in the West and the severe social and political problems that plague Western nations, Arab women aspire to a more genuine form of liberation than that promised by current forms of Western-style modernity.

More important perhaps is the fact that the concept of modernization has not been very useful analytically, nor has the modern/traditional contrast yielded much insight into the complex issue of women's status. Arab researchers have, in general, tended to emphasize the co-existence of modernity and tradition in their society, insisting that the challenge is to determine their exact expression in any given context. Writing of Saudi Arabia, Fatin Shaker says that 'modernization does not necessarily entail destruction of traditional structure, but rather it allows for wide margins of coexistence between traditional and modern forms. On the other hand, tradition does not constitute a uniform, static system antagonistic to modernity. Tradition was found to have a sufficient degree of flexibility and diversity to accommodate modern patterns. Modernization is thus a continuing process in which the cultural and historical experience and the national goals of the country concerned interfere to set their "choice" of the margins of coexistence between tradition and modernity.'[15]

One area where traditional attitudes have persisted in the face of modern structural changes is that of women and fertility. In fact, this is a good case which illustrates the complexity of the issue especially as it relates to women's status. In an important article on status and fertility patterns, Nadia Youssef, an Egyptian sociologist, attempts to understand the high fertility rates of Muslim women.[16] These rates, it must be emphasized, are high even when compared with the fertility rates of non-Muslim women from countries of comparable socio-economic development. Although Youssef includes Iran, Pakistan, Turkey and Indonesia in her survey, her analysis is primarily directed at the Arab countries of the Middle East and North Africa. She points out that in all of these countries, and contrary to trends elsewhere, women's reproductive behaviour seems to be unaffected by changes in the economy and by an improved standard of living.

Youssef seeks the answer in the specifics of women's status in Muslim society: 'The critical point is to relate the fertility levels of Muslim populations to women's status and position.' This latter is measured in terms of five indicators: female literacy rates, sex differential in literacy rates, female income-earning activities, and the timing and incidence of marriage. What emerges from her analysis of these variables is an interesting assessment of women's status and a clear indication of how it relates to reproductive behaviour. In her well-developed essay, Youssef argues that women, who occupy a clearly subordinate position in the social, political and legal domains, none the less derive great respect and a measure of power from their marriage and maternal-related roles. It follows then that women will not easily risk giving up the one role where their status is high, namely, that of mother. 'Muslim women are fully cognizant of the need to attain marital position and motherhood for commanding respect and status in their own kin group and community. They are not about to de-emphasize willingly the only role that now gives them a bargaining position in the social structure. Children represent much more than a form of social insurance against the threat of divorce or polygamy, for women derive status from motherhood even when divorced or rejected for a second wife. Hence, we may expect women to continue childbearing activities throughout their repro-ductive years.'[17]

Youssef acknowledges that highly educated Muslim women may be ready to explore alternative sources of prestige and status besides motherhood and that the increased participation of women in the labour force may have its impact on the reproductive behaviour of women, and their perception of their role within and outside the family. None the less, she cautions against undue optimism, at least for the immediate future. As she writes, 'The current status of women in Muslim society has its impact on their reproductive behavior by way of the interplay between prohibitions imposed informally by males which restrict women to marital and maternal roles, and the resistance of women to claiming their "rights" in the suprafamilial world. This interplay has persisted, despite initial breakthroughs in economic modernization, for two important reasons: the strong control exerted over women by the kinship group, and the respect and sociopsychological rewards derived by women from their traditional status, which have until now mitigated against the eruption of protest and rebellion.'[18]

This brief and selective overview of the major theoretical approaches utilized and the research activities undertaken to study the status of women in the Arab world should make it clear that much remains to be done before we can begin to change the subordinate position of the women. This much seems to be acknowledged by the Arab women researchers themselves. Whether informed by a feminist, nationalist-socialist or a bourgeois perspective, they all agree on the need for more research and on the need to evaluate present research critically in order to determine its cumulative contribution to the problem of women in the Arab world.

Understanding the position of women is, of course, but a first step to seeking the most effective means to change and improve it. At this stage, however, there does not seem to be any agreed or coherent strategy for action, nor is there any organized pan-Arab movement for the liberation/emancipation of women. Such changes and improvements as do exist fall short of expectations and seem to be all planned and directed by the state, where women have no meaningful representation. As Allaghi and Almana point out in the last part of their survey, Arab social scientists seem to raise problems and criticisms in their work, rather than offer solutions. In fact, such solutions as are offered tend to be reformist in nature, and piecemeal. These include the following: consciousness raising among men and women through schools and the mass media, literacy campaigns aimed specifically at women, job training programmes for women, protective legislation, and a social security system that helps single, widowed and elderly women. Of course, one must not forget that the 'will to knowledge' exhibited by the Arab women researchers is itself a significant step in breaking through the barriers of silence, invisibility and ignorance that have historically kept Arab women in their 'proper place'.

Dramatic changes in the status of Arab women will no doubt provoke strong reactions, especially from the increasingly vocal and powerful Islamic fundamentalist movement. This reaction can be understood only in terms of a complex cultural tradition, one that defines male prestige and status largely in terms of men's control over women. A radical change in role relationships will require that men, as well as women, redefine their social reality in terms of a new and revolutionary consciousness—by no means an easy undertaking. Given the political and economic realities of the Arab world today, it is likely that women will continue to be the hostages in the conflict between the security of tradition and the aspirations for full human dignity and liberation.

NOTES

1. See the Final Report of the Meeting of Experts on Multidisciplinary Research on Women in the Arab World. Unesco SS–81/CONF. 804/11. Paris, November 1982.
2. There are a number of bibliographies available, such as: A. Al-Qazzaz, *Women in the Middle East and North Africa: An Annotated Bibliography*, University of Texas, 1977; also S. R. Meghdessian, *The Status of the Arab Woman: A Selected Bibliography*, Greenwood Press, Westport, Connecticut, 1980. A good bibliography is also to be found in L. Beck and N. Keddie (eds.), *Women in the Muslim World*, Harvard University Press, Cambridge and London, 1978.
3. These approaches are explored more systematically, especially in relation to the issue of women and development, in the article by C. Elliot, 'Theories of Development, An Assessment', in *Women and National Development: the Complexities of Change*, the University of Chicago Press, 1977, pp. 1–9.
4. As quoted in Reuben Levy, *The Social Structure of Islam*, Cambridge University Press, 1962, p. 99.

5. See A. Bouhdiba, *La sexualité en Islam*, PUF, Paris, 1975 and F. Mernissi, *Beyond the Veil: Male-female Dynamics in a Modern Muslim Society*, Schenkman, 1975. The relationship between 'Islam' and the inferior status of Arab women is, of course, a very controversial subject and one outside the scope of this paper.

6. F. Allaghi and A. Almana, *Survey of Research on Women in the Arab Gulf Region*. Unesco SS–81/CONF. 804/9. Paris, 1981.

7. See. C. Makhlouf, *Changing Veils*, University of Texas Press, 1979; S. Messiri, 'Self-Images of Traditional Urban Women in Cairo', in *Women in the Muslim World* (L. Beck and N. Keddie, eds.), pp. 522–41.

8. F. Oussedik, *The Conditions Required for Women Themselves to Conduct Research on Women in the Arab Region*. Unesco SS–81/CONF. 804/6. Paris, 1981.

9. A. Belarbi, *Research in the Social Sciences on Women in Morocco*, Unesco SS–81/CONF. 804/7. Paris, 1981.

10. A. Baffoun, *Research in Social Sciences on North African Women: Problems, Trends and Needs*. Unesco SS–81/CONF. 804/4. Paris, 1981.

11. For a discussion of the impact of development planning on women's role and status cross-culturally, see Barbara Rogers, *The Domestication of Women: Discrimination in Developing Societies*, St. Martin's Press, New York, 1979.

12. H. Saffiotti, 'Female Labor and Capitalism in the United States and Brazil', in *Women Cross-culturally: Change and Challenge* (R. Rohrlich-Leavitt ed.), pp. 59–94.

13. F. Mernissi, 'Nos femmes invisibles, rapportent des milliards', in *Lamalif*, no. 103, January 1979. Also unpublished manuscript on the economic roles of women in pre-colonial and modern-day Morocco.

14. Ibid.

15. As quoted by F. Allaghi and A. Almana in their contribution to the present volume.

16. N. Youssef, 'The Status and Fertility Patterns of Muslim Women', in *Women in the Muslim World* (L. Beck and N. Keddie, eds), pp. 69–100.

17. Ibid., p. 86.

18. Ibid., p. 93.

1   Survey of Research on Women in the Arab Gulf Region

FARIDA ALLAGHI and AISHA ALMANA

INTRODUCTION

The women's movement is spreading in every part of the globe; hardly a place in the world has not been touched by its concerns. The women's movement means different things to different people, living in various cultures, under different religious traditions, and at various stages of economic and political development. The one shared message that this movement carries throughout the world is that women should challenge the present status quo, which discriminates against and relegates them to a status of inferiority, submissiveness, and weakness. Sex, the movement's members say worldwide, need not be a barrier to equality, freedom, and opportunity of choice.

The women's movement in the Arab world started in the early 1930s in Egypt. Due to the particular economic and political conditions of the area, however, the movement did not penetrate other Arab countries until the late 1950s and early 1960s. Arab women are increasingly questioning all forms of injustice, refusing their low status, and aspiring to gain their full rights in all sectors of life.

In line with this assessment, one ought to ask: What do we know about women in the Gulf? What scientific 'research' do we have, if any, about women in this region? What future research is required to provide data and information about the situation of women in this region?

The immediate objective here is to review and examine research related to women's status that has been undertaken in the Gulf region, in both published and unpublished sources. The review provides a general profile of women in the Gulf by describing certain historical, economic, educational, and socio-cultural variables, which reflect the conditions of women in the region. The differences between women in different countries of the Gulf are compared. Differences between those who live in bedouin, rural and urban areas are outlined, as well as differences between women of lower, middle and upper classes.

The term 'Gulf region', as Al-Rimehi indicates (Abdulbaset 1975: 307), has been defined in many ways: 'It includes in certain definitions Oman, south of Iraq, and the eastern coastal area of Iran. Other definitions refer to the Gulf only to mean Kuwait, Bahrain, Qatar and the United Arab Emirates (UAE) and totally discard not only south Iraq and Oman, but also the eastern province of Saudi Arabia.'

In this chapter, the Gulf region includes the following Arab countries: Kuwait, Bahrain, Saudi Arabia, the United Arab Emirates, Qatar and Oman. It should be pointed out, however, that the majority of research papers and studies which are reviewed focus primarily, if not exclusively, on women in Kuwait, Bahrain, Saudi Arabia and the United Arab Emirates (UAE). Reference is made, whenever relevant information is obtainable, to women in Oman and Qatar.

Several scholars from the Gulf Region (Musa, Al-Rimehi, Abdulbaset), in papers presented at the First Regional Conference on Women in the Arabian Gulf (1975), have indicated that the historical, cultural, social, religious, economic and political conditions are similar throughout that region. Therefore, where sufficient data are not available, one might assume a similarity in Arab women's status and conditions.

A conceptual framework presents theories utilized to explain changes in the conditions of women in the Arab world. This brief discussion serves as a base for a consideration of research methodology and theories, and lists research questions and needs for future research about Gulf women. We conclude with a commentary on possible solutions to the obstacles currently faced by different classes of women in the region. These solutions are drawn from the various research papers which are reviewed.

A conceptual framework

Any reader of existing literature about Arab women repeatedly encounters two major issues, discussed directly or indirectly by various scholars. The first issue revolves around the process of 'modernization'. The scholars argue that one of the important predicted outcomes of the modernization process, which involves urbanization, industrialization, socio-cultural changes, literacy, and communication, is a change in women's roles and status. Because of modernization, women benefit from increased educational opportunities and acquire new skills, which help them to participate in the productive sector of the labour force. The second issue discussed by scholars revolves around the dilemma of whether or not women in the Arab world are able to strike a balance between certain valued traditions of the Arab/Muslim culture and acceptance of progress and modernization.

A number of contrasting theoretical perspectives exist in the analysis of women's changing status in the Arab world, including the Gulf region. Theoretical perspectives and explanations that have been utilized by Western scientists to analyse the Arab world's process of social change and national development have affected explanations and analysis by both Arab and non-Arab scholars of women's issues. Halpern (1963), Eisenstadt (1966), and Lerner (1964) have chosen a Western model of modernization to analyse the process of social change in the Arab world.

In literature concerning women, modernization is depicted in essentially formal terms and is measured by such formal criteria as education, labour force participation, and political participation, which includes the right to vote and to run for public office. The strong Western ethnocentrism becomes clear in Patai's, Nath's, and Freeth's writings. Patai (1972) asserts that 'all women who fight for emancipation fight for modernism and Westernism'. Nath (1978), in describing the change occurring in Kuwait women, often uses the term 'Western'. In one part of her paper she has written, 'By 1970 the dress and living patterns of the young women had changed enough to be similar to those of their Western counterparts'. Nath also indicates that, 'According to one of the leaders of social change, acceptance of Western patterns of living (which were always considered superior and the thing to achieve) came immediately as we achieved Western standards of income' (1978: 178). Freeth, in her article on Kuwaiti women, talks not only about the Western style clothes that the young Arab women are wearing today but she also calls Egypt and Syria the Western Arab countries, and so does Nath (Freeth 1956: 83). Hence, it is implied from those writings that modernization (the Western way) is the ideal that Arab women should strive to achieve. Those writings also imply that the optimum stage of egalitarianism has been achieved by Western women. Western literature and the women's movement in the West greatly weaken this argument, demonstrating the inequalities and disadvantages of women, and showing that Western civilization has not encouraged women's emancipation and equality.

In identifying modernization with Westernization or Europeanization, Sayigh says:

> The Arab who is critical of the concept cannot but link this concept (and the process itself) with Western colonialism and imperialism, and their contemporary variants. As such, modernization can be seen to have carried and still carry with it painful associations. For one thing, there have been many instances of coercive modernization; even a thing which can be said to be 'good' in itself becomes abhorrent if forced by a colonial agent. Furthermore, the colonialist—partly in self-deception, partly in outright deception and hypocrisy—has often claimed to be the carrier of a civilization mission. (1978: 19.)

In this same vein Shaker wrote, 'Many of the new states aspire toward modernity but on their own terms, and [. . .] modernization does not mean to them Westernization' (1972: 56).

Several scholars, both Arabs and non-Arabs (Khalaf 1972; Shaker 1972; Fersoun 1970; Abu-Lughad 1972), have challenged critically some Western models of modernization and their applicability to the Arab world. These emerging theoretical perspectives on the nature of modernization and its impact on the traditional social structure refute the notion that traditionalism and modernism each stand at opposite poles of a continuum with no convergence between them.

Shaker discusses this issue of the co-existence of tradition and modernity in her study, 'Modernization in the Developing Nations: The Case of Saudi Arabia'. Shaker wrote, 'When modernity and tradition are considered mutually exclusive, the possible interplay between the two becomes obscured. And certain behavioural scientists thus assert, 'whoever wants modernity must get rid of tradition' (1972: 41).

The same author states:

> Modernization does not necessarily entail destructionof traditional structure, but rather it allows for 'wide margins' of coexistence between traditional and modern forms. On the other hand, tradition does not constitute a uniform, static system that is antagonistic to modernity. Tradition was found to have a sufficient degree of flexibility and diversity to accommodate modern patterns. Modernization is thus a continuing process in which the cultural and historical experience and the national goals of the country concerned interfere to set their 'choice' of the margins of coexistence between tradition and modernity. (Ibid., xii.)

Ibrahim and Hopkins in their recent book, *Arab Society in Transition*, observe that 'the contemporary urban family is reluctantly but steadily moving in the direction of egalitarianism. It is not totally modern in the Western sense.' A few other studies have proved that traditional values can generate and facilitate modernization. The interaction between tradition and modernity could be a viable conceptual framework for the study of women in the Arab world including the Gulf region.

The effect of socio-economic changes and the overall process of modernization and development on the situation of women is another major issue, which is increasingly drawing the attention and interest of several social scientists and researchers throughout the Arab world. Their interest stems from increased evidence in the literature (Boulding 1976; Boserup 1970; Buvinic 1976; Dixon 1978; Tinker 1976; Huston 1978; Mickelwit *et al.* 1976), which demonstrates that modernization and development may further lower, rather than elevate, the status of women, especially those in rural areas and in poor urban slums.

In the Gulf region, modernization has improved the lot of certain women, especially in terms of providing accessibility to education and employment. For rural and nomadic women, the literature that will be reviewed indicates that modernization has had an adverse impact. Female peasants, nomads, and poor city workers have increasingly lost their productive role, because the goods they make are being imported. While working urban, rural, and tribal women probably lose out in productive role and status with the growth of a market economy, the position of the upper class urban groups generally improves.

REVIEW OF RESEARCH LITERATURE ON WOMEN
IN THE GULF REGION

A historical overview of women in the Gulf

A general historical profile of women in the Gulf, drawn from the studies under review, will provide a basis for understanding the socio-economic conditions of the region and the roles played by women in various classes. Al-Rimehi's study, 'The Reality of Women in the Gulf' (1975), describes in general the past conditions of women in the region as a whole. The Bahraini National Student Union (BNSU) study, 'Women in Bahrain and the Arabian Gulf' (n.d.), is a major theoretical study, which provides an extensive description of the past status and roles of Bahraini and Gulf women in different classes.

Nath, in her study, 'Education and Employment among Kuwait Women' (1978), provides a brief overall description of the past status of Kuwaiti women. Taki's study, 'The Bahraini Woman in Education and Labour' (1975), describes the overall conditions in Kuwait and Bahrain prior to the discovery of oil. Almana's study, 'Economic Development and its Impact on the Status of Women in Saudi Arabia' (1981), provides a description of the past roles of women in the bedouin, rural, and urban areas of Saudi Arabia.

In his description of past conditions in Kuwait and Bahrain, Taki indicates that the Kuwaiti and Bahraini people were not living in total isolation before the discovery of oil. Men from these two countries, especially rich merchants, were travelling from the first half of the nineteenth century. There were a few educated people within this class who later held key positions in the political system and encouraged women's education.

The study by BNSU provides a different description from that by Taki on past conditions in Bahrain. The study indicates that even though education started in Bahrain in 1919, when the first school for boys was opened, the country remained totally isolated from the impact of modern civilization. No form of modern transportation, electricity, health facilities, or running water existed. Although there were no major differences between the urban and rural areas, the situation was harsher for the latter.

Nath provides a somewhat similar description of Kuwait: until the oil boom began, Kuwait had been a poor and technologically undeveloped sheikdom of about 100,000 people who eked out a living as fishermen, pearl divers, animal herders, and carrier-traders. There was hardly any agriculture, and all food had to be imported. Even water was brought by boats. Almana, writing about the economic situation of Saudi Arabia prior to the discovery of oil, states that it was extremely poor and that the majority of the population were nomadic tribes living a subsistence life. Abdulbaset, in describing the history of the education system in the United Arab Emirates, implies that the past economic conditions there were no better than in the other neighbouring countries. In

'Unknown Oman' (1966), Phillips's description of the lifestyles and conditions of the people reflects the very difficult economic circumstances prevailing in the country.

The socio-economic hierarchies of Saudi Arabia, Kuwait, and Bahrain were quite similar. Almana, in describing the hierarchy system of Saudi Arabia prior to the discovery of oil, mentions four groups: the royal family, the merchants, the nomads of the desert, and the farmers. In Kuwait, the class system was composed of sheiks, or members of the ruling family, and relatively rich merchants at the top; bedouins, fishermen, and pearl divers in the middle; and slaves at the bottom (Nath). Al-Rimehi and BNSU do not differ from the above-mentioned researchers in their classification of the class system in the rest of the Gulf countries. The conditions of women in the Gulf were correlated with the conditions of their men.

The studies provide a description of women's activities in the past. These activities reflected the class structure in which the women lived. Three major classes of women were identified. Wives of fishermen, boat builders and pearl divers represented the poorest Gulf class (Al-Rimehi). These women lived in the coastal areas of Kuwait, Bahrain, Qatar and Oman. They shared with their husbands the hardships of life. In order to contribute some income to help their families, these women sold water, which they brought from long distances, and fish in the market; raised chickens and sold eggs; and worked as servants in the homes of the rich merchants. The wives of the pearl divers, due to the long absence of their husbands at sea, took full responsibility for managing family affairs (BNSU). Al-Rimehi says that the wives of the divers in Abu Dhabi would dive when economic conditions demanded it. The rejection by these women of poverty, exploitation and hard life was expressed in their poems and songs.

Rural women represented the second exploited class in the Gulf. Despite the active roles that rural women played in the agricultural sector, they were never economically independent. In addition to their home responsibilities, women in the Gulf rural areas tilled the land, irrigated the farms, collected dates, raised chickens and other animals, sold vegetables and eggs, made straw baskets, and during the summer season worked as servants for farm landowners (BNSU, Almana, Al-Rimehi, Nath). The tribal women, however, were primarily engaged in food production. They herded animals, mainly goats and sheep. Bedouin women engaged in food processing, making dry milk curds and oil for cooking. They also wove carpets and made tents and containers to carry their possessions. The women bartered these goods in the marketplace for rice, coffee, tea, clothing, and utensils (Almana).

Women of the ruling class and of the rich and merchant families formed the third group described in some studies. Al-Rimehi, in his description of middle and upper class Gulf women, indicates that although their materialistic needs were met, these women in relation to men were inferior human beings, exploited, and not given any power. Their lives were always threatened with the fear that their rich husbands would marry other women, as they often did. Women from this class were kept invisible in order to protect their 'honour' and preserve the image of the family. The study of the BNSU students is critical of the rich women and those of the ruling class. The study explains that the only responsibility of those women was to supervise the housework, which was done primarily by the servants. The only power they exercised was over a large group of women and slaves who were serving them. These women were totally idle and kept in their isolated harem.

After the Second World War, the Gulf region faced radical social and economic changes as a result of the discovery of oil. These changes have directly affected the status of women. The two major variables that were considered to affect the status of women in the region were education and employment. It is argued by many researchers that the increased participation of Gulf women in education and employment is a clearcut indication of their new, emancipated status.

Women and education in the Arab Gulf region

All the studies under review have dealt in one way or another with the variable of education. Education is considered by all the researchers whose work is reviewed here as an important variable that will eventually help change the situation of Gulf women and guarantee them a better future. Four of the studies reviewed, those of Altagheb (1975), Nath, Alkotob (1975), and Almana, utilized the survey method for measuring the attitudes of Gulf men and women regarding women's education.

Almost all the studies deal with women's education in the urban areas. There is a very brief description by Almana of the attitudes of a sample of nomadic and village women concerning their daughters' education.

Algadi, in his study, explains the meaning of the word *elm* in Arabic, which he says, '. . . has many interchangeable meanings. But primarily, it means sciences, knowledge, and/or education. *Elm* appeared in the Quran 854 times. Never has it been used to deprive women of education. On the contrary, it has been used to persuade them to educate themselves' (1979: 56).

In their descriptions of past opportunities of female education, the researchers Taki, Algadi, Abdulbaset, Almana, and Nath indicate that young girls before they reached puberty went to 'Alkutab', which is a school-home designed primarily to teach children the Koran and religious education.

Kuwait is considered today to be the leading Gulf country as far as women's education is concerned. Statistics show a picture of rapid educational expansion. By now the vast majority of Kuwait children attend at least primary school, and the proportion of boys and girls is almost the same from kindergarten to secondary level. Today, the University of Kuwait has over 7,528 students, of whom

4,185 are women. The high proportion of females is in part explained by the relatively large number of males who pursue their university studies abroad. Existing vocational and technical training opportunities for women in Kuwait are rather limited (United Nations Development Programme Mission Report, 1979: 150).

Abdulbaset (1975) indicates that women in Kuwait have entered the teaching professions since 1937. From 1957 to 1970 the increase in literacy has been 50 per cent; primary education increased 61 times between 1965 and 1970. Graduates from secondary school from 1957 to 1970 increased 52 times, and university students between 1965 and 1970 increased seven times. Despite these progressive changes in the educational system in Kuwait, Azzam (1979) indicates that illiteracy rates are still high, especially among women. In 1975 the illiteracy rate among women was 52 per cent, while that of males was 32 per cent.

Women's education in the urban areas of Bahrain started in 1928. In 1932 education was established in rural areas for men, followed by women's education in 1958. Abdulbaset indicates that from 1963 to 1973 there was a 179.2 per cent increase in female education in primary schools. In secondary schools, the increase of females was higher than that of males. The first secondary school for females in Bahrain was founded in 1951 (Mujahed 1976). However, despite this increase in female education in Bahrain, the gap between males and females is still striking (Mujahed, Taki, BNSU), and higher education is still not found in Bahrain. Higher education, therefore, remains the privilege of upper class women, who can afford to travel overseas. The illiteracy rate in 1965 was 81.8 per cent among females and 63.9 per cent among males (Azzam).

Algadi and Almana provide interesting analyses of women's education in Saudi Arabia. Mass public education of girls is a relatively new phenomenon in Saudi Arabia; it is barely twenty years old. Limited private education of girls, however, was available before the present ruling Saudi dynasty existed (Algadi).

Algadi mentions that though the education of girls in Saudi Arabia officially began only in 1960, by 1974 there were 177,464 literate women 10 years of age and over, or 0.7 per cent of the female population and 0.05 per cent of the total population—a remarkable achievement in girls' education. Almana states that the policy of women's education has been to train women to be good housewives and mothers, therefore depriving girls of some kinds of education. Accordingly, as Algadi states, the two dominant areas of study for girls during the years 1969 and 1975 were arts and education. Medicine, science, agriculture, pharmacy, engineering, and petroleum were fields of study available in Saudi Arabia only to boys. Despite these inequalities, Saudi women are strongly interested in obtaining higher education. Almana proves this by indicating that the women's liberal arts college in Dammam had over 1,000 applicants in 1979, but could admit only 350 with regular status.

One of the major problems faced by the Saudi government is the high illiteracy rate in the country. In 1974 the government reported that 66.2 per cent of the native population ten years and over were illiterate (Algadi). Azzam states that in 1974 the illiteracy rate was 65 per cent among Saudi males and 98 per cent among Saudi females. Almana states that in 1978-1979 the illiteracy rate was estimated to be 89 per cent for females and 52 per cent among males.

Education in the United Arab Emirates (UAE) until 1953 was traditional education, primarily religious in the Kutab. The first school, which was founded in 1953, had 450 male students. In 1964-1965 there were 31 schools, two of them for females. In 1972 compulsory primary education for both sexes was created. In Abu Dhabi in 1971-1972, 85 per cent of the school-age children were enrolled in schools. After the creation of the United Emirates in 1971, the government encouraged higher education, and several scholarships were given to female students to continue higher education, especially in Kuwait (Abdulbaset). Several social centres have been created in the Emirates, among them a settlement scheme. Their main objective is to train women in some handicraft skills, and the provision of education and extension programmes is related to their needs and responsibilities (UNDP Mission Report). In a seven-year period, 1968-1975, the illiteracy rate among women in the UAE dropped considerably. The rate was 91.1 per cent in 1968, and in 1975 it was 61.9 per cent (Azzam).

Female illiteracy in both Oman and Qatar in 1975, according to Azzam, was 98.0 per cent. This high rate is an indicator that female education in these two countries is still in the premature stages. Table 1.1 reflects the evolution of the educational system in the Gulf countries. The findings of the survey studies indicate that there is strong encouragement for women's education, especially among urban, educated, and young Gulf men and women.

Altagheb, in his study, 'The Perception of the Kuwaiti concerning the Status of Women in the Contemporary Society', interviewed a sample of 526 people representing 341 familes; 48 per cent of the interviewees were women. Altagheb found that 96 per cent of the respondents agreed about the need for educating women. The 4 per cent who disagreed were illiterate. Seventy-one per cent of the respondents wanted women to finish university and higher education, 23 per cent thought that women should finish secondary school, and 6 per cent thought they should complete primary school.

Alkotob, in his study, 'Perceptions of Female Students from the Countries of the Arab Gulf in Kuwait University Concerning Certain Social and National Issues', interviewed 519 female students: 50.6 per cent were from the college of arts and education; 29 per cent were from the college of commerce, economics, and political science; 16.4 per cent from the college of science; and 3.3 per cent from the college of law and Sharia. Of the students, 69.8 per cent were Kuwaitis, 22.8 per cent were from Bahrain, 2.0 per cent from Qatar, 2.6 per cent from Saudi Arabia, and 2.8 per cent from the UAE. Seventy per cent of the interviewees indicated that the suitable educational degrees for contemporary Gulf women to obtain are masters and doctorates. Concerning equality of education for men and women, 79.4 per cent of the students strongly

Table 1.1 Per cent of females enrolled in school and the female-to-male enrolment ratios by age group in the Gulf Arab countries

Country	Aged 6-11			Aged 12-17			Aged 18-23		
	% females enrolled		F/M ratio	% females enrolled		F/M ratio	% females enrolled		F/M ratio
	1970	1975	1975	1970	1975	1975	1970	1975	1975
Bahrain	69	71	0.87	61	72	0.89	6	7	0.47
Kuwait	58	62	0.92	61	60	0.88	15	24	0.89
Oman	1	26	0.49	–	6	0.26	–	1	1.00
Qatar	78	100*	1.00	51	100*	1.00	8	29	0.78
Saudi Arabia	16	24	0.52	10	20	0.62	1	5	0.31
UAE	43	86	0.91	15	46	0.63	1	7	0.58

*Original percentage over 100 reflecting an error in population or enrolment counts.
Source: Unesco, *Trends and Projections of School Enrolment in Arab Countries* (ED–77)/ MINED ARAB/Ref. 3, Paris, 1977; Azzam 1979.

agreed that there should be full equality. Eighty per cent of the interviewees indicated that university education should be co-educational. When asked about the priorities of education or marriage, 94.8 per cent of the students indicated that women should first be educated before they are married. Women's education should not be limited to home economics or arts majors, 94.2 per cent indicated. However, despite these progressive ideas, 66 per cent of the respondents agreed that the husband's education should be higher than that of his wife.

In her study of a sample of 100 women from nomadic, rural and urban areas in Saudi Arabia, Almana found that the majority of the women interviewed expressed the wish that their daughters would complete their education up to university level. This was especially true among the urban and recently settled groups. Even though the illiteracy rate is high among the recently settled, 58 per cent expressed a desire for their daughters to go to university. In the rural areas, among the farming and nomadic communities, the respondents did not know of nor understand the differences among the educational levels. The nomads would always respond that 'a girl's school is in her herds'. This, Almana concludes, suggests the belief that governmental policies regarding education are primarily targeted for training men. In summary, although women's education in the Gulf region is becoming increasingly popular, and the statistics show that tremendous gains have been achieved, equality and opportunities between men and women in the educational system in most of the countries are still far from being realized. Also, women's education in the rural and isolated communities is still a distant goal to be achieved. In evaluating the functions of education, Shaker says, one must keep in mind that it functions in a milieu of political, economic and cultural forces.

Al-Rimehi rightly observed that education in its beginning has undoubtedly given Gulf women the first push to challenge different social obstacles.

Women and work in the Arab Gulf region

Work, like education, has been one of the most important variables examined by different researchers in their studies of Gulf women. Although each study focused more or less on one, two or three countries in the region, the conditions, problems and solutions concerning women's work were very similar.

The concept of a working woman, Algadi states in his study, cannot be thrown into any society as a concept independent of or irrelevant to other issues. Various scholars (Almana, Al-Rimehi, Algadi, Altagheb, Shilling (1975), Taki, Abdulbaset, and Alkotob), who dealt with this concept, also discussed the issues that are relevant to and directly affect women's work in the Gulf. Such issues include the variables of education, demography, politics, religion and social and cultural factors.

Abdulbaset indicates that despite the educational revolution in the Gulf region and the requirements for labour that have led to a high influx of foreign labour, women as potential contributors to the labour force are still neglected and their resources untapped. According to Abdulbaset, two main reasons contribute to this negligence: the strong traditional beliefs about women's primary role, namely that of a housewife; and women's lack of financial need, especially in Kuwait and the UAE. In Bahrain, however, the demand for a highly skilled labour force is prohibiting not only women, but also men, from working.

Abdulbaset mentions that two factors in the long run will ease women's entrance into the labour force. These are the spread of education, and the need for both skilled and unskilled labour to carry out the extensive projects that are under construction in every Gulf country.

Algadi and Almana have found that participation of Saudi Arabian women in the labour force is still minimal. According to Azzam, in 1975 Saudi Arabian women represented only 2.6 per cent of the labour force and their percentage in agriculture was 5 per cent. The percentage of imported foreign labour in Saudi Arabia reached 65 per cent in 1978–1979 (Almana).

Several studies indicate that many of women's economic activities are excluded from traditional measures of the gross national product. The example that Almana provides in her study reflects the statistical distortions concerning the participation of the female labour force in Saudi Arabia, and especially that of rural women. A labour force survey that included nomadic and herding communities was conducted in Saudi Arabia in 1977 and reported that Saudi participation in the labour force was 32 per cent. Only 6.5 per cent of that labour force percentage was female, and 95.8 per cent of the females were classified under 'housework'. An agricultural survey indicates that Saudi labour involved in agriculture (excluding the herding communities) equals only 650,671 people and that the females in this sector constituted 33.2 per cent.

It is clear from these statistics that the real number of working women in all sectors of the Saudi economy is known only vaguely and not adequately reported. Almana in her field study describes the work of a sample of women who live in three different geographical areas of Saudi Arabia: nomadic, rural, and urban. In Sharora, bedouin women collect camel and sheep wool, spin it into yarn, and use it to make mats, tents, dividers, and sacks (Krooge). Occasionally they sell some of their finished products or spun yarn for cash, but these products are produced primarily for family use.

The sample of Saudi Arabian rural women in Alhasa's study indicates that they engage primarily in housework. A few widows and older women engage in money lending, and some young and middle-aged women in sewing. Of working women living in the urban areas of Dammam, most work primarily as teachers. All these working activities are performed within an exclusively female environment. Women are also engaged in real estate, but they do this by telephone from their own homes. The few Saudi women who work with men are employed by the Arab American Oil Company (ARAMCO). Women typically are confined to their homes, and any activity outside the home is restricted. Women go to the market to buy their supplies, but they cannot engage in any kind of work.

Algadi sums up the constraints and difficulties that are facing working women in Saudi Arabia:

Family restrictions. A woman might face a husband who commands her not to work, or to leave her work; her father or brother might do likewise.

Lack of transportation. Women, Saudi Arabian and non-Saudi Arabian alike, are not allowed to drive in Saudi Arabia, and often their husbands, brothers, or fathers will not drive them to work.

Fear of rumours. Jobs that require a woman to work with men are looked down on and considered 'unsuitable jobs for women'.

Limited opportunities. Saudi Arabian women commonly hold such public jobs as teachers, doctors, social workers and administrators, but only in the female sector.

Lack of child-care facilities. Women face difficulties finding child-care facilities at their work or outside their work. Problems are eased, however, by extended family co-operation.

Lack of economic incentives. Women, married or single, are not required by the

Islamic Sharia to earn the family income, which is considered the man's responsibility. Another reason is that some families do not need additional income.

Another major problem, according to Algadi, which working women face is that cultural heritage tends to dictate the division of labour between the sexes. Most, if not all of these difficulties and problems, with the exception of the second, affect working women not only in the rest of the Gulf countries but throughout the Arab world. Algadi also says that while formal legislation does not restrict women in Saudi Arabia from seeking public jobs, the *de facto* law does.

Saudi Arabian planners should remember that according to the census in 1980, 4.1 million of the population are women. Forty-five per cent of the total population are between the ages of 0 and 14; 45 per cent between 15 and 49; and only 10 per cent are 50 or over. With this demographic distribution, Almana stresses that women should no longer be discouraged or prohibited from joining the labour sector and from contributing to their country's overall development.

According to Mujahed, Bahraini women did not contribute effectively to the labour force, 'the paid sector', until they had the opportunity to be educated and later on to enter the teaching profession, which was followed later by possibilities for employment in nursing. Between 1965 and 1971 the number of Bahraini working women increased from 955 to 1,848. Taki discusses the evolution of the female labour force. In 1971, 5 per cent of Bahraini women were in the labour force. In 1975 the estimate was between 7.1 per cent and 10 per cent. The total number of female government employees in Bahrain reached 21 per cent of the total employees.

Alzayani in her study, 'Women in the Field of Employment and Production', also provides some statistics comparing female and male participation in different sectors of the labour force in Bahrain. Alzayani reports that in 1971–1972 there were 847 females employed in education, compared to 1,182 males. There were more females in nursing (241) than there were males (128). In the agricultural sector only three women were reported to be actively involved, compared to 3,119 men. Azzam reports that less than one per cent of the females in Bahrain are employed in agriculture. This low percentage, according to Azzam, is due to the fact that Bahrain, like Kuwait, Qatar and the UAE, has a significant urban sector. Undoubtedly, these statistics greatly underestimate the contribution of women to the agricultural labour force. Musa (1975) did indicate in his description of the Kuwaiti and Bahraini female labour force that the participation of rural women is still neglected and not reported in labour force statistics in these two countries. Musa recommends that this situation be corrected.

According to Taki, in a country such as Bahrain, which suffers from a lack of labour, the entrance of women into the labour market will help Bahrain meet its needs. Employment has also become an economic need, especially for poor women, in view of the low per capita income and the high cost of living.

Work offers a woman respect as an independent human being who does not have to depend totally on a man. Alzayani and Mujahed argue that women's employment should no longer be a debatable issue. What should be considered are the solutions to all the major problems facing working women and the facilities and services which should be provided for them, especially day-care centres. Alzayani suggests that husbands and children must share in home responsibilities in order to ease the housework burden of working mothers.

The UAE population is a young population similar to that of the rest of the region. Forty-two per cent of the population are between 0 and 14 years old, and 50 per cent are between 15 and 49, while 8 per cent are 50 or over (UNICEF World Data Sheet). The economic sector in the UAE is expanding and almost all the development plans are carried out by foreigners. Although there is a vital need for the contribution of women in the labour sector, Abdulbaset states that as in Kuwait, two major factors are prohibiting women from effectively contributing to the labour force. The social factor could be seen in the role of traditional beliefs and societal constraints on women's freedom to seek employment. The economic factor is that the educated, especially married women, have no need of money; they are educated only for social status, but rarely for obtaining a job. Azzam reports that 5.8 per cent of the UAE labour force were women in 1975, with 94 per cent of these working in the tertiary sector. Kuwait is considered to be the most progressive country in the region concerning women's contribution to the labour force. However, the percentage of the active female labour force indicates that women represent a minority when compared with the total number of the labour force. In 1970, females represented 1 per cent of the total labour force in the region and 3.3 per cent of that of the Kuwaitis. In describing the evolution of the female labour force in Kuwait, Azzam reports that in 1961 it was 0.5 per cent, in 1970 it was 6.9 per cent, and in 1975 it was 8.1 per cent. Shilling in her report on the 'Planning Goals with Respect to Women in Kuwait', wrote that:

> Kuwaiti society tolerates women's employment; it does not encourage it except in those cases where it directly contributes to substitution for foreign labour and then only jobs which are socially acceptable by Kuwaiti standards. Thus, women's labour is accepted neither to fill a need nor for the economic reward it produces. It seems primarily to be accepted to give educated girls something to fill time, between graduation and marriage, or for Kuwaiti to be modern, and theoretically, to provide Kuwaiti substitutes for non-Kuwaiti employees. (1975: 10.)

Despite all these difficulties and perceptions related to women's work in Kuwait, appropriate planning, combined with a genuine desire by Kuwaitis for change, will help women to be integrated fully into the various labour sectors.

Table 1.2 Economically active females in selected countries of the
Arabian Gulf, 1975

Country	Female population (in thousands)	Active females (in thousands)	Percentage of active females to total female population	Percentage of active females to total female population aged 15 years and above	Percentage of active females to total active population
Bahrain*	121	3.249	2.7	2.7	5.4
Kuwait	492	26	5.3	5.1	8.1
Qatar	68	1.8	2.7	–	2.2
Saudi Arabia	4,431	113	2.6	2.4	4.7
UAE*	171	9.961	5.8	5.7	3.4

*ECWA, *Statistical Abstract of the Region of the Economic Commission for Western Asia*, Second Issue: Part I, Beirut, 1978.
Source: Unless otherwise specified, ILO, *Labour Force Estimates and Projections, 1950-2000*, Vols. I and II, Geneva, 1977; Azzam 1979.

The situation of working women in Qatar is similar to that of the UAE, although their percentage in the labour force is lower than that of the United Arab Emirates. Azzam reports that in 1975 the active female population in the labour force in Qatar was 2.7 per cent, and 99 per cent of those worked in the tertiary sector. Oman is the only country in the region where the female labour force in agriculture in 1970 was reported to be 78 per cent (Azzam). Table 1.2 summarizes the number of economically active females in the countries of the Arab Gulf region, 1975.

Alkotob and Altagheb examined the attitudes of women (Alkotob) and those of both women and men (Altagheb) in Kuwait concerning women's work. (For more information on the studies see the previous section.) Alkotob's study found that respondents generally agreed that the teaching profession is the most suitable profession for Gulf women, because it does not require them to mix with men. Teaching was followed by social work and then medicine. Seventy-five per cent of the respondents indicated that they would like to work with the government. When the interviewees were ask for their opinion concerning the claim that women are not capable of job responsibilities, 85 per cent of them strongly opposed the statement. The idea that the natural place for women is their homes and that work is the men's responsibility was opposed by 70.3 per cent. When asked if women should stop working when they have children, 54.1 per cent of the respondents answered positively. Of the women respondents,

78.8 per cent indicated that they do not agree that their entrance into the labour force reduces the opportunities of men. Of all the interviewees, 43.4 per cent also said that there are no opportunities for women in the Gulf in high-level decision-making positions.

The statement suggesting that women who work in a mixed environment will not be able to protect their honour was opposed by 86.7 per cent of the respondents. Gulf women were asked whether they should seek jobs that do not demand their mixing with men, in order to protect their honour, and 52.8 per cent opposed the idea.

Altagheb in his study found that of the men interviewed, 58 per cent supported the idea of work for women, while 82 per cent of the women interviewed opposed it. It should be noted, Altagheb says, that the majority of the sample was composed of housewives whose educational background was less than high school. Ninety per cent of the respondents indicated that women should be working in the government, especially in the teaching profession; 53.1 per cent of the males chose this profession for women. When the interviewees were asked which was more important for women, work or home, the majority said home, and only 13 per cent of the women and 2 per cent of the men said work. Altagheb indicates that this answer shows that men in the Gulf region remain conservative concerning women's employment. Part of this conservatism is due to the strong social and cultural forces persisting in the region.

Social and cultural conditions of women in the Arab Gulf countries

In addition to male dominance, cultural values and social attitudes related to women's seclusion and restricted mobility characterize all societies of the Gulf region. According to Al-Rimehi, the major indicator of the cultural subordination of women in these societies can be seen in the way most of the homes are built. Special entrances and special sections of the homes are provided exclusively for women. This social isolation has confined Gulf women to their private world, which has its own traditions, rituals, and norms, and differs totally from the men's world. This social isolation also has various negative social and economic consequences for women.

The cultural and social situation of women in the Gulf region has created certain social relations and patterns of behaviour; major among them is *Hijab*, the veil. Algadi asks what is *Hijab* (the veil)? 'Allah (God) never intended to specify what he means by *Hijab*; no verse has ever specified what a modest look is. The Sunnah, however, had said that a woman can expose only her face and hands.' Al-Rimehi, Almana, and Algadi all indicate that *Hijab* is a product of social life rather than of the teaching of Islam. For instance, Algadi wrote:

> Ironically enough, *badu* (nomad) women do not veil as non-*badu* (urban) women do in the cities. Moreover, *badu* women drive pickups on the country

roads while urban women do not. Although seclusion and segregation are observable to some extent among them, *badu* women are more mobile and more aggressive than their urban counterparts. For example, while it is extremely difficult for an urban woman to sell some products on a sidewalk in a bazaar, it is customary to see *badu* women engaged in income-producing occupations outside the home. (1979: 42.)

Abureda, in his study presented to the Regional Conference on Women in the Gulf, entitled, 'Women in Islam from the Quran and the Hadith' (1975), indicates that *Hijab* in Islam does not necessarily mean the exclusion of women from participating in public life and contributing to production in order to benefit her society and herself. Women, according to Abureda, are allowed in the Islamic religion to work in all professions. Algadi states that God praises those who get paid for their work. God says, 'How excellent a recompense for those who work'. Moreover, God equalizes both sexes in work. God says, 'Never will I suffer to be lost the work of any of you, be he male or female'.

Altoriki indicates that 'literal interpretations of Koranic verses and Islamic philosophical and theological literature have sometimes misread or read out of context statements relating to the personal status of women in Islam and, more often, naively accepted ideological imagery as cultural reality' (1977: 277). Shaker's study, 'The Status of Women in Islam',

found a great difference between the Quranic norms on women's status and the actual behaviour in Saudi Arabia. Ideally, Muslim women are found to enjoy higher status in marriage, divorce, legal rights, education, activities of political nature than their actual status and role in Saudi Arabia. Testify to the latter the fact that women's education was legalized in Saudi Arabia only in 1960. In addition, arranged marriage without the consent of the bride, the demand for high dowry, lack of any judicial control over men's right to divorce and the institution of polygamy are all instances that stand contrary to the ideal. (1972: 323.)

Kuwait is considered to be the progressive country in the Gulf region concerning the relative freedom and emancipation of its women. However, Shilling and Nath, in describing the status of women in Kuwait, point out the social and cultural restrictions that are still faced by them.

All the studies reviewed concerning the socio-cultural status of women in the Gulf show the subjection and powerlessness of women.

Altorki, in her study on the 'Family Organization and Women's Power in Urban Saudi Arabian Society', refers to the informal power exercised by women in Arab societies and challenges what she calls the traditional Western view of sex-role relationships in the Middle East. Her study describes the power relations between men and women of élite familes within the organization of domestic groups in Jeddah. She notes that:

The data show that women have always exercised significant control over the decision of their male agnates relating to the arrangement of marriages. Given the particular social, political and economic role of marriage in Arabian society, this control, in turn, has had consequences beyond the realm of domestic relations. Among the families studied, their frequent and prolonged residence abroad and the education of their daughters in foreign schools have strengthened the informal power of the women and initiated their emancipation from the jural tutelage of their agnates and husbands. (1977: 277.)

General observations on the studies reviewed

All studies of Gulf women demonstrate, like numerous studies conducted in other parts of the Arab countries, that although definite changes are taking place, problems and conflicts are still found in the situations, needs and lifestyles of Gulf women.

The studies about Gulf women that have been reviewed can be classified into two major categories:

1. Research that is purely descriptive. These studies describe the existing situation of women and offer explanations which neither challenge nor criticize the present situation.
2. Writings that are descriptive and also analytical. These studies propose changes, some through reformist means and others through more radical ones.

The research reviewed reveals that Gulf women do not feel that they are given opportunities to contribute equally in their countries' development. They are analysed primarily in subsidiary roles, with their identities forged through men, and their opportunities and choices extremely limited. Studies furthermore indicate that although bedouin and rural women in the Gulf always have worked alongside their husbands in different activities outside the home, their efforts have gone unnoticed.

Most of the studies focus upon urban middle class and upper class women. Very little information is available about rural and bedouin women and about lower class urban women. Only two studies have dealt with the variable of class. The three studies that utilized questionnaires and direct interviews in data collection report their findings in percentages. None of the studies reviewed utilized any sophisticated statistical tools in testing their hypotheses.

Out of a total number of sixteen studies reviewed, ten were written in Arabic. Analytical research into Gulf women's problems is badly needed. This does not discount past research: descriptive studies, with all their weaknesses, form a useful foundation for more rigorous work. However, in future the question of why, rather than of what, should dominate.

With all the shortcomings of the reviewed descriptive studies, they are important in that they represent the first studies in which the status of Gulf women is examined as the main focus of the study; they have shown that women are contributing, not only in family life but also in public life, and they will lead the way to the development of further research relevant for the region and Arab women.

METHODOLOGICAL AND THEORETICAL CONSIDERATIONS

All the studies reviewed emphasize that planners must develop and implement programmes, which will enhance and alter the situation of Gulf women. Before planners can do this, scientific studies, research, and relevant data, both quantitative and qualitative, should be made available, and, methodologically, should be analysed from the perspective of development. Only then will planners be able to design projects that include women as equal beneficiaries.

Social scientists in general and those in particular who are concerned with women's research in the Gulf region and throughout the Arab world have not yet gained a wide recognition for their research. This is due to several interrelated difficulties; however, it does not imply that no attempts are being made to overcome these difficulties.

The methodological and theoretical confusion that dominates the field of research about women throughout the world is its major drawback. If this is not discussed, analysed and clarified, research about women will never be able to provide the sound, scientific data necessary for effective planning.

Scholars and researchers concerned with the situation of Arab women believe that these women have been victims of many biases on the part of outside researchers, primarily Western. Several cultural assumptions about the lives of these women have led these 'outsiders' to develop traditional definitions, leading to the development of certain conceptual and methodological tools that are not relevant to women's status in their respective countries. It has also been noted by Arab scholars that models and hypotheses based on women's lifestyles in Western countries have been tested without adaptation to the conditions of Arab women. Several concepts used in Western women's literature, such as liberation, equality, and freedom, have to be questioned and redefined to reflect the Arab woman's reality. In sum, the Western model of women's liberation has been considered the ideal model, and the standard by which the status of Arab women has been analysed.

Researchers also have been faced with the fact that social science research in the Arab world, however limited it may be, starts with a frame of reference that neither considers the sex of an individual as a major variable, nor describes women's needs or issues related to them. As a solution to this difficulty, it has been proposed that Arab social science researchers should consider the role and status of Arab women, to prevent sexist analyses.

Besides these basic difficulties, two other theoretical issues—the development of universal hypotheses related to women's status and the theoretical framework upon which women's research in the Arab world should depend— are increasingly debated within the circles of Arab scholars concerned with research about women. These two issues will not be analysed extensively in this chapter. The reason for raising them is merely to generate more discussion, analysis and comments, which might help clarify the vagueness still surrounding the debates. It is argued that if research about women worldwide aims to develop theoretical insights and refined methodological tools, which eventually will attain universal validity, universal hypotheses and concepts should be tested in a variety of societal cultural contexts.

This universal aim, one of the arguments states, can never be reached until social scientists in various cultures, who are engaged in research about women, contribute to the build-up of a conceptual framework at the micro level. Universal hypotheses will be based upon those micro-level and culture-specific hypotheses. However, one of the critical questions that is still debated, especially among sociologists, is how different sociological perspectives can be applied to subnational units, or whether they can be adapted. It is argued that some conceptual frameworks can meet the criterion of regional relevance. Adding or subtracting a particular paradigm will not affect the central argument that a regional analysis of women's situation requires and stimulates a new look at available theoretical resources.

Arab researchers concerned with the status of women also question whether the theories and concepts related to research on women should be related to theories and concepts utilized to understand Arab society as a whole, whether they should strive to develop concepts and theories related to women's issues around the world, or a combination of both.

The following methodological and theoretical considerations aim to pinpoint some critical strategies that may help generate relevant and significant data concerning women's issues both in the Gulf and the rest of the Arab world:

1. The review of studies has indicated that different interacting variables contribute to women's inequality in the Gulf region. Accordingly, any theoretical framework that is utilized to explain sexual differences in the Gulf region should account for the historical, religious, educational, cultural, political and (above all) economic variables. As long as the above-mentioned independent variables are not taken *in toto*, any explanation of the problem will remain vague.

2. Traditions, customs, values and male attitudes have also been reviewed as being explanatory variables for sexual inequalities in the Gulf region; despite the fact that they are indeed important variables, they are not enough for

a conclusive explanation. Very little in the studies traces how and why this situation was generated.

3. A thorough understanding of the real situation of women in the Gulf must depend neither on classical traditional theories, nor on radical ones, because both distort many facts. Radicals must not deny the success, however small, that has been achieved by the reformists in some Gulf countries, nor should reformists avoid raising some radical questions to challenge the status quo.

4. Research on women in the Gulf should not be considered as an isolated field task. Links between research on women and other larger societal, political, legal and economic issues, which face different segments of Arab society, will help bring recognition of and legitimacy to the seriousness and importance of the subject. Such links will also make whatever policies are recommended relevant in most project analysts' minds.

5. Women in development research are increasingly becoming the concern of social scientists, both in the Arab world and the Gulf region. Accordingly, for researchers who are or will be working in this field, the primary objective should be utilizing research data in the implementation of effective programmes to facilitate women's active participation. Research for the sake of research is a luxury which has no place in the Arab world.

6. The various research methods that currently exist in the social science field, 'scientific approach compared with the humanistic one, statistical versus case-study, quantitative versus qualitative, and so on', have caused much controversy among researchers. Whatever research methods used to study Gulf women, they should fit the reality of the subject studied. The problem does not lie in which method is better or more effective but rather in what effect the utilized method has on the study of women.

7. Research concerning women in the Gulf should never treat them as if they are a homogeneous group, especially when the class structure is so evident. However, researchers should also be aware that in the Gulf region, middle and upper class women, who are protected and isolated, endure a strong inequality that is not purely economical but is sexual, social and psychological.

RESEARCH PRIORITIES AND NEEDS FOR THE STUDY OF WOMEN IN THE GULF

As the previous discussion indicates, all kinds of data on the different strata and classes of women in the Gulf must be collected. Project planners, if they are not provided with these data, may ignore the social facts and develop projects that are either alien to the target population or not relevent to their needs.

Different methods exist for establishing priorities to carry out research about Gulf women. To emphasize answers to questions that have been neglected is just one of these priorities. Many of the questions which come out of the studies are cited in regard to issues and problems and constitute a list of researchable questions. This list does not constitute a definitive list of all research priorities and needs applicable to Gulf women. It should also be pointed out that each Gulf country must develop its own priorities as far as the ordering and content of the following specific priorities and needs are concerned:

1. Studies reviewed reveal that conflict exists in the region about traditional role expectations and actual life experience. Research should explore how newly-educated and emancipated women in the region are at odds with their roles, and how people subsequently perceive women who deviate from their expected behaviour. Studies pertaining to the cultural restrictions upon women would pinpoint these restrictions and provide steps to overcome them and bring about positive change.

2. Research should explore whether or not the rapid socio-economic changes which are sweeping the region have fundamentally affected the status of women in different geographical locations and social classes, especially with regard to the division of labour, decision-making power within the household, and increased choice opportunities.

3. Research related to Gulf women and, in turn, the Arab world, must seek explanations about how a balance can be achieved between continuity of certain roles, values, and traditions that are considered 'good', and change of others which impede progress and improvement.

4. Country profile studies should be directed to encourage and develop empirical assessment of the different roles of women in different geographical locations. These studies should also concentrate on the collection of demographic data on rural and bedouin women, which are still largely lacking. Such studies should help in designing action programmes through which women can actively participate in solving the problems of the family, community, and the nation.

5. The reviewed studies reveal a total lack of data and information about rural and bedouin women. Research should focus on such variables as the type of work performed by bedouin and rural women and men outside the household. Findings from this kind of research will indicate which tasks are performed by women in the agricultural sector and within the tribal communities. It also will show what kinds of skills women already have, allowing plans to be developed to build upon and refine the existing skills. These kinds of studies will also encourage planners to recognize the vital roles which rural women play in the agricultural sector and the bedouin women perform in their tribes.

6. Research pertaining to infrastructure building (roads, water, electricity, health, education) should go hand-in-hand with projects pertaining to women, especially in the remote rural and nomadic areas. Other researchers in other parts of the world have shown that if this does not happen, any effort directed towards women, without the supporting infrastructure, will be doomed to failure.

7. Research related to Gulf women should explain regularities, variations and interdependence of social, psychological, cultural and demographic variables. It should also list the indicators chosen to describe the overall situation of all women in all social classes and geographical locations.

8. Research should focus on the felt needs of women themselves. The projects designed to benefit women will be accepted if they address locally-perceived needs.

SUGGESTED SOLUTIONS TO MAJOR OBSTACLES FACING GULF WOMEN

Although more problems were discussed in the studies reviewed than solutions proposed, some researchers have suggested a few solutions. Perhaps some are superficial, reformist, or vague, but others are meaningful, radical and specific. Several studies have emphasized the need for fighting illiteracy among women in the Gulf as a primary solution to the various problems they face. The BNSU study calls for co-education in order to overcome the psychological obstacles between the sexes. The only paper that proposes the introduction of women's studies in the educational system in the Gulf was by BNSU. The paper states that 'women's studies will teach both females and male students about the real potentials of women and help correct wrong and stereotyped ideas about women's primary roles and responsibilities'. Altagheb suggests that educational policies should be planned to encourage more women to join scientific and vocational fields and not continue to be concentrated in the fields of humanities and social sciences. Al-Rimehi states very specifically that 'education for both sexes is the major solution for providing better life for the Gulf individual'. Shilling indicates that programmes to alter women's self-image, expand their options, and motivate them to improve themselves can help overcome the obstacles faced by Kuwaiti women.

Al-Rimehi and Taki both indicate that women in the Gulf must consider their liberation as a national liberation. 'If the obstacles that women face should ever be solved, their problems should not be dealt with in isolation from all sources of exploitation that dominate the Gulf region.' Musa, Al-Rimehi, Almana and Algadi suggest the need for providing women with equal opportunities in the job market. Musa indicates that one major solution in overcoming the obstacles that women face in the job market is appointing them to different jobs according to their skills, educational background and capabilities and not according to their sex.

BIBLIOGRAPHY

Abd Al Rahman, Sad. *Studies on the Status and Perceptions of the Kuwaiti Women*, Kuwait, Dar Al Siyasa (in Arabic), 1971.
Abdulbaset, Ahmed A. 'On Working Women in Kuwait and the Gulf', a paper presented at the First Regional Conference on Women in the Arabian Gulf, Kuwait (in Arabic), 1975.
Abdulkader, Soha. 'Review of Research Literature on Arab Women', 'Draft', Unesco, Paris, Division of Human Rights, 1979.
Abu-Lughad, Janet. 'Urban-Rural Differences as a Function of the Demographic Transition: Egyptian Data and an Analytical Model', *The American Journal of Sociology*, 69, pp. 476-90, 1964.
Abureda, Mohamed A. 'Women in Islam from the Quran and the Hadith', a paper presented at the First Regional Conference on Women in the Arabian Gulf, 21-24 April, Kuwait (in Arabic), 1975.
Algadi, Adnan A. 'Utilization of Human Resources: The Case of Women in Saudi Arabia', Master's thesis, Sacramento, California State University, 1979.
Alkotob, Ashak. 'Perceptions of Female Students from the Countries of the Arab Gulf in Kuwait University Concerning Certain Social and National Issues', a paper presented at the First Regional Conference on Women in the Arabian Gulf, 21-24 April, Kuwait (in Arabic), 1975.
Almana, Aisha. 'Attitudes of Saudi Arabian Students Toward Working Women and Religion', Master's thesis, Arizona State University, 1972.
Almana, Aisha. 'Economic Development and Its Impact on the Status of Women in Saudi Arabia', Ph.D. dissertation, Boulder, University of Colorado Sociology Department, 1981.
Al-Rimehi, Mohammed. 'The Reality of Women in the Gulf', a paper presented at the First Regional Conference on Women in the Arabian Gulf, 21-24 April, Kuwait (in Arabic), 1975.
Al Sultan, Najat. 'The Kuwaiti Professional Women', a paper delivered at the Conference on Development in the Arab World, New York, 1-3 October, 1976.
Altagheb, Fahed. 'The Perception of the Kuwaiti Concerning the Status of Women in the Contemporary Society', a paper presented at the First Regional Conference on Women in the Arabian Gulf, 21-24 April, Kuwait (in Arabic), 1975.
Altorki, Soraya. 'Religion and Social Organization of Elite Families in Urban Saudi Arabia', unpublished Ph.D. dissertation, Berkeley, University of California, 1972.
Altorki, Soraya. 'Family Organization and Women's Power in Urban Saudi Arabian Society', *Journal of Anthropological Research*, V. 33, No. 3 (Fall), pp. 277-87, 1977.
Alzayani, Faiza. 'Women in the Field of Employment and Production', Bahrain Ministry of Labour and Social Affairs (in Arabic), 1973.

Assad, Soraya. 'Role Demands and Professional Women in Jeddah, Saudi Arabia', Master's thesis, Portland State University, 1977.

Assalah, Othman A. 'The Rights of Gulf Women in the Public and Private Law', a paper presented at the First Regional Conference on Women in the Gulf, 21-24 April, Kuwait (in Arabic), 1975.

Azzam, T. Henry. *The Participation of Arab Women in the Labour Force: Development Factors and Policies*, Geneva, International Labour Organization, 1979.

Bahraini National Student Union. *Women in Bahrain and the Arab Gulf, Kuwait* (in Arabic), n.d.

Bint al Jazirah, Samirah. *The Awakening of the Saudi Arabian Women*, Beirut, Maktab Tijari, 1963.

Boserup, Ester. *Women's Role in Economic Development*, New York, St. Martin's Press, 1970.

Boulding, Elise. *Women in the Twentieth Century World. Studies on Women and Development*, Boulder, Colorado, Sage Publications, 1976.

Buvinic, Mayra. 'Women and World Development'. Washington, D.C.: Overseas Development Council, 1976.

Calverley, Eleanor J. 'Beauty for Ashes', *Moslem World* 10, pp. 391-401, 1920.

Calverley, Eleanor J. *My Arabian Days and Nights*, New York, Crowell, 1958.

Cole, Donald Powell. *Nomads of the Nomads*, Chicago, Aldine Publishing Company, 1975.

Dixon, Ruth. *Rural Women at Work. Strategies for Development in South Asia*, New York, Johns Hopkins Press, 1978.

Eisenstadt, S. N. *Modernization: Protest and Change*, Englewood Cliffs, N.J., Prentice-Hall, 1966.

Farsoun, Smith K. 'Family Structure and Society in Modern Lebanon', in *Peoples and Cultures of the Middle East*, Vol. 2 (Louise E. Sweet, ed.), Garden City, N.Y., The Natural History Press, 1976.

Freeth, Zahra. *Kuwait was my Home*, London, George Allen and Unwin, 1958.

Halpern, M. *The Politics of Social Change in the Middle East and North Africa*, Princeton, Princeton University Press, 1963.

Hansen, Henry H. *Investigation in Shia Village in Bahrain*, Copenhagen, National Museum of Denmark (Ethnographical Series), 1967.

Hansen, Henry H. 'The Pattern of Women's Seclusion and Veiling in a Shia Village', *Folk* 3, pp. 23-42, 1961.

Harfouche, Jamal. *The Family Structure in the Changing Middle East and the Pre-school Children*, Beirut, UNICEF (PSWG/PSC/14), 1968.

Huston, Perdita. *Third World Women Speak Out: Interviews in Six Countries on Change, Development, and Basic Needs*, Washington, published in Co-operation with the Overseas Development Council, 1978.

Kannisto, V. *Social Indicators for Bahrain*, Ministry of Labour and Social Affairs, Social Development Section,

Kay, Shirley. *The Bedouin*, New York, Crane, Russak and Company, 1978.

Khalaf, Samir. 'Adaptive Modernization: The Case for Lebanon', in *Economic Development and Population Growth in the Middle East* (Charles A. Cooper and Sidney S. Alexander, eds.), New York, American Elsevier, 1972.

Lerner, Daniel. *The Passing of Traditional Society: Modernizing the Middle East*, New York, MacMillan, 1964.

Mickelwit, R., M. Riegelman, C. Sweet. *Women in Rural Development*, Boulder, Colorado, Westview Press, 1976.

Mujahed, Hoda. *The Role of Women in Social Development*, Bahraini.Ministry of Labour and Social Affairs, Section of Social Development (in Arabic), 1976.

Musa, Ali. 'The Role of Women in Development', a paper presented at the First Regional Conference on Women in the Arabian Gulf, 21-24 April, Kuwait (in Arabic), 1975.

Najim, W. Taha. 'Women's Contribution to Arab Literature', a paper delivered at the First Regional Conference on Women in the Gulf Area, 21-24 April, Kuwait (in Arabic), 1975.

Nath, Kamla. 'Education and Employment among Kuwaiti Women', in *Women in the Muslim World* (L. Beck and N. Keddie, eds.), Cambridge: Harvard University Press, 1978.

O'Dea, Thomas. 'Saudi Arabian Profile: Problems and Prospects', an unpublished paper prepared for ARAMCO, 1962.

Parssinen, Catherine. 'Women's Enlarged Role in Saudi Arabia', a paper presented at the King Faisal Conference, Santa Barbara, Middle East Center, University of Southern California, 1978.

Patai, Raphael. *Women in the Modern World*, New York, Free Press, 1967.

Phillips, Wendell. *Unknown Oman*, New York, David McKay Company, 1966.

Reint Jesus, Hortense. *Die Soziale Stelluing der Frau bei den Nordana Bischew Bedouinen*, Bonn, Selbsverlag des Orientallischen Seminars der Universität, 1975.

Sayegh, Kamal S. *Oil and Arab Regional Development*, New York, Praeger, 1968.

Shaker, Fatin Amin. 'Modernization in the Developing Nations: The Case of Saudi Arabia', Ph.D. dissertation, Purdue University, 1972.

Shilling, Nancy A. 'An Analysis of Planning Goals with Respect to Women in Kuwait', an unpublished paper submitted to the Women's Affairs Work Force at the Kuwait Planning Board, Kuwait, 1975.

Taki, Ali. 'The Bahraini Woman in Education and Labour', a paper presented at the First Regional Conference on Women in the Gulf', 21-24 April, Kuwait (in Arabic), 1975.

Tinker, Irene. *Women and World Development*, Washington, D.C., Overseas Development Council, 1976.

Toy, Barbara. *A Fool Strikes Oil: Across Saudi Arabia*, J. Murray, 1957.

Traini, R. 'Arabia Saudiane: Associazone per L'elevezione della donna. La Prima Donna Jiornalista Saudiane', *Orient Moderno*, 43, pp. 492-3, 1963.

United Nations Children's Fund (UNICEF). 'Education of Women in Saudi Arabia', *Moslem World* 46, pp. 366-7, 1956.

United Nations Children's Fund (UNICEF). *Report on Women's Status in Kuwait*, Commission in Charge of Women's Affairs, 1975.

United Nations Children's Fund (UNICEF). *A Sociological Study of Housewives Living in Poor Neighbourhoods in the Cities of Dammam, Jeddah and Riyadh, Saudi Arabia*, 1977.

United Nations Children's Fund (UNICEF). *Characteristics of the Kuwaiti Women in the 1957, 1965, 1970, 1975 Census*, Working Group Concerned with Women's Issues,

United Nations Children's Fund (UNICEF). *World Women's Data Sheet of the Population Reference Bureau Incorporated*, 1980.

United Nations Children's Fund (UNICEF). *World Data Sheet*, 1980.

United Nations Development Programme. *Integration of Women in Development in Six Arab Countries: Tunisia, Egypt, Sudan, United Arab Emirates, Iraq, Kuwait*, New York, United Nations, 1979.

2 Research in the Social Sciences on North African Women: Problems, Trends and Needs

ALYA BAFFOUN

GENERAL INTRODUCTION TO THE STUDY OF NORTH AFRICAN WOMEN

Preliminary remarks

Before embarking on an investigation into the position of social science research on the problems of women in present-day North Africa, we should like to draw attention to a number of points that are essential to an understanding of what we have to say.

1   We believe that all social relations of dependence and oppression, of which the subordination of one sex to the other is only one example, take their origin exclusively in economic domination.

2   In the effective organization of such oppression, the superstructure plays an important role of camouflaging and whitewashing brought about by those in power (a social group or the state). Accordingly, it is necessary to study not only that oppression, but also the prevailing social institutions and ideological authorities and their influence on the organization of the family, the rules governing sexuality, and the status of women.

3   In present-day societies, the study of the status and influence of women as perceived in everyday life reveals that for the first time in the varied and complex history of feminist militancy, the women's movement is no longer the exclusive initiative of a small group or an *élite* (working class, middle class or whatever) but is becoming a worldwide phenomenon, making it one of the most significant political forces of our time. The broadening of the movement to include a great many women who together form a 'front line of revolt' must be related to the present stage in the development of international capitalism and to the changes that have occurred in its patterns of organization. One of the salient characteristics of this development is the impressive number of women now employed in the production process. This new historical and economic factor explains the primary concentration of the women's movement in certain regions of the industrialized world (Italy, Spain, and the United States of America, for example), which have a patriarchal and class structure.

4   It must be remembered that within a class-structured society, women do not constitute a class in the Marxist sense, and the man–woman relationship cuts across class barriers. For this reason, the women's movement must be studied in the light of the real status of women in male-dominated civilization. This last point indicates the complexity of the problem of the subordination of women who, while they are the last and the most numerous human colony to be liberated, are nevertheless a colony whose frontiers cannot yet be clearly discerned.

5   In the Arab countries of North Africa, the majority of which are economically dependent on international capitalism, the status of women, while displaying certain specific characteristics of its own, is undergoing changes, because these societies have recently subscribed to the dominant mode of production, and are imitating the culture attached to it, passed on through the still powerful French language and purveyed, in particular, by the mass media (television, newspapers, the cinema, etc.). The conflicts and contradictions accompanying the emergence of the new North African society should be viewed within this frame of reference.

A critical methodological approach

From the numerous attempts to analyse studies of the family, marriage and women in North Africa and to explain the existence of a strong sexual imbalance in men's favour, we can single out two methodological lines of interpretation:

(a) The first, which is past-oriented (salafism i.e. traditionalism, integrationism, fundamentalism) originates either in juridico-religious ideological thinking, or in the ideology of hegemony, especially an anthropological version of this (research on exotic cultures). In both cases, women are defined in terms of a policy of 'seclusion'; and in this context the justification for subordinating one sex to the other would appear to have its foundations in an unshakeable fatalism, built into biogenetic human nature and erected into an immutable code by religions. Anthropology, meanwhile, was at pains, for a very long time, to highlight the 'perennial' and 'exotic' aspects of North African societies. Whether deliberately or not, such anthropology (excessively influenced by ideology) reflects a state of affairs in which a large part of mankind was rendered defenceless against the remainder (Lévi-Strauss). The only schools of thought that were free from the tendency to argue in terms of the innate and unchangeable nature of the 'male establishment' were certain reformist religious movements (T. Haddad in Tunisia), which very soon attracted persecution, and a new trend in cultural anthropology (G. Tillion 1966).

(b) The second, and most recent approach, although supported by relatively few studies as yet, and suffering from an absence of theory, nevertheless shows promising signs of an objective and scientific interpretation of the status of women in North Africa. It introduces a dynamic aspect, in that it urges a return to the scrutiny of observable social patterns and their comparative impact on the structure of the family, women's access to employment and women's status within society. The method used here is either historical, or else empirical, based on field studies and surveys which have been designed to prevent any 'intuitionist' and subjective interpretation that is not founded in fact: 'practice is more important than theory, for any practice that is fundamentally sound helps to correct partially erroneous theories, whereas the converse is not true' (S. Amin 1974).

According to this approach, the pseudo-scientific arguments and theories seeking to support the 'innatist' thesis must themselves be seen as the historical outcome common to all patriarchal social patterns based on private property, the safeguarding of inheritance through the male line, and economic oppression of women. The existence of private property leads, for purposes of manipulation and class domination strategy, to the control and management of sexuality according to a given 'sexual economy', which is nearly always highly repressive. The research work that has been done, mainly by women, makes very little impact on the societies concerned, for the establishment opposes it.

Let us observe, finally, that in many cases research on North African women has been unable to avoid the fundamental epistemological and theoretical stumbling-block encountered by research in social sciences in our regions. This research has in fact been unable to evade the epistemological domination of Western knowledge, which has in many cases remained Europe-centred, for 'this middle of the road Western-style preconceptual approach is sectoral. It has sometimes incorporated material from dependent countries and peoples, but as objects, never as subjects' (A. Abdelmalek). Nor has it been able to avoid the opposite extreme, i.e. taking refuge in ideas of 'specificity' and 'the right to be different', for very often these concepts are played up 'in order to disguise the machinery of systematic exploitation to which the peoples of the Third World are subjected as a result of the present rules of the world market, dominated as it is by dictatorial imperialism' (F. Stambouli 1979).

STATE OF THE ART AND TRENDS IN RESEARCH ON
WOMEN IN NORTH AFRICA

Setting aside religious and legal writings on the status and position of Arab women, which are plentiful and belong within a tradition of exegesis, we find that very little has yet been accomplished in the field of scientific research.

For example, in a review such as *Temps modernes*, we find that out of 37 articles on North Africa in the special issue of October 1977, there is not a single article on North African women. This shortcoming (or, rather, this significant lapse, as we think it is) cannot be attributed to the non-existence of specialists on the matter; the publication of a book entitled *Women in the Muslim World* (1978), in which the situation of women in North Africa is established through a series of articles by various authors, shows clearly that the problem lies elsewhere.

For our part, we have tried, on the basis of existing research in the social sciences, to confirm a few fundamental facts about women in North Africa, by referring in particular to specialized publications such as the North Africa Directory (*Annuaire de l'Afrique du Nord*), and to a great deal of recent research carried out by both individuals and teams. We have been able to determine the present state of research on this issue and to make an initial quantitative assessment. Interpretation of these basic data has provided us with ample clues to the overriding concerns of this research and the form that it usually takes. The section on 'the state of the art and trends in research on women' is the outcome of this investigation.

We were able to determine the trends and the 'peaks' of research in this field by conducting an analysis of content, indispensable to any understanding of the problems of women in North Africa today. Much of this research has been done by women writers, an appreciable number of whom are non-nationals. At this initial stage of research on the situation of women in our region, we welcome all contributions from, and co-operation with, specialists concerned about these questions, and we hope that this research will finally emerge from its early or 'prehistoric' phase, thanks to joint and complementary efforts.

Sample survey based on the North Africa Directory (1968-1976) and interpretation of the data

The North Africa Directory is a very important basic tool, invaluable for gathering information about virtually everything that happens in the Maghreb region (Algeria, Morocco, Tunisia, Mauritania and Libyan Arab Jamahiriya). There is nevertheless a remarkable and revealing gap where research on women is concerned. For example, of 300 bibliographical titles dealing with the Maghreb area and listed in the most recent Directory (1976), no more than fifteen or so deal with women.

With regard to Algerian, Tunisian and Moroccan women in particular, we have nevertheless succeeded in gleaning a few basic facts on current trends in research from the ten-year bibliographical index. We have classified present trends in work and research under eight main headings. Some of these headings have been grouped together for convenient breakdown into themes and sub-themes that are regarded as closely related. The eight headings listed in Table 2.1 cover the main lines of most of the work carried out, and this table shows the numbers of studies on each of these themes between 1968 and 1976.

Table 2.1 Thematic quantitative breakdown of studies published 1968-1976

Theme	Year and number of publications (1968)	1968-1972	1972-1976	Total
History Anthropology			4	4
Law Marriage Divorce Filiation Custody of children	2	10	5	17
Family	6		2	8
Work	1	2	5	8
Modernization Rural-Urban Politics	2		4	6
Sexuality Prostitution Delinquency		1	1	2
Family planning		6	1	7
Emigration Population Shift		1	2	3
Total publications	11	20	24	55

Source: Annuaire de l'Afrique du Nord, 1968-1976.

Interpretation of findings and development of the thematic structure

Most of the quoted studies on women have been done by men, especially those under the headings 'law' and 'planning'. A good many have taken the form of doctoral theses submitted by researchers, or as the conclusions of papers presented at various national seminars. This is true, for example, of studies under the heading 'work', under which half the publications are doctoral theses, or the category 'family', which has been the subject of a great many seminars.

The survey, the questionnaire and the interview are often found side by side with attempts at theoretical interpretation that are not always supported by reliable paradigms. There is very little research that shows an attempt to build up a general theory in a comparative context (such as the work of Germaine Tillion). Apart from this piecemeal structure of research and the lack of a comparative angle of approach, the general picture is often abstract and remote from any practical usefulness, with a few exceptions (F. M'rabet 1979, F. Mernissi 1978 and J. Minces 1972).

Furthermore, despite the quantitative increase in research on women (which doubled between 1968 and 1976), it is still inadequate in comparison with other sectors of social reality. This relative scarcity is to be explained, we think, by a certain reluctance, unconscious or otherwise, to examine a 'taboo sector', and by the discouragement and disapproval forthcoming from the traditional patriarchy, on the defensive and opposed to any attempt, even a scientific one, to question the assumptions that determine the situation of Arab women in general and North African women in particular. Even in Tunisia, where the status of women is most advanced, the Islamic revivalist movements are steadily increasing their pressure against women's representation and freedom, thereby jeopardizing the inestimable progress made just after national independence.

A first glance at the data reveals a high peak corresponding to the heading 'law', followed by the headings 'family' and 'work'. This observation should, however, be qualified, for there seems to have been a development in the order of priority of research themes over the 1968–1978 period. For example, until 1968, the theme 'family' was in the lead, and accounted for more than half the publications. From 1968 onwards and until 1972, the dominant themes concerned 'legal' matters (more than fifty per cent), while at the same time the heading 'planning' emerged. Lastly, from 1972 to 1978, the heading 'law' (marriage, divorce, custody of children, etc.) remained at the same level and reached ninety per cent for Algeria. At the same time, two new themes emerged: modernization and emigration, which are connected with an expanding area of social pathology (delinquency).

These two new themes are obviously connected with the problems of urban sprawl and the top-heaviness of North African capitals as a result of a large-scale population drift from the land. Difficult living conditions in a deteriorating urban environment are described with increasing frequency. The following titles speak for themselves: 'Women and housing', 'Women alone in Algerian society', 'Urban women and health problems'. Women's emigration is at last beginning to attract the attention of researchers (M. Lacoste Du Jardin 1975; H. Brahimi 1980).

Comparative assessment of present trends in research on women in North Africa, on the basis of case-studies and content analysis

Tunisia

After systematically searching through the Bibliographical Index of the Journal of the Economic and Social Studies and Research Centre of the University of Tunis (for the years 1964–1979), we were in a position to describe the state of the art of research on women in Tunisia and its main trends, as shown in Table 2.2.

Table 2.2 Research on women in Tunisia, 1964–1979

Heading	Number of publications	Discipline involved
History Anthropology	3	History Sociology
Family	10	Sociology
Work	7	Sociology
Sexuality Prostitution	3	Sociology
Family planning	35	Demography
Total	58	

Family planning

The issue of family planning takes the lead in the volume of research carried out (60 per cent). This means that women are studied from the narrow angle of their traditional role as mothers, which has, however, been reversed today in terms of a policy against an increased birthrate. The large amount of research carried out reflects the concern shown by international organizations and national authorities for the practice of birth control, and Tunisia is one of the North African countries to take the keenest interest in this issue. It should also be pointed out that the status of women in Tunisia is one of the highest in the Arab world (note the prohibition of repudiation, abolition of polygamy, right to divorce for the woman, and possibility of retaining custody of children). This status is further strengthened by a bold policy on a woman's right to terminate pregnancy by abortion or to restrict births by the use of readily available contraceptives.

This new and unprecedented right of the Arab woman to take control, without interference, of her own body and her sexuality will call for future study of its manifold socio-cultural and psychological repercussions. For the time being, however, research in this field seems to be concerned mainly with the effectiveness of birth control and with changing attitudes and opinions relating to it.

Family

This theme is nearly always discussed by sociologists in contrast with the preceding theme, on which demographers have a monopoly. The research often focuses on changes in family structure and in the status and roles of members of the family in a society in transition. Some surveys stand out from the mass by virtue of their scientific rigour (for example, C. Camilleri 1967).

Work

This theme is one of the most recent, dating from approximately the mid-1970s, and it is often studied by women. Although Tunisian women have always participated in the country's economy, their access to paid employment and skilled occupations is recent. The acceleration of the urban growth rate (47 per cent of the Tunisian population lives in the towns), and the enactment of the Law of April 1972 concerning subcontracting firms, have encouraged the emergence of a female proletariat recruited for the most part in the new textile sector (80 per cent of the labour force is female and unmarried, aged between 15 and 25). The rate of employment of this labour falls as the rate of marriage rises, as we see that the home is still in competition with employment in society (N. Karoui 1975).

Most women workers are unqualified and have had only a few years' schooling. Most are the bread-winners of poor families, and they are usually of rural origin. The studies carried out in Tunisia confirm the data already gathered in other regions of the Third World with regard to certain characteristics of women's employment: women are concentrated in lowly occupations (49 per cent are manual workers, 34 per cent are office workers), especially in poorly-paid occupations of the non-structural sector: crafts, domestic service, small trades, prostitution, etc.; 28 per cent of working women are domestic cleaners in Tunisia.

In some parts of the secondary sector (food), women's employment is sporadic and of an impermanent nature (because work in this sector is often seasonal). Generally speaking, the development of employment over the past twenty years in Tunisia has benefited men rather than women. For example, 75 per cent of educated girls are seeking work.

In the non-formal sector, that of domestic service (28 per cent of all working women), we have at present no information that might enable us to discuss aspects peculiar to this category of women. Future research should strive for more accurate coverage of the female population concentrated in the lowest grade and least sought-after types of work, for here are to be found the exploited and silent majority of women (Amal Rassam) who will show astonishing potential for social regeneration in times to come. Furthermore, the impact of women's work on the crisis affecting the institution of the family should provide material for future research, not in an ideological or moralizing vein, but of a more scientific and substantial kind, related to structural changes in society as a whole.

Libyan Arab Jamahiriya

The very small amount of work that we have been able to examine on the Libyan Arab Jamahiriya does not concern women directly, but mentions in passing that their status is a crucial problem. We find that their participation in working life is virtually nil, and that this society is extremely dependent on imported foreign labour (F. Mernissi 1978). Furthermore, there is an Islamic revival among women themselves, due to their problems of status in a society supposedly founded on the levelling out of inequalities (*North African Directory*, 1972).

Mixed marriages of Libyan men with foreign Arab women, mostly Egyptians, are a blow to the dignity of Libyan women. There is a recrudescence of polygamy, following the 'economic oil boom' phase. Indeed, the distribution of incomes from oil, because of the non-adult status to which women are confined, has primarily benefited male society. In this way, high incomes are paradoxically increasing women's subjugation in this region.

Women react to this situation by seeking to take refuge in such sectors as Islam and theology. Nevertheless, the social and family problems caused by polygamy and divorce, and the reduction of women to passive and consenting victims, are producing a state of unrest that future studies on women in these regions should investigate further in order to understand them and to bring them under control.

Algeria

On the whole, published research emphasizes the failure of the revolution to achieve true liberation for women as Fanon understood it; there has been a steady erosion of their status. In 1964, the Charter of Algiers was a pioneering piece of writing which was rapidly abandoned. In the national Charter adopted on 27 June 1976, which maps out Algerian socialism's ideological shape and purpose, only one page deals with the problems of Algerian women (J. Minces 1978). The emancipation of women seems all the more superfluous in that Algeria is moving towards a highly technological industry and cutting down on manpower. The influence of conservative religious groups is strong. The status of Algerian women is far lower than that of Tunisian women. The government seems to be sacrificing the struggle for women's liberation in order to win broader support from the mass of the people and buttress its authority (Minces 1978; F. Diabi 1980).

Some research attempts to attribute the failure of the revolution for women in Algeria to the lower-middle class nature of the Algerian State (J. Minces), whereas others emphasize the gap between an advanced and capitalist-dependent economic development model and a cultural sphere in which tradition still holds sway (A. Baffoun 1979).

Morocco

Interesting studies have been carried out in this country against a background of new and dynamic research (V. Maher 1978; F. Mernissi 1978). These studies seek to deal differently with women according to the socio-economic level and social groupings to which they belong. They discuss the role of magic, religion and the re-emergence of certain sects as a counter-culture used by women as a reaction against their exclusion from the formal economic sector appropriated by men (Fernéa 1972; Mernissi 1978; Rosen 1978).

Most research criticizes the traumatic nature of the dominant development model. It emphasizes its undesirable repercussions on the already precarious economic circumstances of the female population, and its influence on socio-cultural structures (exemplified by the increase in divorce and prostitution rates).

Features of women's employment in North Africa—current research trends (1980): Morocco, Algeria, Tunisia

Current research findings, particularly about North African women's role as active members of society and as workers, are highly relevant to the social sciences for accurate diagnosis of women's position in these emergent societies.

If access to employment and to paid work is a pointer to a society's development, it is apparent from the various studies that the North African region is still well below acceptable standards, especially where women's employment is concerned. For example, in Algeria, the rate of women's participation in the working population is one of the lowest in the world, and its rate of increase is slow (rate of employment: 1.82 per cent in 1966 and 2.61 per cent in 1977). For Tunisia and Morocco, where the rate of women's employment is increasing rapidly (6 per cent in 1966 and 18.7 per cent in 1975 for Tunisia), identification of this population and its hierarchical ordering on the scale of increase is difficult, for most working women, both in the agricultural sector and outside it, are still not wage-earners.

Study of the data on women's share in the working population in North Africa prompts the following preliminary remarks:

(a) The female working population was mainly agricultural until the 1960s, but there has been a sharp falling off as a result of the destruction of the countryside. Even the 'green revolution' in Algeria, which has had extremely encouraging results in the sphere of agrarian reform, has been unable (particularly because of the strong technological pull that it exerts) to stabilize the

Table 2.3 Comparative rates of women's participation in employment in various regions of the world

Developed countries 1966	Underdeveloped countries 1966	West Africa 1966	Morocco 1976	Tunisia 1975	Algeria 1977
26.8	22.9	38	26	18.5	2.61

work-force, including the female work-force (23.35 per cent in 1966; 5.71 per cent in 1977): this plummeting rate of employment for women coincides with the choice of 'self-management' and the invasion of rural areas by male wage-earners.

(b) However, for North Africa as a whole, the erosion of women's employment in the agricultural sector should be seen in the light of a statistical underestimation of rural women who, for the most part, do not receive wages. The greater part of women's farming work in rural areas remains invisible and is not recorded, because it nearly always takes place on the family farm, or as impermanent seasonal work.

(c) Since the decline of agriculture, the non-agricultural sector has developed considerably in North Africa, and is still the leading source of employment for women. Its expansion has been encouraged by girls' access to schooling, and it is increasing more rapidly than male rates of employment in this sector (in Morocco and Tunisia).

However, women's work is still 'urban', is concentrated mainly in big cities, and is channelled into two sectors of the economy: the service and administration sector; and the industrial sector (subcontracting). (See Table 2.4 below).

Favourable circumstances for private initiatives have led to the establishment of processing factories (especially textiles), eager to employ skilled young women, especially in Morocco and Tunisia. The rise of the industrial sector has been encouraged by a code of investment granting tax relief to firms which create new jobs, and as a result, more than half the female labour force is employed by industry in some cases (Morocco). However, for both Morocco and Tunisia, industrialization is proving to be still incapable of satisfying all the job-seekers, whether men or women.

In Algeria, the majority of women are employed in administration and services (70 per cent); however, it is not impossible that the establishment of electronics factories, as shown in the development plans, will boost women's employment in the industrial sector to a much greater degree in the future.

Throughout North Africa, the increase in the number of wage-earners is to be found mainly in the service sector (ninety per cent of permanent wage-earners) and not in industry, which shows too high a proportion of trainees and apprentices.

Table 2.4 Comparative breakdown of the female working population in
North Africa by branch of economic activity (percentage)

	Morocco 1976	Tunisia 1975	Algeria 1977
Agriculture	11.6	11.3	5.7
Water, electricity, energy, factory work	0.4	0.7	–
Building, public works	0.3	0.9	2.05
Processing industry	52.3	35.5	17.25
Transport, communications	0.6	2.4	–
Commerce	4.2	7.3	–
Service	21.7	41.8	69.29
Administration	9.9	–	–
Other	–	–	5.71

Sources: data supplied by M. Abzahd for Morocco, F. Hayder and F. Diabi for Algeria, and 1975 census for Tunisia (see bibliography).

(d) Even in the non-agricultural sector, where the rate of women's employment is relatively well-defined, we find it impossible to identify more precisely this working population and its hierarchical structure in a particular occupation (see Table 2.5).

A more detailed and hierarchical account of the occupations and incomes of women in North Africa is needed, for it could illuminate and render more conspicuous the 'pockets of economic activity', most of them non-formal, which cater more particularly for the deprived urban fringe of the North African female population.

In short, although the labour market in North Africa is beginning to provide some employment for women, the proportion seems ludicrous, since it does not even amount to one million for the three countries together (139,000 in Algeria, 690,000 in Morocco and 116,000 in Tunisia), and is characterized by an extremely narrow range of skills (factory work and services). Furthermore, wage-earning, which is an indicator of development and of a society's economic take-off, is limited, and women's share in wage-earning is still meagre. Some research reveals (Tunisia) unemployment of intellectuals among women, affecting a sizeable proportion of women in the professions.

As for the great majority of non-wage-earning women, outside agriculture (approximately 47 per cent in Tunisia, 38 per cent in Morocco and 6 per cent in Algeria), they remain in an economic 'no man's land' that the statistics show under the headings 'independent' and 'home helps' (see Table 2.5).

For the sake of improved understanding of women's work and of the

Table 2.5 Comparative distribution of the North African female working
population by occupation (percentage)

	Morocco 1976	Tunisia 1975	Algeria 1977
Employers or proprietors	0.6	–	–
Independent	31.2	31.5	2
Wage-earners	54.5	40.6	94
Home helps	6.7	24.2	4
Apprentices	7.0	3.4	4

sociological content of North African society, it is necessary to define more
clearly in future the various characteristics of this non-wage-earning situation
among working women, and its manifold implications.

It would seem that North African women have overcome the formidable,
age-old barrier that hitherto kept them out of the world of work, the office, the
street and the school, thereby attaining an improvement in their status; now,
they must go a stage further and gain access to a broader spectrum of occupations and to posts of responsibility, this being the *sine qua non* of a harmonious
and equitable society.

Priorities for scientific research on women in North Africa today

Any scientific work on the status of women in North Africa today must necessarily start from the following methodological premises:

(a) North Africa consists of social groupings which have developed unevenly,
and which have been determined by the expansion of a dependent, capitalist-
inspired pattern of production. This general structure is apparent in all the
workings of society, and causes its specific features. No sector of social reality
can escape this overall determination.

The state of economic dependence in particular, and the unequal terms of
trade between the societies of North Africa and the developed and dominant
countries, imbue every level of practical living in North African society with
its characteristic historical flavour. For example, in order to analyse such phenomena as shanty-towns, unemployment, prostitution or the revival of tradition,
it is necessary, from the methodological point of view, to see them in the light
of the master plan for the form of development which, in the last analysis, is
what determines them; i.e., the dependent, capitalist-inspired pattern of development. The phenomena mentioned above were brought about by the dismantling
of the rural and urban economy, the weakening of the original bonds that held
tribes or villages together, and the violent intrusion of commercial relations

competing with relations honoured by custom. Hence the need, with a view to reconstructing the particular historical causes of such a process of social change, for an effort of imagination and a revitalized theory in order to rethink, along critical lines, such concepts as development, progress, evolution, women's liberation, etc.

(b) To this first general methodological approach made necessary by the structure of dependence, must be added a specific approach to the biological differences between men and women, which have served as a pretext for sexual inequality and the double moral standard (what a man can do and a woman must not do). In this context, the subordination of North African women to men poses the same theoretical and practical problems (of substance) as the problems posed for women in the modern developed world. All studies conducted in this field in the West are therefore of great value here.

Aspects (a) and (b), then, map out the general theoretical framework for any scientific research on women in North Africa today. Taking this framework as our starting-point, we recommend three priority areas:

1   Encourage all work of scientific renewal, and in particular construct paradigms or theories of medium scope, capable of revitalizing research on women.

2   Promote *ad hoc* research (empirical and practical) designed to provide more detailed practical information about women and their lives. It would be worthwhile to direct some of the research towards the North African woman's self-image and experience of the world in which she lives. By this means, certain hypotheses can be invalidated or confirmed.

3   These basic facts and their comparison (by region, social class, age-group, etc.), should lead to better knowledge of the problems of women in North Africa today. One might also draw up a list of suggestions or priorities, in education, health, and social or legal matters, so as to improve, on reliable foundations, the status of women and their position in modern society.

We are now able to single out priorities for future research:

(i) Compilation of a basic bibliography on the theoretical and conceptual aspects of women's problems in general.

(ii) Setting up of a data bank and a specialized bibliography on North African women.

(iii) Studies aimed at better knowledge of new forms of oppression and exploitation of women in North Africa. Along these general lines, several topics may already be suggested:

the socio-historical development of women's status in North Africa (on the basis of analysis of common law, in contrast with current legislation);

the role of superstructure and ideology in perpetuating the 'innatist' image of women, conducive to their subordinate status (with reference to literary and artistic output, the mass media and the theatre, and everyday official writings);

the various forms of violence against women in North Africa. A list of these, assessment of their extent and causes (e.g. verbal aggression, rape, physical assault), and the passive or active reactions of women (suicide, divorce, delinquency, prostitution and mental illness);

the special case of women in rural areas;

women in the non-formal urban sector. The female proletariat. Domestic service (28 per cent of the working urban population in some cases). The non-formal clandestine sector;

emigration to other countries and its impact on the status and circumstances of women;

sexual repression in North African society in its various guises, and repercussions on the present status of women;

women and social class.

This list is only an outline. It nevertheless gives some idea of a series of research priorities, whose accomplishment would be so many milestones on the road to recognition for North African women.

Concluding remarks

In the case of North Africa, it would seem that the independence movement has not culminated in full liberation of the economic and social structures of the Maghreb area, which remain tethered to the old colonial mother country and to the rest of the capitalist world. Nevertheless, the lure of the capitalist model is still present for North Africa and, verbally at least, it associates the emancipation of women with the development of society.

Moreover, the proposed emancipation of women stems, at best (Tunisia), only from deliberate action on the part of the state, and not from the demands of the rank and file. This blueprint is centred on the need to improve women's legal status (in this respect, Tunisia is ahead of its North African neighbours). Thus the drive for universal schooling aims to reach a statisfactorily large proportion of both girls and boys. Indeed, if the facts are studied, they reveal that the traditional order impinges on the new code of conduct, and customs nearly always fall short of the law (C. Camilleri 1967, F. Mernissi 1978, M. Tessler).

The working, wage earning female population is still very small. It represents 5 per cent of the working urban population in Algeria, 15 per cent in Morocco and 20 per cent in Tunisia (J. Minces); in positions of authority, women are virtually unrepresented (N. Karoui 1976, Oufriha 1980, F. Diabi 1980).

The need for 'liberation' of the African woman is therefore twofold: at work she is exploited by her employer, and in the family she is exploited by male domination which steadily endures, against all the odds. Everything seems to indicate a desire to punish the working woman and make her feel guilty. As for the housewife (3.5 million women of working age stay at home in Algeria), the family code, in the event of repudiation, leaves her totally destitute from the economic point of view (Morocco, Libyan Arab Jamahiriya and Algeria). Most research (Libyan Arab Jamahiriya, Morocco, Algeria and Tunisia) further emphasizes the phenomenon of the resurgence of tradition and its 'retrograde' effects on the few improvements achieved in the status of women in this region (Tessler 1978).

Furthermore, the ambivalent emancipation of women is not achieved without conflict. Recent studies (F. M'rabet (1979), N. Kacha (1979) for Algeria and Sleim Ammar (1974) for Tunisia) emphasize the neurotic reactions that such a situation causes, with their repercussions on the family unit initially, and later on society as a whole. Suicide rates are steadily increasing, as are rates of mental illness and psychosomatic disturbances. In 1964, in the city of Algiers alone, 175 suicide attempts due to forced marriages were recorded. In Tunisia, since 1970, there have been three suicide attempts by women for every one attempt by a man. F. M'rabet relates: 'It is as if, at the time of the liberation, girls were forward-looking and filled with extraordinary hope: they were sure of changes. But nobody answered their hopes, and nothing has changed; in their disappointment, they have given up, and are taking their revenge in this way.'

More recent studies (N. Kacha 1979) carried out in Algeria confirm that psychopathological disorders are becoming more acute. For example, the number of women psychiatric patients is greater than the equivalent figure for men, and has been steadily growing since this society's attainment of its independence. It is especially within the new social stratum of young, urban, working women (aged between 24 and 29) that records show most clinical depression, brought about by a situation of conflict between opposing values, incompatible with the new status of women.

When these young women have attended primary and secondary school, they are more sensitive to frustrations than illiterate women of the same age, and more vulnerable to psychopathological disorders. It is among working-class women in towns that the highest rates of deviance and 'disturbance' are to be found: prostitution, thieving, alcoholism and adultery—the consequences of the breakdown of the tribal, patriarchal family and the contradictions resulting from the new structure of the emergent society, which is still inegalitarian and sexist.

BIBLIOGRAPHY

Abzahd, M. 'Dispositif d'enquête-période sur l'emploi urbain au Maroc', IVe Colloque de démographie maghrébine, Hammamet (Tunisia), 1980.
Adamson, K. 'Perspectives on the position of women in Algeria', University of Leeds, 1975.
Amin, S. *Féminisme et luttes des classes*, Editions de minuit, 1974.
Ammar, S. 'Le suicide en Tunisie', University of Tunis, 1974.
Anonymous 'No easy exit from slavery behind the veil in Algeria', in *Arab Society in Transition*, Cairo, AUC, 1977.
Baffoun, A. 'Femmes et développement dans le Maghreb moderne', in *Socio-analyse de l'origine de l'inégalité*, IDEP, Dakar, 1977.
Belloumi, A. *Le salariat en Tunisie en 1975*, Tunis, INS, 1980.
Borrmans, N. *Statut personnel et famille au Maghreb de 1970 à nos jours*, Paris, Mouton, 1977.
Brahimi, M. 'L'émigration des Maghrébines', IVe Colloque de démographie maghrébine, Hammamet (Tunisia), 1980.
Camilleri, C. 'Modernity and the family in Tunisia', *Journal of Marriage and the Family* 29, 1967.
Chaliand, C. and J. Minces. *L'Algérie indépendante*, Paris, Editions Maspéro, 1972.
Chateur, S. *La Tunisienne—citoyenne ou sujet*, Tunis, 1977.
Dammak, R. *La main-d'oeuvre féminine dans l'industrie de l'habillement*, Tunis, 1976.
Diabi, F. 'L'emploi féminin en Algérie', Chantilly Symposium (France), CNRS, May 1980.
Fanon, F. *Sociologie d'une révolution*, Paris, Editions Maspéro, 1959.
Fernea, R. 'Variation in religious observance among Islamic women', in *Scholars, Saints and Sufis: Muslim religious institutions in the Middle East since 1500* (N. R. Keddie, ed.), Berkeley (Calif.), 1972.
Hayder, F. and R. Ait Hamon. *Quelques données sur l'emploi en milieu urbain et rural*, Algiers, AARDES, 1980.
Hilse Dwyer, D. 'Women, Sufism and Decision-making in Morocco Islam', in Keddie and Beck, 1978.
Kacha, N. 'La situation et les aspirations de la femme algérienne', Thèse de 3e cycle, Sorbonne, Paris, 1979.
Karoui, N. 'Famille et travail: les ouvrières de Manzel Bourguiba', *RTSS*, No. 45, 1976.
Keddie, N. and L. Beck (eds.). *Women in the Muslim World*, Cambridge, Mass., Harvard University Press, 1978.
Maher, V. 'Women and social change in Morocco', in Keddie and Beck, 1978.
Mernissi, F. *Country Report on Women in North Africa*, United Nations, 1978.
M'rabet, F. *Les Algériennes*, Paris, Editions Maspéro, 1979.
Oufriha Bonzina, F. Z. 'La place de la femme dans l'activité économique en Algérie', IVe Colloque de démographie maghrébine, Hammamet (Tunisia), 1980.
Ottaway, D. and M. *Algeria: the politics of a socialist revolution*, University of California Press, 1970.
Rosen, L. 'The negotiation of reality: Male–female relations in Sefrou, Morocco', in Keddie and Beck, 1978.

Stambouli, F. *Some characteristics of urban immigrant society in the Maghreb*, Binghamton University, 1979.
Tillion, G. *Le harem et ses cousins*, Paris, Editions du Seuil, 1966.
Zghal, A. 'Reactivation of tradition in post-traditional society', in *Arab Society in Transition*, Cairo, AUC, 1977.

Documents

Annuaire de l'Afrique du Nord (North Africa Directory), Paris, CNRS.
Fourth Maghreb Demography Symposium on 'Labour and employment in the Maghreb countries', Maghreb Association for Population Studies, Hammamet (Tunisia), 9–13 June 1980.
National censuses of 1966 and 1975, Tunisia, National Institute of Statistics.
Review of Economic and Social Studies and Research, Tunis, Study and Research Centre.

3   Research in the Social Sciences on Women in Morocco
AICHA BELARBI

Research in the social sciences is so closely related to the development of society that it is necessary, first, to define the aims of research in clear terms, establish priorities and make choices among the various possible lines to follow, and, secondly, to regard development in a new way, as an integrated process with man as its centre, i.e. both its source and its goal.

In Morocco, however, research in the social sciences enjoys only marginal status. The Institute of Sociology was closed down in 1971, and sociology became merely an optional subject in the philosophy section of the Faculty of Letters, despite the fact that the problems confronting people in such a profoundly changing society demand a planned and coherent policy of scientific research in this field.

Research in the social sciences on women has developed differently according to the historical period and even the region in question. Such writings or studies as have been produced have, moreover, been the work of individuals and institutions, native or foreign, with widely differing points of view and aims.

A critical bibliography on the subject of women in Morocco is, then, urgently needed. It is a long-term task requiring years of work by interdisciplinary teams, for, as has already been said, the texts are of various kinds and scattered among different publications and universities. There is a mass of information and of studies on women waiting to be brought together, codified, analysed and placed in the relevant historical, political and social context.

This bibliographical research will enable us to throw light on the subject itself of our study: the position of women in Morocco. We shall accordingly identify the various bibliographical trends—i.e. the areas that have been studied in depth, and those that have been either merely touched on or neglected altogether —and in conclusion indicate lines for further research.

Studies on the position of women in Morocco range from straightforward impressions, comparisons and value judgements to genuine scientific studies.

The studies carried out while Morocco was still a protectorate were rudimentary, limited and often ethnocentric. Their object was to gain knowledge of family life and the position of women in Morocco in order to help incorporate Moroccans (men, women, the younger generations, and so on) more effectively into the stream of French culture and the system of capitalist production, while preserving the exotic element represented by Moroccan culture itself. Independence, the crisis in structures, and changes in theory of development led later

researchers to concentrate more on economic and political studies, with sociological research often restricted to rural life. No particular need was felt for
work on women and the family. It was not until around 1969–1970 that some
teachers and students began to be interested in these themes, and made them the
subject of theses and newspaper articles published on such occasions as elections,
International Women's Year in 1975 and the International Year of the Child in
1979.

The lack of interest in the question of women, reflected in the rarity of
serious studies on the subject, is evidence of the survival and enduring nature
of a prevailing ideology of conservatism which confines women to the home and
the sort of work connected with it, isolating them from the active and productive outside world even when they actually form part of it. This ideology,
internalized and accepted by most men and even most women, and implying the
exclusion of the latter at all levels—political, economic, social and cultural—is
one that we come across again in the field of research.

We do not claim here to provide an exhaustive bibliography on the subject of
women in Morocco, but we will attempt, through the list established and the
works consulted (certain early works no longer exist and others are not available
on loan) to identify the various trends and reveal the ideological basis of the
authors. It will show a surprising lack of studies in Arabic. There were very few
of these during the protectorate, apart from some newspaper articles. In the
period following independence the subject was frequently dealt with in theses
presented in the faculties of letters and of law, at the higher teacher-training
college (Ecole normale supérieure) in the training school for senior personnel in
the Ministry of Health, in the National School of Public Administration, and so
on. To cover the whole field would require a longer and more systematic investigation than is possible here.

HISTORICAL AND SOCIO-POLITICAL CONTEXT

Period I: Before the protectorate

For this period we shall confine ourselves to certain nineteenth and early
twentieth-century works, nearly all travel books, which contain scraps of information about Moroccan women. From these accounts four themes emerge.

The inaccessible world of Muslim women

When he wanted to paint or sketch figures during a visit to Morocco in 1832,
Eugène Delacroix encountered great reluctance on the part of the Muslim population. According to Roland Lebel,[1] 'unable to paint people unhindered because
they shied away, Delacroix fell back on horses'.

While Muslim women were unapproachable both at home and even out of doors whenever they ventured forth, Jewish women seemed much more free, because they were not veiled and thus more accessible to the eye. It was his glimpses of them that enabled Delacroix to paint his 'Jewish Wedding in Morocco'. André Chevrillon, who was introduced into a rich Jewish family, gave a minute description of the beauty, dress and mild submissive manners of the women.

Pierre Loti and Gabriel Charmes explained at length that women could be seen properly only in their own environment, cut off from the outside world, on the terraces of their houses. Delacroix, denied this access, said: 'The jealousy of the Moors is extreme. . . . They are people that belong to the past. . . . This life outside the home, these closed-up houses, these cloistered women'.

The exotic appeal of the woman's world

This unapproachable, invisible, unknowable world stimulated the imagination of foreign travellers, who gave extravagant descriptions of the dresses of the women they had glimpsed on the terraces of their houses, their stately carriage beneath all those layers of clothes, their haunting and provocative smiles. Some visitors even claimed to have established a liaison with them via the terraces, but one is inclined to be sceptical about these boasts.

Glimpses of the world of the women

These travellers, especially those who stayed in the large towns, were very intrigued by the life of the women of the harem. R. Ladreit de Lacharrière, probably the only woman to travel all over Morocco before the protectorate, describes the harem of the pasha of Marrakesh, noting that it included Turkish women. She gives a detailed account of this world of women as objects, covering dress, activities, relationships and so on. While R. Ladreit actually entered the shadowy world of the women, other travellers had to rely on the inhabitants, or on Algerian and other foreign residents, for information about prostitution, the quarters where it was practised, and the part played by old women in these matters.

Education and culture

Feminine culture as reflected in these accounts is mainly traditional, with considerable emphasis on magic and superstition.

Reference to the education of girls is rare, for few of them went to the Koranic schools of the period, and those that did left at the age of eleven or twelve. R. Ladreit reports that the daughters of the pasha of Marrakesh were given some religious instruction within the palace up to the age of twelve. Other accounts mention modern Jewish education, and the Jewish women teachers who came and shut themselves up in the *mellah* or Jewish quarter in order to civilize the Jews and help the women towards emancipation.

This cocooned world of the women, hardly known and little understood, was approached differently under the protectorate, which possessed the material, psychological and methodological means of penetrating and bringing influence to bear on the Moroccan environment. The Moroccan people reacted against this interference, but the constant cultural contact with the other presence nevertheless produced changes.

Period II: 1912-1956—Under the protectorate

The years 1943-1944 mark a turning point in the history of the French protectorate in Morocco. Up till 1934, the year of the 'pacification', the prevailing policy was the bloodthirsty and repressive one derived from that of General Lyautey, which denied direct rule and refused to respect Islam, the Makhzan or native Moroccan administration, the religious confraternities or their centres, the Zaouias. Both policies aimed at one goal: to get an insight into Moroccan life so as to bring influence to bear on it more effectively. In 1944 this approach was succeeded by a more liberal central policy which tried to bring the 'Moroccans' into the public and political life of their country. Furthermore, with the economic crisis which widened the gulf between the exploiters and the exploited, and as a result of the growth of both Moroccan and Arab nationalism, the people of Morocco openly called for the decolonization of their country.

The change in colonial policy in 1944 was not intentional, but rather the result of internal struggles and of external pressure and influences, in particular the United Nations decisions on decolonization.

First phase: 1912-1944

The scientific mission set up in Tangiers in 1904 and subsequently directed by Michaux Bellaire was, as he said, designed to 'seek documentation available on the spot which would lend itself to the study of Morocco and the reconstitution of its organization and way of life, not only through books and manuscripts but also through oral information and the traditions of tribes, confraternities and the family'. Areas of inquiry included more especially the family, with its structures, organization and internal relationships, and the customs, values, etc. governing those relationships. A not inconsiderable place was accorded to women in these studies.

The research was socio-ethnological in character; specifically sociological studies were rare. But for reasons of clarity we shall consider as sociological studies all those that dealt with women in relation to social and domestic organization and with the evolution of the position of women. Ethnological studies deal with such subjects as women's dress, tattooing and beliefs.

The following themes emerge from these studies.

Dichotomization

The predominance of studies of this kind is in accordance with the colonialist maxim of divide and rule. A division was established between rural and urban women, Berber and Arab women, proletarian and bourgeois women, as if there were no common factor linking them all, and no such thing as the Moroccan woman herself. This distinction was part of a wider division of the whole Moroccan population into Arabs and Berbers which was reflected in the Berber dahir or royal decree of 1930.

The distinction between rural and urban women only confirmed the separation between Arab and Berber; the following passage from G. Hardy is very explicit on the subject:

> To this liberty [that of women in the country], to this active and public role, the peasant woman owes her robust personality. She is coquettish, probably preoccupied with her looks. . . . But she is not just a harem doll. She is a strong character, proud in her bearing, brave, even indomitable, and ready if necessary to rush into the fray. [The women of the towns] are women bent under the yoke of laws [those of Islam] and customs, and seem to have been stripped for ever of freedom and dignity.[2]

Domestic organization and women's place in society

Family organization was often examined, with the emphasis on the patriarchal structure of the family, the excessive authority of the father and the total submission of the women and children. From the cloistered women of the town to the unveiled women of the country, none escaped masculine power. The stress on feminine submissiveness and the lower status of women in these texts helps to point out their ethnocentricity. Although they supply minute and detailed description, they fail to provide any analysis in depth and make no attempt to seek out the informal structures and the latent feminine authority which played an important role both in the family and in society.

Another aspect which interested these colonial writers was polygamy and the life of the harem. The relations between co-wives was often described, together with the intrigues and the use of witchcraft involved. The popular tales recorded reflect this situation. Life in the harem was seen as slow, idle and monotonous. The women got used to it, and manipulated things in the hope of one day achieving some power.

Prostitution was often dealt with, together with the changes introduced under the protectorate, when the activity was subjected to rigorous discipline and health regulations.

Women and class

Two socio-economic levels appear to predominate in these studies: the proletariat and the ordinary middle classes. This was because the upper middle classes were still inaccessible, and little attention was paid to women living in the country.

The women of the proletariat were represented by those who worked as domestics in French families. A maid was almost always a newcomer to the city who retained her links with her rural background. What emerges from the chapters in these monographs devoted to the subject of these 'maids' is France's civilizing mission, one combined with paternalism and a limited generosity. The authors paint a general picture of the birth of the female proletariat in Morocco —a proletariat manipulated and exploited by France. The religion, beliefs and superstitions of these women are brought to the fore, mainly with the idea of showing the pagan and magical dimension still lurking behind Islam.

The women of the ordinary middle classes were studied only in the town of Fez. But the detailed description given of them is ambiguous. Sometimes they are represented negatively as superstitious illiterates, and sometimes positively, as intelligent, resourceful and active within their limited sphere.

Ethnography

This type of study deals either with women's adornment, dress, jewellery, tattooing, etc., or with beliefs, myths and witchcraft.

Much attention was devoted to women's dress. Berber costume was studied according to region, urban costume according to town and socio-economic level. The *haik* (an outdoor garment rather like a *burnous* worn in the towns) puzzled many foreign observers, who were surprised by the bright and garish colours. Tattooing was presented as an integral part of Moroccan folklore, a tourist attraction. Small wonder that official tourist brochures carried illustrated articles on body tattooing, often classified as one of the native arts.

Women emerge as illogical, superstitious, the guardians of tradition, according to the documentation collected by Mrs A. R. de Lens on the subject of medicine as understood and practised by the natives of Morocco, by the women. Through access to people's homes, information was obtained from both old and young women about practices relating to medicine, witchcraft and beauty. At this period, women did play an important role in the care of the sick, and they were often hostile to the prescriptions and recommendations of European doctors, attempting to neutralize them by the use of their own practices and beliefs.

French 'action' in Morocco as regards women

There is a mass of statistical data on education for girls and aid to women in childbirth. Modern schooling for girls and hospital maternity services were both new departures introduced by the protectorate. But both innovations met with resistance; the people felt safer in their own institutions.

Women and the law

These texts favour Berber customary law relating to women. Islamic law is referred to only for purposes of comparison, and is represented as inferior to Berber customary law, primarily on the subject of repudiation.

Change

The contact between French and Moroccan culture produced some shocks and some adjustments, with cultural traits being exchanged in both directions.

The first change affecting women came through the acceptance of various imported articles such as fabrics and ornaments. The second change came through the education of girls, the 'modern school' teaching them housewifery and child care, and through the paid employment of women, although this was on a limited scale.

The school enrolment of girls and access by women to paid employment were key factors in changing the situation of women in Morocco; the changes that occurred disrupted family life and relationships to the extent that the patriarchal family structure came under attack.

Second phase: 1945–1956

French penetration of Morocco, with the imposition of a new economic system and a new cultural policy, although these were not accepted in their entirety or were assimilated imperfectly, had a destructive effect on Moroccan society. It brought about changes in the smallest social unit, the family, and this had both direct and indirect effects on the position of women.

The crisis which hit Morocco after the Second World War, the development of a proletariat and a subproletariat, together with the growth of the nationalist movement and of Moroccan private schools, led the representatives of the protectorate to introduce partial reforms in favour of the inhabitants as regards both employment and education.

It was during this period that Robert Montagne conducted an extensive and important survey on the Moroccan proletariat, including more than eighty studies on the rural exodus and life among newcomers to the towns.

The following themes emerge from these studies.

The female proletariat

Many studies were made at this period on the proletarian family, its composition, contradictions and expectations. In 1950, under the direction of Robert Montagne, A. M. Baron carried out a survey of the proletarian family which revealed maladjustment, instability and failure to adapt among families which had emigrated to the city of Casablanca.

Women's entry into the world of paid employment and economic independence gave them a certain amount of power within the family; they sometimes managed the whole household. This was a source of marital conflict and instability. The changed living conditions arising from emigration and paid employment led to new attitudes and behaviour among women which were reflected in their relationship with men—for example in their choice of a husband and the age at which they married. A new family structure appeared among the proletariat: that of the conjugal family. But this change brought problems with it, the most obvious being the challenging of parental and marital authority, a series of divorces and the setting up of one new family after another.

Broken marriages

Family disunity was a result of an imposed change as yet imperfectly assimilated by the people concerned. It was also the consequence of an acute material crisis which turned the woman into a potential worker in support of the home, often manipulated by the man. The fragility of marriages and the ease with which they were contracted was often noted among the poor, and entailed chronic family instability. In rich families where there were more possessions to be safeguarded, marriages seemed stronger and more durable.

Social classes in the face of modernization and the evolution of women

While family structures were greatly disrupted among the proletariat, where women emerged as an important element in social change, in the middle classes (according to some authors) women acted as a brake on change. A. Adam observed that the advancement of the middle classes in general and their aspiration towards modernization was to some extent hindered by the backwardness of the women and the survival of patriarchial family structures.

The bourgeoisie in the big towns seemed to be changing rapidly. Great changes were noted among the women as regards clothing, infant care, etc. But this progress was only superficial, and the old families, with their rigid principles, prevented women from embarking on out-and-out modernization. The only real factor of change resided in the schools, which after 1947 began to attract many more girls. This trend was encouraged by progressive moves on the part of the monarchy and of the nationalist party.

The position of women changed gradually from generation to generation. Changes were mostly superficial, and affected only a very small part of the population (women in country areas seem to have been left out). Even in working class circles, where the women seemed to enjoy more freedom in the form of outdoor excursions, visits to the cinema with their fiancés, paid employment and so on, this liberty disappeared with marriage and childbearing or when their husbands found a permanent job, giving place to complete submission to the traditional demands of married life.

Women and ethnography

Studies of this kind continued to flourish, their authors still laying emphasis on tattooing and its more recent interpretations. The exotic appeal of Moroccan women was often suggested through the songs and costumes which reflected their way of life.

French 'action' in Morocco in relation to women

Studies on this subject concentrate on two themes, health and education. The authorities of the protectorate seem to have been increasingly concerned about mother and child care. Studies of the period refer to centres set up in the villages and rural areas. The class distinction to be seen in education, with its schools for the daughters of leading citizens and its vocational training for the daughters of humble or poor families, was encountered again in the realm of health. The centres were of three kinds: working-class centres for mother and child care and health education; family and child welfare centres; and rural centres for maternal and infant welfare.

The first aimed at giving mothers some idea of hygiene and housewifery, and catered for the masses. The second kind of centre was for the wives and daughters of leading citizens and aimed at imparting basic knowledge to help them adapt to modern life. The third, set up in the country areas, provided medical supervision for expectant mothers and young children, and distributed layettes and baby food. The texts reflect French interest in traditional midwives and methods of training them, and also in infant nutrition.

In education, the main problem confronting the protectorate authorities was how to keep Muslim girls at school. But at about this time there was an important turning-point in Moroccan attitudes, resulting in a certain acceptance of education for girls and to their going on to secondary studies.[3] But tradition was still the predominating influence, and the girls themselves, when they could not proceed to their final examinations, insisted on the continued provision of instruction in manual skills and infant welfare.

Women and the law

The legal position of women is dealt with in many studies. Muslim law on women gave rise to contradictory but often negative opinions. Comparison with Berber customary law is less explicit. We may note the work of Jacques Berque comparing the morphology of Seksawa marriage and that of orthodox marriage.[4]

Most of the studies carried out in this phase are based on a more precise methodology and attempt to show the modifications that have come about in Moroccan society. They record the various changes in family life, dwelling on the degree to which the women have advanced, seeing them as sometimes the driving force of change and sometimes a factor restraining it.

Young men, as depicted in these texts, seem much more advanced than the women, producing an *élite* which called for the modernization of the situation of Moroccan women and their initiation into French language and life. This implies that French habits and customs and the French way of life had been internalized and assimilated by the young men of Morocco, who were trying to find a way of getting them accepted by the women too. But the authors of these accounts leave out the reluctance of these young men, including the *élite*, to contemplate the advancement of women, employment for women, the right of women to pursue their studies, etc. The main aim was to change women within the prescribed framework, i.e. the family.

Another factor which emerges from these studies is the domination attitude of France, which under cover of a camouflaged paternalism aimed at incorporating the younger generation of Moroccans into French culture and the Moroccan proletariat into capitalist production. A. M. Baron is explicit on the subject: 'The Moroccan people will repay with trust the understanding we have shown them, for they are favourably disposed towards us, and I think they really expect us to direct them towards the ideal which our presence has introduced into Morocco'.[5]

Period III: After independence

Women played an important part in Morocco's struggle for independence. The women's liberation movement was part of the liberation movement of the country. Women threw off their veils in the streets and took part in demonstrations, breaking with the traditions and customs which had shut them up at home for centuries. Political consciousness-raising made them more aware of their own position, which they rejected in favour of ever-increasing emancipation.

Such feminine pressure following independence, whether formulated explicitly or not, gave a new impetus to research about women, and although other fields were given priority, this one was not neglected. Sociological studies on the family and on women were cautiously carried out by both Moroccan and foreign researchers. Studies on education, culture and social class regularly included a chapter on women.

The newspapers reflected this drive towards partial and as yet unorganized emancipation, and a controversy grew up between the 'modernists' and the 'traditionalists'. Another attitude developed soon after independence among young men and women, showing various complexes on both sides, including feelings of inferiority and superiority, and revealing that they often saw one another as enemies. Women in rural areas do not seem to have shared this attitude or been drawn into the argument. The call for emancipation was an urban phenomenon, and it was not until later that women in the country began to echo it under the pressure of capitalist, paternal or marital domination and exploitation.

The bibliography of this period demonstrates several themes.

Women in the family

Some studies on women approached the subject through the family, because any change affecting the family influences all its members, including the women, and because any change in women's attitudes and opinions acts directly or indirectly on family life.

Research studies on women in the family were conducted in different regions or urban districts. Studies on the habitat, budget and general living conditions of these families reveal the difficulties of women's lives, the failure of women immigrants from the country to adjust to urban life, and the material crisis which forced women and children into a world of exploitation, insecurity and want.

Access for women to paid employment

Up to 1956 the world of modern production was closed to the vast majority of women. Those who did enter it were restricted to minor jobs, were often badly paid and constantly liable to dismissal.

Although the female proletariat had grown considerably by independence, it is clear that there were very few women employed in middle management, and none at all in higher management. The prevalence of illiteracy among women, the limited education available to girls,[6] together with the taboos and prohibitions concerning female employment in general and in particular, combined to discourage women from entering the world of paid employment, or even to exclude them from it altogether, except when marital difficulties in the family forced them to take jobs.

Attitudes to women's employment were varied and often contradictory, especially in relation to certain jobs. Nelly Forget's survey[7] shows that some activities were accepted and others rejected. The attitude of the women themselves was sometimes positive, work being seen as a liberation (this view was found among the newly prosperous classes and women students), and sometimes negative, work being regarded as a constraint and a burden and not a real function (this view was found among the traditional bourgeoisie, and among unskilled workers and women in low grade posts).

In the decade 1970–1980 an important change took place in the attitude of Moroccan society to paid employment for women. The economic crisis, the rising standard of living, the stability of wages, the needs arising from a longer period of schooling for children, etc., made it more and more common and sometimes even vitally necessary for wives to go out to work in order to keep the family going. This produced a new approach in studies relating to women, with sectoral surveys devoted to the problems of working women. Studies appeared on women civil servants, women domestic servants, women in crafts, women in factories, and so on. It was no longer a question of whether or not women should be in paid employment, but of how women were to be integrated into the economic and social development of the country.

In the towns there was no longer any opposition to sending girls to school and letting them go on to further studies. Change in the position of women could come about only through the spread of literacy and schooling, which led not only to the possibility of employment outside the home, with the prestige that conferred, but also to modifications in the roles, attitudes and behaviour of women.

Girls' education

Studies on differential socialization show that equality of the sexes will not be achieved for some time, because both girls and boys internalize models which will eventually make them more or less like their parents. The survival of certain practices shows the persistence of a patriarchal and conservative ideology which holds back women's advancement and liberation.

Women, motherhood and family planning

The question of family planning, which did not arise during the protectorate, was cautiously embarked upon in the early years of independence. In 1965–1966, population growth became a major problem and was recognized as an obstacle to development. The continual growth in the number of young people needing to be fed, educated, given health care and provided with employment, added to rural exodus and urban encroachment and led the authorities to seek new solutions to the problem of the imbalance between population and development through the establishment of a family-planning institute. International experts and advisers were called in, surveys were carried out and pilot experiments initiated in various regions. Moroccan and foreign publications tried to show the advantages of family planning. A special association was created, the AMPF.[8] Surveys showed that attitudes to family planning varied according to the educational and socio-economic level of the women involved.

Family planning, as it is being developed in Morocco, is not the result of a popular choice but rather something imposed, which the people accept to varying extents, or totally reject. Opinion surveys carried out after 1970 demonstrate the failure of family planning and the many obstacles it encounters, economic, social, cultural and so on.

The sociological side of motherhood (childbirth, feeding of babies) has attracted less attention from researchers. Studies on the medical, especially the gynaecological and obstetrical aspects of the subject, have been produced in considerable numbers in the Faculty of Medicine, particularly since 1970.

Women and the law

In this area, studies have concentrated on that part of the legal code which deals with the individual, drawing attention to the provisions concerning women. The problems considered most frequently are divorce, broken marriages, and desertion; i.e. exceptional situations which disrupt the family. Other studies go deeper and deal with articles in the code relating to women's right to engage in business, reciprocal rights and duties between marriage partners, etc. These bring out the contradictions which exist between the law and the facts, and the way the law acts as an impediment to the real liberation of women.

It becomes more and more necessary to analyse the position of women: the fact that they are dominated and marginalized can no longer be ignored or concealed. While the problem of women's access to paid employment and of their advancement in general has appeared less acute since 1970, and while under the law women are now recognized as citizens with as many rights and duties as men, all this is merely external. Negative attitudes and prejudices about women and their potentialities, including their ability to contribute to economic development and the creation of a national culture, still survive and continue to impede the real liberation of women. More and more critical studies of this situation appear, often written by committed women intellectuals who see the only solution in a transformation of the thinking of women and men alike in relation to women and to all other dominated groups. Such a transformation calls for parallel changes in political, economic, social and cultural structures as a whole.

RESEARCHERS AND METHODS

Institutions and individuals alike have taken an interest in Morocco, and research was undertaken on tribal and family life and the Makhzan (Moroccan administration under the protectorate), with the object of gaining a better knowledge of the environment for the purpose of effective action directed towards a clearly defined goal.

Before the protectorate, this research was done mostly by individuals, such as those accompanying ambassadors or military missions. Explorers, merchants and tourists also wrote about women and family life in Morocco. These texts varied in form and content, ranging from slight impressions and mere descriptions to more realistic accounts.

Studies belonging to the early part of the protectorate were not usually founded on any precise methodology. They rarely defined their concepts; sampling procedures were not properly worked out, and techniques lacked precision. Such studies were often based on general information supplied by the inhabitants or on very hasty observations on the part of the writer. The following quotation illustrates these methods:[9] 'a fortnight is not long to get to know a foreign country, but thanks to the visits which allowed me to go into Arab homes and to the books I have read on the subject, I think I have understood how poetical is the life of a woman of the East'. Such observations were often made at different times: notes on a particular subject might be made in the course of two or three different visits, separated by several years.

Studies on families or individuals were numerous. They called for some knowledge of a Moroccan dialect, and for the special conditions needed to make interviewing women possible (the subjects of the interviews might be, for example, maids working in French families, or women employed by the protectorate authorities for such jobs as teaching girl apprentices). These studies were often carried out by women.

The development of social science methodology has had an important effect on the development of sociological research in Morocco. The years 1945–1950 saw the introduction of a new approach, based chiefly on research in the field. Robert Montagne was an enthusiastic exponent of this method, as were his colleagues. The result was that superficial description was superseded by a somewhat deeper investigation of the environment. Observation grew more exhaustive and scientific. With regard to tattooing, for example, the work of J. Heber was based on direct observation and examination of women in hospitals, clinics, prisons and so on. Some thousands of cards were indexed and analysed for his work *Le tatouage du corps chez la marocaine* ('Body Tattooing among Moroccan Women').

While individuals with different approaches and different methods devoted their attention to Morocco, the development of research as a whole was greatly influenced by the Institut des Hautes Etudes Marocaines. Its object was to establish a scientific policy for Morocco, and to prepare suitable analytical tools and teams of specialists in various fields. It should be noted that large-scale studies carried out by the Institut were initiated and designed by foreigners. Despite the fact that this work was often not really scientific, it remains a valuable source of documentation for national Moroccan researchers.

After independence, neither individuals, national institutions nor international bodies gave priority to studies concerning women. Most of the work done at that period concentrated on current socio-economic problems. But both Moroccan and foreign researchers (not only French, but some Americans too) who were preparing theses on Morocco often dealt with the problems of women, the changes in their role and status, and the contradictory reactions to these changes. Researchers from the Maghreb, for their part, took more and more interest in the position of women, and used meetings, seminars and conferences to analyse the subject as an integral part of the problem of development in general.

Young Moroccan researchers, especially students aware of the changes affecting the family, men, women and children, often chose these subjects for their theses and doctorates.

Women's political societies have always laid stress on the position of women in Morocco, but the studies they produce tend to be political rather than feminist in nature. The Association of Moroccan Women, founded in 1970, has only a sporadic activity and has not contributed to the advancement of research on women. The legal side of the question, which seems to interest the Association, cannot be approached openly, for fear of conflict with orthodox religious authorities. The women's sections of the progressive political parties did not embark on any effective action until 1974, because of the political situation up to that time. Since then, new sections have been founded, creating a forum of ideas which reveals all the inconsistencies of Moroccan society and all the oppression and repression to which women were subjected. Various government ministries have taken an interest in research on women to a greater or lesser degree. The Ministry of Health stands out above the rest, with various surveys including one on family planning. Research carried out on this subject by international bodies has multiplied, and the Moroccan Society for Family Planning has played a not inconsiderable part here.

As regards methodology, field surveys have increased since 1956, especially studies carried out among educated young people (secondary-school pupils, boys and girls and students of both sexes) in order to ascertain attitudes and behaviour relating to the family and the education and employment of women. These surveys are often limited in both time and scope. Field surveys are popular as theses, but they are very restricted, consisting of general observations that constitute an introduction to research rather than research itself. It is worth noting that the number of women writing such studies is still limited, though in recent years women teachers have led research groups in an attempt to give a wider dimension to research on women.

SOME SUGGESTIONS FOR FURTHER RESEARCH ON WOMEN IN MOROCCO

Both Moroccan and foreign researchers who have written on the subject of women have tended to concentrate on the role of women in the family, on women's employment, and on the rights of women. Other areas of research have never been examined, or only partially. There is a great lack both of more profound theoretical studies and of large-scale empirical research.

A scientific study of the position of women in Morocco calls for the following:

1 The inclusion of research on women within an overall research policy.
2 The selection of priority areas of research.
3 An appeal to specific bodies to carry out such research and to influence university work in this direction.
4 The use of a suitable methodology.

At the last seminar (8 October 1980) organized by the Moroccan Centre for the Co-ordination and Planning of Scientific and Technical Research, the committee on health and population stressed the importance of research on women and the family in the understanding of current social changes and their significance. The positive aspect of the seminar was the participants' awareness of the almost total lack of scientific research on women, and of the need to work out a long-term research policy on the subject.

I. *Sociology of the family*
typology of the family in Morocco;
function of the family;
role and status within the family, roles old and new, role conflicts;
pathology of the family caused by change.

II. *Sociology of reproduction*
the sociological determinants of reproduction;
marriage age;
fertility and motivation of fertility;
family planning.

III. *Special studies on women*
education and employment of women and the effect of these on the patriarchal structure of the family;
legal status of women;
images of women in society.

To these main research themes we would add certain others which seem to the present writer indispensable and which complement those laid down by the committee.

1   Socio-historical evolution of women in Morocco, with emphasis on change and resistance to change.
2   The integration of women into development, the processes and methods of this integration, and the effective participation of women in the development plan.
3   Women and politics: their interest in politics and degree of political consciousness, and the level of their political participation.
4   The question of women's liberation in Morocco. What liberation? Its causes, meaning and driving forces.
5   Differentiation in education as an impediment to women's liberation.
6   The different forms of violence against women, and their reactions.
7   The problems of girls, their status, conflicting images with regard to them.
8   Women in rural areas, and their confrontation with the modernization of country life.
9   Virginity and sexual repression; pathological reactions produced.
10 Prostitution in all its forms, its causes and consequences.
11 A blueprint for society enabling women to take an equal part with men in all areas of public life.

These lines of research are only suggestions, but they show how much remains to be done in the field of research on women. But such studies can be tackled only within the context of an overall development policy, one that is centred on individuals, is promoted by them, and is designed to ensure the well-being of men and women and their adjustment to change.

NOTES

1. Lebel, Roland. *Les Voyageurs français au Maroc*, Paris, Librairie coloniale Larose, 1936.
2. *Le Maroc*, Paris, Librairie Renouard, 1930.
3. October 1945 saw the Inauguration in Rabat of the first class of the secondary course for Muslim girls. It was attended by ten primary certificate holders. A similar course was instituted in Fez two years later. See *Bilan 1945-1950—La Direction de l'instruction publique au Maroc*, Rabat, Ecole du Livre, 1950.
4. Berque, J., *Les Structures sociales du Haut Atlas* (chapter on the family), Paris, PUF, 1950.
5. Baron, A. M., 'La famille prolétarienne', *Cahiers des faits et idées*, no. 1, 1950.
6. In 1955, only 150 Muslim women had primary-school leaving certificates. Fourteen had secondary-school leaving certificates. Bilan 1950-1955, *Bilan de l'instruction publique*.
7. Forget, Nelly, 'Women and Professions in Morocco', *International Social Science Journal*, Unesco, Paris 1962, XIV No. 1.
8. AMPF: Association Marocaine de Planification Familiale.
9. Leysel, M. 'Les deux cloches de la vie féminine telle qu'elle apparaît de part et d'autre du mur', *Bulletin de l'enseignement public*, Morocco, October 1936.

BIBLIOGRAPHY

Period before the protectorate

Charmes, Gabriel. 'Une ambassade au Maroc', in *La Revue des deux mondes*, 1886.
Chevrillon, André. *Un crépuscule d'Islam. Fès 1905*, Paris, Librairie Hachette, 1925.
Doutte, Edmond. 'L'organisation domestique et sociale chez le Haha', *Bulletin du Comité de l'Afrique Française*, January 1905.
Ladreit de Lacharrière, R. *Le Long des pistes maghrebines*, Paris, Editions Larose, 1913.
Lebel, Roland. *Les Voyageurs français du Maroc*, Paris, Librairie coloniale et orientaliste Larose, 1936.

Period of the protectorate
First phase: 1912-1944

Sociological studies

Bendaoud, M. and L. Brunot. 'Histoire de deux épouses', *Bulletin enseignement public du Maroc*, July 1933, pp. 297-303.

Bendaoud, M. and L. Brunot, 'L'orpheline et sa marâitre', *Bulletin enseignement public du Maroc*, September-December 1933, pp. 364-70.

Delance. 'Protection de la femme et de l'enfant indigène', *Maroc médical*, No. 63, 1927.

Goichon, A. M. 'La femme dans le milieu familial à Fès', Mission report, in *Collectives supplémentaires à l'Afrique Française*, May 1929.

Goichon, A. M. 'La femme de la moyenne bourgeoisie Fassia', *Revue des études Islamiques*, Vol. 3, No. 1, 1929.

Hardy, G. *Le Maroc* (chapter on women), Paris, Librairie Renouard, 1930.

Lamazière. 'Chez les recluses des harems', *La Volonté*, 17 January, 19 February, 1930.

Léger and Décor. 'L'assistance aux femmes en couche à la maternité indigène de Marrakech', *Bulletin de l'Institut d'hygiène du Maroc*, No. 2, 1932.

Lens, A. R. *Le Harem entrouvert*, Calmin Lévy, 1922.

Lens, A. R. *Pratiques des harems marocains, sorcellerie, médecine, beauté*, Paris, Genthner, 1925.

Le Tourneau, R. 'Evolution de la famille musulmane en Afrique du Nord', *La France Méditerranéenne et Africaine*, Pt. 3, 1938.

Marmey, Ch. and J. Marmey. 'Statistiques générales de la maternité de Rabat: contribution à l'étude de l'obstétrique au Maroc', *Bulletin de L'Institut d'hygiène au Maroc*, No. 5, 1933.

Montagne, Robert. *Les Fassis évolués et le problème de la famille*, Paris, Harlman, 1938.

Morère, C. *Vie de Fatma Bent Mohamed—la Sociologie et l'école*, Charles de la Cour, Recueil de textes, Librairie Félix Alcan, 1939.

Peyronnie, M. 'La prostitution dans la loi musulmane', *Maroc médical*, No. 22, 15 October 1923.

Saule, M. 'Jeux de fillettes musulmanes à Fès Djedid', *Bulletin enseignement public*, September-December 1933.

Ethnographical studies

Besse, G. and H. Aioun. 'La femme et la parure en Afrique du Nord', in *L'Afrique du Nord illustrée*, 21 March 1936.

Bons, G. F. 'Tatouages des femmes berbères', in *La Vie marocaine illustrée*, Syndicat d'initiative du tourisme, 1932.

Demagistri, F. 'Curiosités marocaines, la signification primitive des tatouages chez les femmes des tribus berbères du moyen Atlas', *Tribune de Genève*, 11 March 1940.

Jouin, J. 'Le costume féminin en Afrique du Nord', *L'Anthropologie*, 1936.

Rousseau, G. *Le Costume au Maroc*, Ed. de Boccard, 1938.

Sbihi, A. 'Proverbes inédits des vieilles femmes marocaines', *Hespéris*, Vol. 14, 1932, pp. 104, 108.

Women and the law

Bruno, C. 'Etude du droit coutumier berbère. La rupture du lieu conjugal par la volonté de la femme des Aït Atta du Rteb', *Gazette des tribunaux du Maroc*, Casablanca, 16 October 1943.

Capitant, M. 'Contribution à l'étude de la situation juridique de la femme berbère/coutumes des Aït Ammar, *Supplément de l'Afrique Française*, March 1966.

Khelladi, M. 'Notes sur la dot/Sadak et le trousseau choura chez les musulmans de Rabat-Salé', *Bulletin économique du Maroc*, 1939.

Second phase 1945-1955

Sociological studies

Alerini, A. and P. Mange. 'Evolution de la famille traditionnelle et patriarcale dans la tribu de Thezrane, de l'annexe d'Ahermoumou', *Cahiers des faits et idées*, No. 1, 1955.

Baron, A. M. 'La famille prolétarienne', *Cahiers des faits et idées*, No. 1, 1950.

Baron, A. M. 'Mariages et divorces à Casablanca', *Hespéris*, 1953.

Berque, J. *Structures sociales du Haut Atlas*, Paris, PUF, 1955. Chapter on the family.

Boucetta, O. 'La femme marocaine, sa condition actuelle préface à son évolution', *Maroc médical*, 1951.

Caltez, P. 'La famille patriarcale. Afrique berbère', *Etudes sociales Nord Africaines*, Cahier 7-8, Paris, 1950.

Cauvin, F. 'La protection maternelle et infantile au Maroc', *Maroc médical*, January 1950.

Costalat, P. and Charbonneau. 'L'allaitement maternel en milieu musulman: enquête menée sur l'allaitement maternel à Fès', *Maroc médical*, 1954.

Daleas and Cismigiu. 'Les accouchements négligées dans le milieu musulman', *Bulletin de la Société de Gynécologie et d'obstétrique*, 1952.

Décor, A. 'Vingt années d'activité d'une maternité en milieu marocain urbain', *Bulletin de l'Institut d'Hygiène du Maroc*, 1946.

Escourou, P. 'Accouchements et maternité au Maroc', Doctoral degree thesis (medicine), Paris, 1949.

Etienne, Jean. 'Une famille marocaine', in *L'évolution sociale du Maroc—cahiers d l'Afrique et de l'Asie*, Edition Peyrounet, circa 1950.

Féline, P. *Les deux femmes de Moulay Ali. Scène de la vie marocaine*, Algiers, Imp. Bacorier Frères, 1947.

Igert, M. 'La privation des soins maternels', *Maroc médical*, 1952.

Jouin, J. 'Invocations pour l'enfantement', *Hespéris*, XL, 1953.

Ladreit de Lacharrière, R. 'En pays de l'Islam, le voile et ses accrocs', *Outre mer/mond collective illustré*, France, February 1948.

Lalu, P., 'Le mythe de l'enfant endormi—occasion d'examen gynécologique, Documents Nord Africains, Paris, January 1954.

Lalu, P. 'Le nourrisson et sa mère au Tafilalet', *Maroc médical*, 1948.

Mathieu, J. and R. Maneville. *Les accoucheuses musulmanes traditionnelles à Casablanca*, Institut des Hautes Etudes Marocaines, 1952.

Panque, L. P. 'La famille musulmane au contact de l'Occident, Aperçu d'évolution comparée', *Les cahiers des faits et idées*, No. 1, Rabat, 1955.

Sefrioui, A. 'Les rites de la naissance à Fès', *Maroc médical*, 1952.

Villeine, Louis. 'L'évolution de la vie citadine à Fès', in *L'évolution sociale au Maroc—cahiers de l'Afrique et de l'Asie*, Paris, Edition Peyrounet, circa 1950.

Ethnographical studies

Besance, N. J. 'Parures féminines Nord Africaines', *Le Magazine de l'Afrique du Nord*, 1949 (+ photos).
Heber, J. 'Le tatouage de la face chez la marocaine', *Hespéris*, Vol. 33, 1946.
Heber, J. 'Les tatouage du cou, de la poitrine et du genou chez la marocaine', *Hespéris*, 1949.
Heber, J. 'Les tatouages du bras chez la marocaine', *Hespéris*, 1951.
Roux, A. 'Quelques notes sur le langage des musulmanes Marocaines', OR bis 1952.

Studies on law

Filali, A. 'Condition juridique de la femme dans le mariage au Maroc', Thesis, Grenoble, 1951.
Lapanne, J. 'La reconnaissance de paternité de l'enfant issu du concubinat légal', *Revue Marocaine de Droit*, 1 April 1952.
Malka, E. *Essai sur la condition de la femme juive au Maroc*, Paris, Librairie générale de Droit et de Jurisprudence, 1952.
Pesle, O. *La Femme musulmane dans le droit, la religion et les moeurs*, Rabat, Les éditions La porte, 1946.

Period after independence

Sociological studies on women and the family in Morocco

Adam, A. *Une enquête auprès de la jeunesse musulmane*, Aix-en-Provence, 1963.
Adam, A. *Casablanca, Essai sur la transformation de la Société marocaine*, CNRS 1972 (chapter on the family).
Alami Merrouni, H. 'Hygiène et grossesse', *Mémoire de l'Ecole des Cadres de la Santé*, Rabt 1972.
Aujard, R. 'Problème de l'habitat rural dans la province d'Agadir—La cellule rural familiale', *Bulletin économique et social du Maroc*, Vol. 21, January 1958.
Badraoui, Batoul. 'Mariage et changement social', study carried out for Unesco, 1974.
Bargach, A. 'Budget familial du Douar Doum'. Degree thesis, Rabat, 70.76.
Belarbi, Aicha. 'Femmes, mobilité et transformations sociales', Séminaire, Association marocaine de prospective, Beni Mellal, March 1980.
Belghiti, Malika. 'Les relations féminines et le statut de la femme dans la famille rurale dans trois villages de la Tessaout', *Bulletin économique et social du Maroc*, No. 114, July–September 1969.
Belghiti, Malika, Najat Chraibi and T. Adib. 'La ségrégation des garçons et des filles àl la campagne', *Bulletin économique et social du Maroc*, No. 120, 121, January 1975.
Bellout, A. 'Une étude sur quelques budgets familiaux de paysans moyens dans le région de Sefrou', Faculté de Droit, Thesis, 1975.
Blan, A. 'L'évolution intellectuelle, morale et sociale de la jeune fille musulmane', *Revue de psychologie des peuples*, No. 13, 1958.
Chène, M. R. *La Vie des familles dans les fondouk des médinas de Rabat-Salé*, Rabat, Ministère de la Santé Publique, 1968.

Chraibi, A. 'Les dépenses des familles du bidonville de Sidi Othman', Faculté de Droit, Casablanca, Thesis, 1975.

Donath, D. 'L'évolution de la femme israélite à Fès', Faculté de Lettres, Aix-en-Provence, 1962.

Inabi, H. 'La crise du logement et ses répercussions sur le budget familial', Thesis, Faculté de Droit, Rabat, 1977.

Jonbin, O. *L'Intégration des femmes musulmanes à une société moderne 2 exp. Tunisie-Maroc*, Paris, Bibliothèque Sorbonne, 1965.

Khalil, Lamrani. 'Le corps de la femme dans la société endogame, Le Maroc', Doctoral degree thesis, Paris VII, 1976.

Lahlou, A. 'Etude sur la famille traditionnelle de Fès', *Revue Institut de Sociologie*, Brussels, 1968.

Mas, M. 'La petite enfance à Fès', *Annales de l'Institut d'Etudes Orientales*, Algiers XVIII, 1959.

Mernissi, Fatima. 'Quelques références concernant la femme et la famille dans le monde arabe et au Maroc en particulier', *Revue de la Faculté de Lettres*, No. 1, January 1977.

Mernissi, Fatima. 'Virginité et patriarcat', *Lamalif*, No. 107, June–July 1979.

Mernissi, F. and M. Belghiti. *Etudes de cas socio-culturels pour l'éducation en matière de population*, Unesco, August 1979.

Mesri, F. 'Rôle de l'assistance sociale dans la promotion féminine au Maroc', Rabat, Mémoire de l'Ecole des Cadres de la Santé, 1972.

Pascon, P. and M. Bentahar, 'Ce que disent 296 jeunes ruraux', *Bulletin économique et social*, Rabat, January, June 1969.

Radi, A. 'Adaptation de la famille au changement social dans le Maroc urbain', *Bulletin économique et social*, No. 135, 1977.

Ziou Ziou, F. and Naima Abdessadak. 'Enquête sur la femme tétouanaise', Thesis, Faculté de Droit, 1978–1979.

Women and Work

Abaussalim, N. 'La femme marocaine fonctionnaire', Mémoire de l'Ecole des Cadres de la Santé, Rabat, 1970.

Baddou, K., N. Guedira, and B. Boulouiz. 'Les obstacles à l'intégration de la femme au developpement', Thesis, Faculté de Droit, 1977.

Belahcen, M. 'Salaire féminin dans la conserve de sardines à Safi', Thesis, Faculté du Droit, 1974.

Benouiss, K. 'Le travail des femmes de ménage au Maroc', Thesis, Faculté de Droit.

Forget, N. 'Women and professions in Morocco', *International Social Science Journal*, Paris 1962, Unesco, Vol. XIV No. 1.

Hassar Zeghari, L. 'La femme marocaine et sa préparation à la vie familiale et professionnelle', *Confluent*, September–October, 1962, No. 23-24.

Immanssar, F. 'Les femmes dans la fonction publique', Mémoire du cycle supérieur de L'ENAP, Rabat, 1978.

Martensson, M. 'Attitudes *vis-à-vis* du travail professionnel de la femme marocaine', *Bulletin économique et sociale du Maroc*, XXVII, January–March 1966.

Mernissi, F. 'Women excluded from development' (Irene Tuiker and Michel BoBramsen, eds.), Office of International Science, Washington, 1967.

Mernissi, F. *Historical Insights for New Population Strategies. Women in Precolonial Morocco*, Unesco, Division of Applied Social Sciences, 1978.

Nouaceur, Kh. 'Women and professions in Morocco. The changing status of women and the employment of women in Morocco', *International Social Science Journal*, Unesco, Paris, 1962, Vol. XIV. No. 1.

Family planning, gynaecology and obstetrics

Addouh, S. 'Les problèmes des accouchements au Maroc', Mémoire de l'Ecole des Cadres, Rabat 1968.

Alaoui, H. 'La planification familiale au Maroc', Thesis, ENAP, Rabat, 1977.

Alj, L. 'La limitation des naissances et la femme marocaine', Thesis, Faculté de Droit, Rabat, 1973.

Bennani, M. A. 'Planification familiale et état d'esprit au Maroc', Thesis, Faculté de Droit, 1970.

Benomar, L. 'La planification familiale dans le Province de Fès', Thesis (medicine), Rabat, 1977.

Bouzidi, K. 'Les maisons d'accouchement au Maroc', Mémoire de l'Ecole des Cadres de la Santé, Rabat, 1960.

Brown, C. F. 'Moroccan family planning. Progress and problems', *Demography* 5, 1968.

Chalumeau, J. 'Education sanitaire dans les dispensaires de protection maternelle et infantile au Maroc', *Revue de l'infirmière*, 26, 1971.

Cherqui, K. 'Enquète d'opinion sur le planning familial au Douar Nga. Sidi Aíssa du Fouih Ben Salah', Thesis, Faculté de Droit, 1975.

Coale, A. J. and W. Mauldin. 'Rapports présentés au gouvernement marocain sur la planification familiale au Maroc', The Population Council, New York, 1967. Symposium on contraception organized by Maroc Medical in Casablanca, 14 January 1971, No. 548, 1971.

El Amani, J. 'La planification familiale au Maroc, IV', *Journées d'études médicales sur la P.F.*, Tunis, 1971.

El Mahi, F. 'Rôle de l'assistance sociale des centres de santé urbaine dans la planification familiale', Mémoire de l'Ecole des Cadres de la Santé, Rabat, 1967.

El Menjra, D. and A. Lahlal, 'La famille marocaine face à la natalité', Thesis, 1973.

El Yacoub, R. 'La femme et son rôle déterminant dans la réussite du planning familial', Thesis. Faculté de Droit, Rabat, 1973.

Fosset, R. 'Les caractères démographiques, géographiques de la population du Maroc', *Maghreb machek*, No. 5, May–June 1973.

Khatibi, A. 'Etude sociologique sur le planning familial au Maroc', *Journal de médicine du Maroc* Vol. 3, No. 1, January 1967.

Koucham, A. 'Les accouchements à domicile', Mémoire de l'Ecole des Cadres de la Santé, Rabat, 1972.

Laphan, R. 'L'utilisation passée et présente de la contraception chez la femme de milieu urbain et rural dans la plaine du Sais au Maroc', *Revue Tunis de Sc. Soc*, Tunis, 1969.

Laphan, R. 'Family planning attitudes and practice in the Sais plain', *Studies in Family Planning*, 58, 1970.

Laphan, R. 'Planification familiale en milieu rurale: connaissances, attitudes, pratiques', The Population Council, No. 5, April 1971.

Marzak, M. 'Les causes essentielles de l'échec de la planification familiale au Maroc', Thesis, Faculté de Droit, 1975.

Mernissi, F. 'Obstacles to family planning practice in urban Morocco', in *Studies in Family Planning*, Vol. No. 2, 12 December 1976, The Population Council.

Michel, A. 'Planification traditionnelle et planification moderniste dans les familles maghrebines', *Confluent*, 1964.

Pascon, P. 'Paysans et birth control: un dialogue de sourds', *Lamalif*, 1977.

Poulsen, A. and H. Nels. *The Moroccan Family Planning Programme*, Rabat, USAID, December 1970.

Zahi, M. *Aspects médicaux de la planification familiale au Maroc*, Rabat, 1974.

Women and the law

Aboud, Moussa. 'La capacité de la femme mariée marocaine pour exercer le commerce', Thesis, Faculté de Droit, Rabat.

Anderson, J. N. D. 'Reforms in family law in Morocco', *Journal of African Law No. 2*, 1958.

Bellefauds (de) Limont. 'Le divorce pour préjudice en droit marocain', *Revue marocaine de Droit*, No. 10, 1965.

Bormans, M. *Statut personnel et famille au Maghreb de 1940 à nos jours*, Paris, Mouton, 1977.

Bosquet, 'Le droit coutumier des Aït Haddidou des Aït Mellou et Isselalin', *Annales de l'Institut d'études*, XIV, Algiers, 1956.

Chaukh, Zallah. 'Les abandons de foyer', Mémoire de l'Ecole des Cadres de la Santé, Rabat, 1970.

Cherif, Noureddine. 'Les conflicts de lois en matière de mariage en droit international privé marocain', Thesis, Faculté de Droit, Rabat, 1971.

Colomer, A. 'Le code du statut personnel marocain', *Revue Algérienne, Tunisienne, Marocaine de législation et de jurisprudence*, Pts. 4, 5, 6, 1961.

El Jazouli, N. 'Les causes d'instabilité du mariage. Les modes de dissolution du mariage en droit marocain', *Revue Algérienne des Sciences juridiques économiques et politiques*, Vol. V, No. 4, December 1968.

Lapanne, Joinville J. 'Le code marocain de statut personnel', *Revue juridique et politique de l'Union Française*, 1959.

Tahri, Z. 'L'adoption au Maroc', Mémoire de l'Ecole des Cadres de la Santé, Rabat, 1966.

4 Human Sciences Research on Algerian Women

FATIHA HAKIKI and CLAUDE TALAHITE

INTRODUCTION

In the present state of our knowledge concerning university research in the human sciences on Algerian women, and pending compilation of an exhaustive critical analytical bibliography of dissertations and theses on this question during the period 1962-1980, we propose to put forward here a few assumptions regarding the sets of problems underlying such research.

These assumptions will be formulated in terms of a provisional summary typology representing three broad approaches:

1   the dichotomy between traditionalism and modernism;
2   the problems involved in participation;
3   the feminist approach.

An attempt will be made to outline broadly what we consider to be the characteristics of these three approaches to the question of women in Algeria, then each one will be illustrated by a summary review of one or two studies. These studies, selected because they were the most explicit or eloquent illustrations of the methods of approach referred to, cannot be reduced to the aspects set out here. They have other aspects, including theoretical ones, which we shall have to pass over.

This typology will be rather special inasmuch as there will not be any classification of the studies on the basis of the terms in which the problem is stated. It seems to us that the boundaries separating the different approaches referred to earlier are not sufficiently clear and radical—for reasons which we shall attempt to explain—and also that, with a few exceptions, there is actually one basic statement of the problem common to practically all this university research on Algerian women.

THE DUALISTIC APPROACH

This approach is represented by the doctoral thesis submitted by Miss Yamina Bentabet at Paris-Sorbonne, in 1976, and prepared under the guidance of Mrs Germaine Tillion. It is entitled: 'Les lycéennes d'Oran entre la tradition et la modernité, 1963-1973: étude sociologique des rapports entre l'éducation scolaire et l'éducation familiale' (Secondary school students in Oran between tradition and modernity 1963-1973: A sociological study of the links between education in the school and education in the home').

We have used for our study Miss Bentabet's own statement of the purpose, methods and results of her research, to the meeting entitled 'Studies and reflection on Algerian Women' (Journées d'Etude et de Réflexion sur les Femmes algériennes) held in Oran in May 1980.[1]

In this paper the author sums up concisely the dualistic approach, tradition versus modernism, which she adopted for her investigations. She begins by noting the existence of 'two major components in Algeria's present-day cultural system, namely, the system of values which might be called modern, in contrast with the so-called traditional system of values' (p. 129). She connects with 'traditional education' values such as 'authority, honour, mutual assistance, respect, solidarity, conformism, that is, the virtues specific to kinship' and in women 'docility, modesty, obedience, self-sacrifice' (p. 131). As for the values of modern education, these are described as 'responsibility, initiatives, competition, effort, success'. According to her, these two contrasting systems assume concrete form in two institutions: the family and the school.

The author attempts to justify this polarity in economic terms. The traditional system is equated with 'subsistence economy', confined to the household and to its internal management (p. 134). The second system of values is directly connected with industrial economy and takes the form of a rational plan. This is apparent in the aims of the schoolgirls—to take up university studies and enter the professions (p. 135).

This contrasting of two sectors, the so-called modern one and the so-called traditional one, is but a reflection of the theory of dualism—in agriculture or in the economy as a whole—familiar in connection with the economies of underdevelopment and cropping up in analysis in terms of the linking up of ways of production (Pierre-Phillippe Rey) or centre/periphery polarization (Gunder Frank and Samir Amin).

Yamina Bentabet nevertheless tones down this contrast. On page 129 she emphasizes that 'rather than two separate antagonistic systems there are always different combinations of the contributions of each—according to the sphere, the situation, the social conditions, the moment in history, etc.'. Further on (p. 132), she goes so far as to say that 'rather than a dichotomy or duality there is an extremely complex interpenetration of the two cultural systems as a result of the long-standing character and the intensity of the contacts and the various borrowings from the two systems of values involved'. However, her analysis remains fundamentally dualistic. What are the assumptions, or rather the postulates, underlying this approach? They are explicitly stated on page 146, where the author notes that 'Algerian society is in the process of moving from tradition to modernism'. In her opinion, the 'transition from traditional culture to modern culture' is 'central to the whole set of problems involved in the sociology of education in Algeria' (p. 129). Indeed, she considers that 'the sending of girls to school marks a break with the traditional standards. It is the most logical and effective means of bringing about the emancipation of women in Algeria— in the final analysis, a prerequisite for the reorganization of the economy' (p. 148).

This conception (tradition versus modernism), which is widespread in our societies, is in keeping with the way in which the problem of women in Algeria is felt empirically. So this kind of study, instead of calling this stereotyped reaction into question, explaining its origin and putting forward another view of the question of women, only takes over current popular opinion, giving it academic form and pseudo-scientific legitimacy.

The explanation is to be found on page 147, where the author announces that what she calls the 'modern cultural system' is 'of Western type', while the 'traditional' cultural system is prudently referred to as of 'non-Western form or origin'. This way of stating the problem, which stems directly from colonial ethnology and anthropology, is characterized by an ethnocentric or Europe-centred view of Algerian women. The latter are viewed as belonging exclusively to the traditional family with all its 'specific cultural features' (preferably Islamic). The concept of the family refers to a centre of authority, determined by religion and traditions, in which a mythical past is perpetuated. The object of this argument is to imprison women by building for them a dungeon sealed up by tradition.

By way of contrast, the Western 'modern' model is represented as the highway to progress, the most direct route to the emancipation and promotion of women. It is presented unhesitatingly as the only positive alternative. In the last passage of the paper the second approach is prefigured in terms of participation in the state blueprint, which we shall describe presently. The author therefore concludes as follows: 'If this social blueprint is not to be jeopardized, it must be made an integral part of a wider goal and fitted into a set-up favourable not only from the economic and administrative standpoints but also from the legal, social and cultural standpoints' (p. 148).

THE PROBLEMS INVOLVED IN PARTICIPATION

Rejection of the ethnocentric view imported from Europe and relayed at national level has been one of the hubs around which research in the human sciences in Algeria has been organized.

On the theoretical side of the struggle for national liberation, this phenomenon also shows the aspiration for a national intelligentsia which would gradually take over the study of its own society. Does this mean, however, that in respect of studies on women, it is no longer possible to state the question in terms of tradition/modernism? We shall show by means of an example that this

dichotomy still operates as a basis from which to reason and hence still under-
lies the approach to studies on women, even though it assumes a different form
here, and the arguments and supporting references are changed. That is why we
are treating it as a method distinct from the first one.

What can be said about this conception today is that the national intellectuals,
when they replace the colonial thinkers, will at the same time identify themselves with the state and adhere to the latter's declared economic, political,
social and even ethical blueprint. For the most part they will endeavour to
justify it and present it as legitimate. Hence the ethnocentric view can be said to
have been replaced by a position we would describe as 'establishment-centred',
meaning that a research topic is not taken into account unless it can lead to
action on the part of the state, to institutional policies. So the different aspects
of civic life beyond the actual or potential range of direct state intervention
will accordingly remain in the background. Moreover, this is perhaps what will
serve to represent 'traditions' in the dualistic approach, for the term 'traditions'
here obscures the reality of civic life, inasmuch as it puts itself beyond the
control of the state.

The obscurity and the generality of this concept of 'tradition' also serve to
colour the second term, 'modernism'. It merges into the actual and potential
activity of the state, postulated as the assuming of responsibility for human
aspirations to 'progress' and 'promotion'. This manner of stating the problem—
more or less explicit in a great many studies on women produced in recent
years—is taken to extremes of exaggeration in some studies, which are more
akin to propaganda.

To illustrate this approach we selected, however, one of the best studies
published since 1962 on Algerian women: a thesis for a doctorate in political
science, entitled: 'La participation des femmes algériennes à la vie politique et
sociale'. ('Participation of Algerian women in social and political life'). It was
submitted in Algiers in 1972 by Mrs Hélène Vandevelde-Daillière, who prepared it under the guidance of Mr Jean Leca.

We found this study interesting in that, conducted in masterly fashion, it
exhausts the problems involved in participation and, by exploring every possible
aspect, reveals the limitations of this approach. This is particularly clear in the
contrast apparent between the wealth of information yielded by the survey, on
the one hand, and the insignificance of the conclusions to which it inevitably
led in the form of advice proffered to the State—compromises, half measures,
in which the cause of women is prevented from getting off the ground: 'domestic
science, mother-craft, home economics', a few more women in 'representative
institutions', and the like.

For this paper we have used the updated version of Mrs Vandevelde's thesis,
which was published in 1980 by the O.P.U., Algiers, with the title: *Femmes
algériennes à travers la condition féminine dans le Constantinois depuis l'indé-
pendence* ('Algerian Women in the Constantine Area Since Independence').

Already in the Foreword the author places the problem unequivocally in the context of 'development', which she posits as depending 'both on state inter-ventions and on popular support' (p. 8). In the light of this priority, women, 'anxious to come out of their effacement, could help considerably in creating that will for development' (p. 8). So, just as Yamina Bentabet maintained that 'the emancipation of women in Algeria' was 'in the final analysis, a prerequisite for the reorganization of the economy' (p. 148), Hélène Vandevelde begins by accepting development as the goal, then tries to show that the 'promotion' of women is a step in the same direction and is even an indispensable prerequisite. We shall see later on that therein lies the basic difference between this type of approach and what we have called the 'feminist' approach. The latter purports to be a standpoint specific to women and, with the feminist cause placed resolutely in the foreground, it is to be distinguished from the other studies not so much on account of its content but on account of the perspective it adopts.

The development line might be regarded merely as a tactical or 'diplomatic' move intended to convince as many people as possible of the advantages likely to accrue from the emancipation of women. However, there should be no mistake: it is because the author is addressing the State that she thus involves herself in its design, reserving for women a mere adhesion which she would like to see as possible.

For the fundamental questions that she tried to answer are the following:

Why confine them [women] to a subordinate role and a position of in-feriority, which can only delay their adjustment to the imperatives of develop-ment, for which all the forces of the country need to be mobilized? (p. 8) . . . Why this anomalous situation in respect of the female population? How could it be changed? (p. 8).

Are we to believe that if the present situation of Algerian women was, on the contrary, consistent with this development—and such is partly the case—there would be no problem?

The author then finds herself in the position of exhorting the authorities to widen opportunities of participation for women. The term 'participation' is defined as follows: 'taking part in development, hence the extent of women's commitment'; 'partaking in development, hence the extent of social justice in regard to women'.

The dichotomy tradition versus modernism comes to the fore as soon as some content has to be given to this concept of 'development' and a little light has to be shed on the changes expected for women:

Although Algerian women participate very considerably in national reality, since they are even regarded as the custodians of its profound values, to what extent do they participate in the collective building up of the country, or even in the decisions which determine their destiny as individuals? Then again, are they partakers in the same way as men? For instance, is it not less easy for them to gain access to modern life? Do they benefit from advances in development in the same way as men? (p. 9).

Similarly, in regard to the form of the survey and the wording of the questionnaire answered by over a thousand women, the traditional versus modernism dichotomy reduces the scope of the operation, channelling the replies into its narrow categories. On page 213 the author uses the title 'Women's aspiration to modern life', which is actually '. . . a longing to escape (to travel) and to take their destiny into their own hands. Hence the thirst for learning and for more freedom'.

Further on, a question is formulated explicitly, as follows: 'Do you wish to preserve traditional life-styles?'. Here there is no question of proposing an alternative approach. We should like, however, to suggest radically different lines of research, with the help of a quotation from a particularly lucid essay on the 'ideology of development' (and its corollary, 'underdevelopment') and on Third World intellectuals, by the Nicaraguan, Rafael Pallais:[2]

> . . . this ideology of underdevelopment [which] has become at the same time the main source for thousands of would-be ideologists and tens of thousands of militants hankering after pseudo-revolutions of the Third World variety and the best justification in these backward regions for the accelerated development of mercantile alienation, preached by all the local profiteers under the name of *economic development* (p. 9).

THE FEMINIST APPROACH

It is difficult to describe the main lines of this approach, which we have called 'feminist' because, as mentioned earlier, it is put forward chiefly as an attempt to give an independent women's view, from that specific standpoint. Apart from that, since it has as yet no theoretical basis, this position is not represented in published research by clear-cut, thoroughgoing analyses. This situation should be seen in relation to two sets of factors.

The first of these concerns the possibility—or impossibility—of a theory on women emerging in any present-day society, and the difficulty involved. Marie-Blanche Tahon, whose thesis is selected to represent the 'feminist' approach to the problem, clearly puts this question when she says, 'Can a female intelligentsia emerge without a women's movement, without a collective struggle on the part of women?'

The other factor which may be at the bottom of the theoretical weakness of this approach is that, as Tahon remarks in her thesis,

The oppression of Algerian women in everyday life is such that a woman intellectual cannot be recognized and put on show unless she speaks with the voice of the powers that be, that is, unless in the situation of oppression she does not side with the oppressed.

This logic may seem too absolute and implacable. The fact remains, nevertheless, that such is the situation today—that is, if one can refer to 'Algerian women intellectuals' at all, so timid, muzzled, inconspicuous and discreet are the few that exist.

Two studies were selected to give some idea of this approach: 'La femme dans la littérature algérienne contemporaine' ('Women in contemporary Algerian literature'), two volumes, doctoral thesis submitted by Mrs Ahlem Mostaghanemi El-Rassi, in Paris in 1980, and prepared under the guidance of Mr Jacques Berque, Ecole des Hautes Etudes en Sciences Sociales; and 'Des Algériennes entre masque et voile' ('Algerian women between the mask and the veil'), thesis for a doctorate in studies on women, submitted by Marie-Blanche Tahon in 1978 and prepared under the guidance of Hélène Sixous, University of Paris VII.

Classification of the first study poses a serious problem, inasmuch as there is no unity of approach, and feminist positions are found intermingled with legalistic considerations or vindications of the merits of the State. In this the study reflects the real heterogeneity of the 'feminist' approach as it appears in the research which has come to our attention, the absence of any theory, compensated for in a greater or a lesser measure by borrowings from the studies quoted earlier or from certain variations on them.

What is more, when stating the problem, the author shows that her choice is not final. From what she calls the 'sexist-feminist' approach she takes the idea that 'a distinction must be made between literature written by men and that written by women when this appears to be necessary to throw light on certain statements' (p. 10).

Deploring the fact that the 'Marxist approach' reduces 'women's problems to relations between exploiters and the exploited' (p. 11), the author says that she will 'resort to [this] approach . . . whenever it appears to be necessary to elucidate the particular case of a work or a writer' (p. 12). Finally, she comes out in favour of a 'comprehensive social approach', which she sees as taking 'advantage of the analytical methods afforded by the two approaches, feminist and Marxist, while situating [her] study within the framework of a comprehensive social approach' (p. 12).

As if feminism or Marxism consisted of different but complementary *techniques*!

Marie-Blanche Tahon's thesis has more ideological unity and closely follows the pattern of feminism seen as a *movement*. What is more, the author recognizes the gaps in her study and in her knowledge of the question of women in Algeria.

In this connection she alludes to the difficulty involved in being a woman intellectual, to her delicate position as a foreigner, and to the resistance which she has encountered (and which she attributes to the fear of 'feminist neo-colonialism').

This thesis, which is a veritable cry from the heart, manages as such to affect and move the reader, but it does not go beyond the violent denunciation of an unbearable situation. In preparing it, the author has spontaneously resorted to the tradition versus modernism dichotomy, against which she was not cautioned by any strict critical judgement. See the Appendix to this chapter, which consists of an analysis of Marie-Blanche Tahon's thesis. See in particular page 91 in the Appendix, where reference is made to the sociological standpoint adopted by the author in her research on the works of Assia Djebar.

CONCLUSION

Today we have reached the stage where there are enough publications on Algerian women for us to be able to summarize them and make a critical analysis of them. The latter task appears to us to be of primary importance if this research is to move forward without marking time or giving rise to complacent self-satisfaction. Perhaps it is not even possible to produce 'positive' documentation on Algerian women. The answer may be found in Marie-Blanche Tahon's reflection: 'Can a female intelligentsia emerge without a women's movement, without a collective struggle on the part of women?'

NOTES

1. *Cahiers du Centre de Documentation des Sciences Humaines*, No. 3, Oran, 1980.
2. *Incitation à la réfutation du tiers monde*. Pallais, Rafael. Editions Champs Libre, Paris, 1978.

APPENDIX

'ALGERIAN WOMEN BETWEEN THE MASK AND THE VEIL'

This study falls into two parts and is to be read as 'a [dual] incursion into two fields—a description of Algerian women today and an introduction to an Algerian woman intellectual [Assia Djebar] and the novels published by her' (p. II).

The two parts are as follows: (I) Oppression in everyday life; (II) Suffocation.

General plan of the study

The two parts of the study are not artificially linked: 'It would be a simplification to say that the oppression of Algerian women in everyday life is the cause of the stifling of one of them' (p. II). The link is political rather, bringing out a set of problems involving more than just Algeria—the place and the role of women intellectuals in a social group.

The oppression of Algerian women in everyday life is such that a woman intellectual cannot be recognized and put on show unless she speaks with the voice of the powers that be, that is, unless in the situation of oppression she does not side with the oppressed. Djebar is a woman intellectual. Although she has been able to keep at a distance from the seclusion of women, she must, through her writings, contribute to their being walled in more effectively. Between the mask and veil (p. IV).

It must be admitted that to refer to the oppression of women is to take a political stand. To refer to the oppression of women is tantamount to saying that the situation of women is not immutable, that it can change if women struggle and if they struggle together to abolish it. As long as women do not regard themselves as oppressed, as long as they do not get their movement under way, how can a woman intellectual do otherwise than be on the side of the oppressor? Probably not, as long as she remains an intellectual. Can a female intelligentsia emerge without a women's movement, without a collective struggle on the part of women? (p. V).

Part I: Oppression in Everyday Life

The subject of the study, remarks the author, is based not on sensational revelations, but on information that is readily accessible in Algeria. The work entails putting this information together 'in such a way that the oppression of women actually appears as a sociological phenomenon and not as an accident of history' (p. 4).

This oppression is presented as a veritable act of violence. Violence without bloodshed—though crimes of honour still occur—but 'that of which women die slowly and ingloriously. Not martyrs, but worn away' (p. II). Violence exempt from illegality: 'Women can be stifled to death while the texts are observed' (p. 4).

In a brief sociological analysis, present-day Algeria is represented as aiming both at preserving the values of the past and at promoting economic development. These aims are divided on the basis of sex, the former devolving on women, the latter on men. 'The root of oppression is probably not so much Arab-Islamic values as such; it is the fact that women have to be the custodians of those values' (p. 5). Women thus find themselves 'disqualified from the forward march, which is increasing its speed. Accession to political independence has not changed anything for them. They are confined to a role of passive resistance. Men and women do not live in the same century.'

The violence to which women are subjected is represented as political violence 'inasmuch as it is necessary if the society as defined by the present ruling class is to function' (p. 8).

The predominant social argument, based on the Constitution, to the effect that 'all citizens are equal in regard to rights and obligations', denies any need for women to struggle for their emancipation. It defines them as 'citizens'— even when asserting the primacy of the role of mother and the sexual division of tasks. It affirms the need for a promotion of women that is not inconsistent with Arab-Islamic values. Finally, the iniquitous temptation of imitating 'Western' women, represented as completely alienated and exploited by men through capitalism, is held up as a veritable bogy.

The study as a whole is arranged under the following headings: argument; law; seclusion; marriage; maternity; polygamy; prostitution; asexuality.

Part II: Suffocation

Part II, considerably longer than Part I (it covers 293 of the total of 362 pages, compared with 140 pages for Part I), is presented as 'an introduction to an Algerian woman intellectual and to the novels published by her' (p. II). Assia Djebar was selected because many young women regard her as 'the standard-bearer in their emancipation' (p. 143).

The analysis of the novels is preceded by an introduction to the author, based on interviews granted to Algerian and European journalists, her activities as the first woman film-maker, and two articles published in periodicals—'La femme en Islam', in *Algérie—Actualité* No. 175, 23 February-1 March 1969, and 'Le point de vue d'une Algérienne sur la condition de la femme musulmane au

20e siècle' in *Revue de presse* No. 197, July–August–September 1975, which was a reprint from *The Unesco Courier* (August 1975).

Generally speaking, she notes that 'as a woman intellectual, Djebar illustrates the oppression of women and, although she herself is submitted to it, she justifies it' (p. 141).

As a French-speaking novelist, Assia Djebar emphasizes the fact that her main problem is one of language. Building up in French the character of an Arab woman and what is reality to her means introducing a certain distance into the text. However, this is not an essential problem, she says, as it is transitory. 'But it imposes an effort of tension on the author' (p. 147). M.-B. Tahon regrets that the novelist did not go farther and ask the right to question: the tension may also be due to the fact that Djebar 'takes' a female character but describes her in the language of a man. In addition, M.-B. Tahon emphasizes, as a deliberate attitude, what Djebar calls 'dissimulation'—'something like: I write to conceal what seems to me the most important' (p. 150).

In her interviews, A. Djebar first defines the Arab man, then situates women in relation to him. The content of her novels, what she is seeking, is 'the memory of the Arab man'. That is what her female characters express. These women do not have any discourse of their own. They express in 'practical' fashion, with 'a sense of the concrete'—according to Djebar, this is the specific feature of women's language—what the memory of the Arab man conveys. Then again, 'Speaking of women meant restoring their role as relays', the novelist comments. This leads inevitably to the women custodians of the values of the past, according to M.-B. Tahon, who goes on to say: 'Djebar takes up with the official line of the women, but fundamentally she does not mark herself off from Algerian men writers' (p. 154).

Similarly, the film 'Nouba des femmes du mont Chenoua', shows in the main women in their traditional role—the oral transmission of the values of the past. As for the emancipated woman shown in the film, she creates the illusion that there is nothing more to ask for, which is the official line. However, she lives under her husband's steady gaze and this stare arouses a feeling of uneasiness.

According to M.-B. Tahon, A. Djebar is 'driven to the acme of conformism' (p. 195). While in her novels she sometimes expresses revolt, this is immediately relativized. She represents a world in which the liberation of women does not depend on them but on the capacities of society for transformation.

The works analysed were: *La Soif* (1957), *Les Impatients* (1960), *Les Enfants du nouveau monde* (1962) and *Les Alouettes naïves* (1967).

The study is carried out under three broad headings: (I) Women; (II) Mothers; (III) Men.

The progression described is 'a gradual stifling of the voice of the other person' (p. 197). The early novels are marked by introspection with indifference to social questions. The women try to express their aspirations as women and are faced with the problem of their freedom. The last two novels represent the intervention of the war of liberation, and interest in social questions. At the same time we have the emergence of the couple, which is said to be a feature of Djebar's novels. However, 'everything happens as if the interest in social questions arising with the intervention of the war was necessarily bound up with the need for the women characters to stop wondering about their independent futures in order to become integrated in life with a man and finally to live in terms of him' (p. 153).

The development of Djebar's work depicts a gradual stifling of the voice of the other person, which was already not very strong in *La Soif*. This stifling is marked by a gradual realization of the private/public, inside/outside opposition. This opposition is not operative until the heroines become involved in social disquisition. At this point Djebar can compete with men writers. Her 'originality' as compared with them is that she attaches more value to private life' (p. 197).

Under the last heading it is noted that women in a situation such as this are asexual, or rather that they, as a sex, are the custodians of the honour of the family. After being regarded as her father's daughter, a woman is regarded as her son's mother. She is not respected, except in the role of mother-in-law.

This thesis, we think, can be classified in the feminist category on the basis of the following features; first, the researcher is subjectively involved in her text: she expresses the suffering and revolt aroused in her by the reality which she is describing. She makes her own position clear—that of a foreign woman teacher unable to form a research team owing to the dread inspired by 'feminist neo-colonialism'. Second, she observes that 'suffocation is an integral part of this study' (p. V). Third, the study is also an appeal in favour of a collective struggle on the part of women, a political struggle.

5   The History, Development, Organization and Position of Women's Studies in the Sudan

HAGGA KASHIF-BADRI

SUDAN AND SUDANESE WOMEN

Until the end of the first half of this century, which is the period in which this study begins, other areas in Africa were known by the name of 'the Sudan'. Subsequently, however, the term came to be applied exclusively to the area known to the Arabs as 'the eastern Sudan' or 'the Nilotic Sudan'; it is known today as the Democratic Republic of the Sudan.

It is a mainly flat country, with an area of 1,000,000 square miles and a population of 17,400,000. Various peoples of different races migrated to it from many directions at various periods and for different reasons; and the result was a change in the original Negroid population—the predominant type in the whole of sub-Saharan Africa—which was clearly marked in the northern, eastern and central parts of the country, less obvious in the west, and non-existent in the south. Geographical and political reasons also contributed to it. The Nubians migrated to the Sudan at a remote period, so that some historians regard them as sharing a common ancestry with the Negroes. Subsequent migrations brought in Arabs, Egyptians and Ethiopians. These races gradually came together, and the civilizations of the Pharaohs, the Nubians and the Negroes intermingled with that of the Arabs and Muslims. The life of the people was greatly influenced by this, the most powerful influence being the Arab one. This factor began to show when the Arabs reached the Sudan from the north through Egypt and from the east via the Red Sea as traders and pilgrims in the pre-Islamic era. Arab influence grew stronger and crystallized after the advent of Islam as the Arabs arrived in the seventh century A D, bringing with them a concept and a complete philosophy of life, and settled in large numbers in the Sudan.

Most of them came from Egypt, the Hijaz, West Africa and the 'central Sudan' region. They came up against the Nubians and the Beja and made treaties with them, which facilitated Arab penetration into the Sudan until the end of the thirteenth century A.D., when the Christian kingdom of Maqurrah in the north fell. With this event the obstacle was removed, and Arabs poured into Sudanese territory: the northern and eastern parts of the country swarmed with them. Arabs and Islam reached western Sudan from North Africa, Egypt and the 'western Sudan' region, and this played an important role in the spread of Islam in the eleventh and twelfth centuries.

The southern part of the country, on the other hand, was not settled by Arabs, so that the Sudanese tribes south of the 10th parallel were not subjected to Arabic or Islamic influence even after Islamic kingdoms had been established in the central and western parts of the country.

Thus the Arabs settled only in the northern, central, eastern and western parts of the country. On the Nile they engaged in agriculture, while in the flat lands of the Sudan they became wandering herdsmen. They also engaged in trade between upper Egypt and the Hijaz, and in handicrafts such as spinning and weaving. Meanwhile they were living with the native population as neighbours, intermarrying with them, taking them as slaves and so on, and hence they influenced them by the strength of their beliefs, traditions and customs. This influence was strong in some areas and weak in others.

In the north, for example, although that was one of the entry areas for Arabs and Islam, the Nubians to a great extent retained their own languages, customs and traditions. This may be due to the fact that the Nubians had to face the Arab challenge and Arab raids, and so naturally went to war against the incoming Arabs to defend their lands and property. It is also due to the fact that the Nubians were different from the other Sudanese tribes in having their own distinctive civilization, so that it was difficult for them to accept an incoming civilization. Moreover the process of intermingling had been accompanied in the north by a certain amount of distasteful violence, while it proceeded naturally, gradually and peacefully in the other areas, which influenced the aboriginal inhabitants so that their languages, traditions and beliefs and some of their customs vanished.

In the nineteenth century the British entered the Sudan, after courageous resistance to them had failed. Women played a full part in the local revolts and battles that broke out between the inhabitants and the foreign rulers in the north and south of the country, and participated in the popular resistance.

THE NATIONALIST MOVEMENT AND WOMEN'S PLACE IN SOCIETY

After the First World War, women began to progress within the nationalist movement with the formation of the 'Graduates' Movement', which started after the war in the form of a club for graduates of Sudanese schools. It was an idea that originated with the teachers of the Omdurman elementary school in 1914. But its implementation was delayed because of the war, and the club was not inaugurated until the summer of 1918.

There began to be interest in the education of girls: the pioneers of the Graduates' Movement concerned themselves with it, and this made them realize all the more the need for such education to give impetus to the progressive movement. Their concern was reflected in plays and other performances, and in their poetry recitations at the literary soirées organized by the club. There was strong opposition to this trend, and it grew stronger: religious leaders were frightened of the emancipation of women and the British administration also opposed it, sometimes secretly and sometimes openly, putting forward feeble excuses and taking advantage of the backwardness which reigned over the country in the 1920s. The Financial Secretary in his yearly report (referring to the education of girls) said that progress to date had been slow because of the lack of suitable premises. Obviously there was competition to produce excuses! Nevertheless, by virtue of increasing popular pressure, girls' education moved forward.

Sudanese women were attentively watching the whole movement and helping to foster feeling against the British administration from their homes and through their slight participation in public life; the latter was quite ineffectual. But national awareness in the Sudan generally was growing, stimulated by the severity of the British administration and encouraged by world events. In the wake of the First World War the League of Nations was founded, and this filled the Sudanese with enthusiasm and optimism that the world was entering an era in which the rule of law would replace chaos and the role of force.

After the end of the First World War and the outbreak of the nationalist revolution in Egypt, the British administration tightened its hold on the Sudanese. The United Kingdom had emerged from the war financially weakened, and was trying as far as possible to undermine the mutual understanding and sympathy between the Egyptians in the Sudan and the Sudanese. To no avail, however: the conduct of the British administration served only to increase those mutual feelings. The graduates, although few in number at that time, took advantage of the nationalist revolution in Egypt to rouse the feelings of enlightened Sudanese merchants and civil servants against the British administration. Indeed, the behaviour of the British drove them to clandestine activity, and organized secret societies began to operate which attracted large numbers of graduates and high school students. The best known of them were the White Flag Society and the Unity Society.

Women played a unique role during this period from inside their homes, for the secrecy of the meetings, the movements of members of these societies and the organization of encounters depended entirely on them. The graduates understood the women's question well and clearly: they perceived it as part of the problem of the nation as a whole. Hence from this clear vision came the fundamental principle of the women's question. The feminine nature realized that it was an inseparable part of the country's problems—despite the efforts of the British administration and its helpers to implant the mistaken idea that the women's question was a problem created by men, and hence to be channelled into warfare against men.

As a result of this a chasm developed between men and women in society, and some traditional practices helped to widen it. One of the most important tasks of the British rulers was to deepen these divisions, and these ideas dominated their planning for the future of the Sudan. Indeed, this secondary position of women was subsequently codified by the promulgation of laws, decrees and administrative orders, both temporary and permanent.

Nevertheless, the economic progress which the country had achieved against the will of the imperialists, and the beginnings of education, encouraged the increase of national awareness. In addition, both the nascent Sudanese press and the Egyptian press (which represented the Sudan's window on the world) helped to give impetus to the forward movement.

Women began to achieve progress daily, though it slowed down or speeded up with the rise of the tide of nationalism. Then, with the advent of the Second World War in the early 1940s, the Graduates' conference revealed its political face. This confrontation helped to bring pressure to bear on the government to increase the number of schools in general, and hence the number of girls' primary schools and training colleges for women teachers. In addition, a beginning was made with the education of girls at intermediate level. As the number of educated women increased, they began to think of their uneducated sisters, and the result of this was the beginning of literacy work among women, and the beginning of studies to carry that task forward.

Cotton-growing in the Gezira area, the progress of communications and certain other development projects had brought into being a class of workers, peasants and technicians, who had engaged in many struggles with the employers over their wages and working conditions; and those struggles against the employers helped them to form a bloc among themselves and stimulated an irregular form of trade union activity. Socialist and communist ideas were stirring in the world and in the Near East, especially Egypt, and this helped to increase national awareness among the citizenry. Many of them became determined enough and courageous enough to stand up to the imperialist regime and demand, through their organizations, an improvement in their circumstances and the liberation of their country; and some of those who did so were women. These demands contributed to a tendency towards careful, in-depth studies of the conditions of various groups, including women's studies. Thus the first study on the situation of a group of women appeared in a memorandum from the Sudanese Women Teachers' Union.

THE IMPORTANCE OF STUDIES ON SUDANESE WOMEN

Growth affects the lives of all the citizens for better or for worse, and consequently we ought to explain why we are singling out women for particular attention in a development study programme. Although we recognize that an improvement in women's living standards cannot and should not be achieved in isolation from the general objectives of development, nevertheless there are strong reasons for regarding the social and economic advancement of women as an important objective, both on humanitarian grounds and on the grounds of national priorities.

These reasons are three:

1   The role of women is extremely important in national development; in addition, they have a role as productive elements in agriculture, trade, administration, teaching, nursing and so on. They contribute to the growth process as a basic factor in the social system and the achievement of comfortable conditions—that system representing the arena for all developmental activity. For instance, the preparation of food, the protection, moral guidance and emotional support of the family, the care of the sick and aged, the upbringing of the next generation, the spreading of affection and psychological stability, the provision of a closely knit family environment, all these constitute an invisible fabric which is nevertheless important as the background to developmental activity.

2   Development agreements have to a great extent disregarded women. Most development projects in our country still aim at increasing the economic productivity of men. Those projects in which women participate tend to give priority to secondary, complementary services, thus emphasizing women's domestic role, or promote skills that will create only a slight improvement in women's economic level. But there have been a few projects which have devoted noteworthy efforts to direct, complete and effective participation by women in the economic life of the country.

From another point of view, there has been little concern to develop inexpensive technological innovations which could set women free from time-wasting methods that have a negative effect on their productive and domestic activity.

More important, migration to the cities and entry into the money economy and paid work have introduced new dimensions into people's lives and changed the nature of economic relations. The result has frequently been an increase in women's responsibilities, coupled with a decline in absolute living standards and increased financial reliance on the husband, brother or son, and also reliance on governments for monetary support. Increased reliance on the man may in many ways be considered more dangerous than decline in real living standards, for it limits a woman's ability to take decisions affecting her interests and those of her family free from outside pressures.

3   Women's advance towards a share of power has for various reasons helped to give women tangible ways of making their voices heard to express their needs, although in some cases the result has been compromise. Obviously there are many limitations on dynamic participation by women in development, and those limitations are interrelated. The legal position of women, for example, depends partly on the law; but it also depends on economic and social factors which in practice limit women's ability to take full advantage of what the law allows them.

While we recognize all the factors that have a bearing on the matter, we must pay particular attention to the economic factors, because of the way they have been disregarded in the past, especially in development programmes concerning women.

The present proposal arises from the belief that control of the benefits arising from the means of production and the distribution of the fruits of that production is the prime concern of society, and as a corollary that fundamental social relations are bound up with control of production and distribution. Accordingly, we arrive at the view that economic factors can cause the most profound change, and that to improve the economic position of women—as, for example, their ability to command such resources as they need to cope with their responsibilities—will be more effective than other measures in enabling women to assume to the full their role in national life. This does not mean that other factors should be disregarded, namely education, the discarding of hampering customs and traditions, taking advantage of every opportunity available in society, and acting freely in ways that will enable them to participate effectively in public life.

THE HISTORY OF WOMEN'S STUDIES IN THE SUDAN

General conspectus

Women's studies have begun to attract the attention of research workers, especially within the regional and international organizations concerned with providing services for women and children, and of social scientists, particularly women. But such studies are still few and far between and inadequate for the task required of them. Moreover, they tend to be connected with services to women.

Another factor is that these studies are in general academic or superficial in nature. They have shown themselves in most cases inadequate to extend and develop women's economic and social role.

In the Sudan

The history of women's studies (in the broad sense) in the Sudan goes back to the beginning of the fifteenth century AD, with the formation of the Sudanese state in the central Sudan. The historians of that period wrote about the history of Sudanese society[1] and the history of the family in the Sudan; they also discussed the roles of all individual members, including women. Although the work referred to is a historical enumeration devoid of analysis, it is nevertheless useful as the first written source dealing with Sudanese society.

Women's studies in the modern scientific sense began in the Sudan at the beginning of the second half of this century. Political antagonisms and conflicts had broken out between the various nationalist groups and the British Government, which was meeting with resistance from all social groups, workers, peasants and employees. To find an opportunity for action and to clarify their positions, these groups rallied around their own organizations. The first women's organization established in the country was the League of Young Women Teachers, in 1946. While the League's constitution might be regarded as the first study on the condition of women in the Sudan, the first scientific study on this was the Memorandum which the Union of Sudanese Women Teachers sent to the governmental authorities in 1949.[2] The Memorandum contained an exposition and study of the condition of Sudanese women teachers, and also limited general and particular demands. Thus it was a scientific study of the professional, social and political status of women teachers.

During the 1950s, and after the formation of the Sudanese Union in 1952 and other women's organizations thereafter, interest in the women's question grew: and there was considerable activity in studies devoted to the condition of women generally. These studies dealt with educational and health questions as they affected women. They also dealt with the obstacles that stood in the way of women and prevented their participating fully in society. There were also studies dealing with the question of women's work and their opportunities for training and specialization, and their social and political rights. But all or most of these studies were by nature reports, and never went beyond the traditional form of studies and reports.

The link between women's studies and nationally organized action by women meant that the period 1958–1965 was virtually devoid of effort in the field of women's studies, because the military government which controlled the country during that period ordered the dissolution of all social organizations, including women's organizations.

Women's studies in the period from the mid-1960s to the mid-1970s concentrated on political studies. Some of them aimed at achieving political demands, such as the extension of women's right to take part in elections, stand as candidates for political office, serve as representatives on political and administrative bodies, etc.

Once women's organizations had achieved some of their political objectives, a trend emerged towards scientific women's studies dealing with the question of women in the context of the overall development of society. What helped this trend was the idea, inherited by women's studies from the women's movement in the Sudan, of the close connection between the women's movement and the nationalist movement, and also between the women's question and the question of economic and social development.

THE EVOLUTION OF WOMEN'S STUDIES

In the context of these interconnections, and given the emergence of the trend towards scientific women's studies, studies were undertaken through governmental and popular bodies and academic institutions and through the intermediary of individuals, both men and women, interested in the subject.

The subject of women in the Sudan is one of the most important social questions. Women make up over half the population. While the percentage of illiterates in the population at large is high (80 per cent), among women it rises to 90 per cent.

The main paid employment for women is in agriculture and stock-breeding, for the Sudan is an agricultural country; earnings from those two sectors make up 75 per cent of the national income.

Since the spread of education and the availability of training opportunities for women, women have taken part in administrative work to a considerable extent, and have come to occupy senior positions in the civil service. But their participation varies as between the various ministries: while in the Ministry of Health and Communications the number of women is over 20,000, in some ministries such as Foreign Affairs there are only 33 female employees. This variation or disparity in participation is due in the first place to the fact that in some ministries the work is more closely related to women's circumstances than in others. The need in some civil service posts for a high level of education, training and specialization may be another reason. Table 5.1 gives figures for 1970. Participation by women in administrative work has helped to encourage women's studies, especially by organizations concerned with women's work and training. These studies have grown and progressed.

During the past ten years interest has concentrated on women's studies carried out by the women's organizations and the academic and official institutions. This concentration was helped by the United Nations Organization's proclamation of International Women's Year. The preparations for and celebration of this event, and the follow-up work done since, have greatly encouraged and consolidated women's studies, so that they touch upon every aspect of the women's question. Seminars, meetings and conferences have been held to discuss vital issues and decisions and recommendations have been adopted, e.g. on motherhood and childhood, women and work, illiteracy among women and ways of eradicating it, adult education among women, social welfare and women, women and the environment, women and economic and social development, the changing position of women in a changing society,[3] and so on.

THE ORGANIZATION OF WOMEN'S STUDIES

The concern with women's studies is clear from the concern of the various academic and official bodies with the organization of such studies. The women's

Table 5.1 Numbers of women working in ministries and governmental agencies, 1970

Ministry/agency	Number of women	Remarks
Education	4,646	Excluding women working in literacy or nutrition work and doing casual work
Health and communications	10,160	This ministry has very few women employees in the southern region.
Local authorities	782	
Agriculture	290	
Finance	219	
Banks	268	
Information	231	Many women are employed in this field in the southern region.
Service and repairs	191	
Labour	70	
Industry and trade	50	
Irrigation	34	
Foreign affairs	26	
Public prosecutor	23	No women are employed in the legal field in the southern region.

Source: Department of Labour, Statistics Division Reports: *The Labour Force*, Khartoum, 1970.

organization—the Sudan Women's Union—has appointed a committee of men and women specialists in women's affairs and social affairs generally to carry out painstaking scientific studies on the women's question.

Moreover, for the first time in the history of the country, a scientific society for women's studies has been formed.[4] This society, founded by a group of women teachers, works to stimulate and direct women's studies, and this indicates the degree of concern of the voluntary effort with the women's question and its desire to see it dealt with on a scientific basis.

At official level, the National Council for Welfare and Social Development has set up an office for women as one of its departments. That office includes women's studies on its programme, as a basis for the evolution of participation by women in development. It will also act as a technical body undertaking research and study on any project or programme put forward by the political organization.

Among academic institutions, the Centre for Development Studies attached to the University of Khartoum is also concerned with women's studies; it is now arranging a work programme to systematize women's studies, and linking it with development needs in the Sudan.

The Institute of Further Education is endeavouring to make use of a project which was submitted to it, in the form of a one-year course of study; students will graduate with a diploma in women's studies.[5] The course, which specializes in teaching a programme on women's studies, is the first project of its kind in the Sudan. In addition, programmes dealing with women form part of other courses organized by the Institute, such as the course for the Advanced Diploma in Social Service, the course for the Diploma in Adult Education, and the course for the Diploma in Communication.

In the last five years, interest in women's studies has also begun to show itself among students in the advanced studies department of Sudanese universities, as a subject of research leading to higher degrees in science; and this emphasizes the universities' concern with the matter. The Sudanese Library now has many scientific articles on the subject of women.

This established interest in women's studies has already had results in the form of joint projects between the women's organization and the Women's Office of the National Council for Welfare and Social Development, such as the publication of *Al-Mawaū'a al-nisā'īyya* (Women's Encyclopaedia),[6] and the collection of everything written by and about women in newspapers, magazines, periodicals, books and advertisements. This was a huge task, but essential as a beginning and a basis for women's studies.

Furthermore, the interest of the institutions in women's studies has reinforced the idea of establishing women's studies centres in Khartoum, the capital of the country, and in the six provinces of the Sudan.

CONCLUSION

Interest in women's studies is a healthy phenomenon which will assist the process of economic and social development in our country. We may expect that in the institutions and in future women's studies centres there will be flexible programmes covering:

the collection of information and opinions on the women's question;

in-depth research designed to paint a full and complete picture of the life of Sudanese women;

examination of the historical development that led up to the present situation;

research and evaluation of participation by present-day women;

research into how successfully women play their various roles in society;

research into the activities and vitality of family life;

research into men's changing roles in a changing society, and the distribution of work as between men and women;

research into Sudanese customs and traditions and the promotion of what is good among them;

research into the enforcement of laws about women and the extent to which they benefit from them;

the trend towards linking women's studies in the Sudan with women outside the Sudan: in the Arab world, in Africa and worldwide;

research into the establishment of working relations with women's groups and organizations in the Sudan and abroad;

research into the rapid and flexible development of women's studies, to accord with the requirements of the present stage.

Furthermore, social research workers consider that women's studies programmes within existing institutions or future centres will be supplementary tools. The establishment of documentation units is desirable, as such units would represent a basic infrastructure for the introduction of women's studies programmes or centres.

Communication by means of publications and periodicals is essential, together with seminars and conferences to bring up general issues related to the women's question. This would enrich the curriculum and make it more lively and more relevant to events in society. Workshops are also clearly essential to reinforce concentration and training.

Women's studies programmes, and the future women's studies centres, will achieve their effectiveness by running training courses for administrators, politicians and those in charge of education, culture and health in the country. They will be supplementary tools in society, helping towards the understanding and comprehension of the objectives of women's studies. Women's studies will thus achieve their goal: to give women their natural place and enable them to play and enjoy their role in society.

NOTES

1. Muhammad al-Nūr ibn Dayfullāh, *Tabaqāt Wadd Dayfullāh*.
2. The text of the Memorandum is appended to this paper.

3. Examples of recommendations and decisions adopted by some of these meetings and conferences are given in Appendix II.
4. The Ba Bakr Badri Scientific Society for Women's Studies was formed in 1975.
5. See Appendix II.
6. The Encyclopaedia is now in press (in Arabic).

APPENDIX I

MEMORANDUM FROM THE UNION OF WOMEN TEACHERS,
NOVEMBER 1952

To: The Director of Education of the Sudan

Dear Sir,

So that you may be more fully informed about the duties and obligations of women teachers in state schools in the Sudan, in connection with which they meet many difficulties; in order to correct the flagrant inadequacy of the laws under which female civil servants work; and although our sex is an unreliable minority (yet events have perhaps shown that we do the same work as men, and competently within the scope of our work); the Committee of the Union of Women Teachers in state girls' schools, at its meeting on 24 September 1952, instructed me to submit to you the following requests. It hopes that items 7, 9 and 17 may be considered expeditiously. Thank you very much.

Requests:

1   The new 'Mills system' amendment is unfair to women teachers, because it concerns itself with their grades in the context of their conditions of service with the government, and of their compulsory retirement after only a few years—unlike male employees, to whom it is open to continue in the service when of pensionable age. We therefore request the abolition of the efficiency bar and the promotion bar, to ensure that there is no interruption of annual increments.

2   The scale for male employees and teachers is different from that for women teachers, whereas they all perform equal teaching duty in the programme; furthermore it is well known that women teachers do extra work in addition to the teaching of science. This is unjust, and we therefore request equality of men and women teachers as regards scales, increments, stipends and pensions.

3   Since women teachers enter government service at an early age, it is unjust to regard their paid service as beginning at age twenty-one, as with men. We request that the minimum age be set at fifteen rather than twenty-one; this should be applied both to teachers already in service and also to future entrants.

4   In accordance with the general policy followed by the government in sending missions abroad, and in view of the need for an increase in information and general culture, we ask to be sent abroad for periods of study and study visits.

5   In the general interest, and in accordance with the logic of paragraphs 1, 2, 3 and 4 above, we request an expansion of the course at the women teachers' college so that it becomes an institute like the Bakht er-Ruda Institute, which women teachers would enter after completing their intermediate education.

6   So that older women teachers are not put at a disadvantage, we request the preparation of training courses—on the understanding that their duration would be not less than six months—to give instruction in modern methods of education.

7   The system now in force in schools is that four women teachers are pro-vided for each four-grade primary school, which means teaching seven periods a day. We ask that the hours of work be reduced by increasing the number of teachers to five, in order to obviate overstrain: for the teaching profession is an onerous one, and different from other professions. The criterion used in considering this question should not be the average hours of work per week provided for in the government's laws, since women teachers work additional hours doing the preparation and correction in their spare time.

8   As regards the difficulties faced by women extension teachers, we request:
   (a) that their term of service should not exceed one year, out of concern for their health conditions, and that continuation beyond that period should be optional;
   (b) that they be provided with housing and safe drinking water, and that they be made comfortable in various ways;
   (c) that they be given opportunities for rest during their assignments among the villages.

9   Given that women are new to the civil service, we request:
   (a) attention to the conditions of women teachers during transfers;
   (b) that in keeping with Sudanese customs and traditions each woman teacher be provided with a chaperon from her family, and that chaperons be authorized to travel in the same class as their protégées;
   (c) that on transfer or appointment women teachers be entitled to a choice of three duty stations;
   (d) co-operation with community leaders to find solutions based on mutual understanding to resolve differences arising from the Ministry of Educa-tion's treatment of women teachers in matters relating to transfer, appointment, dismissal from the service etc.

10   The headmistress is of course responsible for supervising the teaching and administration in the school in which she works, and we therefore request

that the grade of headmistress be separated from other teachers and that head-mistresses' administration allowances be paid continuously and not stopped during the holidays.

11 When a woman teacher is transferred from a primary school to an inter-mediate school or from an intermediate school to a secondary school, to carry out more important work and bear greater responsibility, she should be moved up a step on the scale.

12 A woman teacher in a boarding school who performs additional duties should be paid an allowance for such duties.

13 Married women should be given an opportunity of earning, if they wish (and not be dismissed solely because of being married), as in the case of foreign women teachers.

14 Since married women teachers have heavy commitments in carrying out their official duties and also acting as wives and housekeepers, we request that a distinction be made between them and their unmarried colleagues, namely that they be not transferred to locations far from where their husbands live.

15 In justice to Sudanese women who have done secondary teaching, they should be substituted for foreign teachers in teaching posts in intermediate schools, to avoid difficulty in understanding Arabic, especially in the case of pupils who have begun their education in English.

16 We request that education in primary, intermediate and secondary schools be made free for all members of the population.

17 In the interests of equality between Sudanese men and women, we request that the percentage of girls educated be raised by increasing the number of primary and intermediate girls' schools to 75 per cent of the number of boys' schools: also that girls be given ample opportunity for university education.

18 Since foreign women teachers are paid an allowance of 50 Egyptian pounds on appointment for the purchase of household furniture, we request that every Sudanese woman teacher be paid an allowance of 50 pounds on her marriage.

19 We ask for the repeal of the Emergency Law, since it restricts trade-union freedoms.

20 In view of the exorbitantly high level of prices and the increase in charges and service costs, we request the introduction of price controls and the abolition of tax on the staple food products.

21 The Union of Primary School Teachers deserves support in its boycott of the Marshall Plan, which would put primary schools under the supervision of the local authorities and make them subservient to them; for we fear that those in

charge in these authorities will disgracefully abuse their power by injuring the reputation of women teachers. This has happened, as the Inspectorate of Girls' Schools would be the first to testify.

22 If a woman teacher wishes to join the civil service in a government department, or her services as a teacher are no longer required, she should be given the opportunity of replacing one of the foreign women employees in the various agencies and ministries.

23 In view of the impossibility of complete mutual understanding with English women, especially those newly appointed, we ask for more Sudanese women inspectors and for their rights with respect to travel and other matters to be provided for, i.e. that they be authorized to travel by first class or by air in remote areas.

These are the just requests which we submit to the Ministry of Education of the Sudan. Since they are just and within the rights of Sudanese women teachers, the Union hopes that they will be considered and decided upon, especially the urgent ones, by 31 December 1952 at the latest.

Respectfully yours
Nafisa al-Malik, President

APPENDIX II

OUTLINE OF A COURSE IN WOMEN'S STUDIES

Introduction

The traditional treatment of the changing role of women in the Arab world always suggests that the position of women is constantly progressing in our modern and contemporary history.

On the contrary, however, careful examination of the position of women reveals the fact that Arab women are still struggling to achieve relative independence in the economic and social field.

As a result of the activity of the women's movement throughout the world, sociological research has shown clear interest and concern on the part of both sexes in improving society.

But concern for sociological research in the Arab world has not encouraged women's studies commensurately with the great and regular need for them in a complex traditional society like Arab society.

It is of considerable importance that any programme of development studies in the Arab world should pay special attention to women. Although we believe that improving the position of women cannot be treated in isolation from the general aims of economic and social development, nevertheless we believe that concentration on improving the economic and social position of women is one of the important aims of improving development.

Why?

1   In addition to the importance of women as an effective element in the labour force, they are also, necessarily, an important element in the structure of society and essential to the flowering of development activities.

2   In most development projects in the Arab world, women have not participated directly or fully in economic life.

3   Although in some parts of the Arab world women have through their organized struggles achieved equal opportunities in education and work, and have held administrative and political posts, yet they have not enjoyed these rights to the full, for many social and political reasons.

One solution to this situation would be to introduce a programme of women's studies to be taught in universities, through schools of social service, departments of economic and social studies, or further education institutes.

Women's studies, after all, have begun to attract the notice of students and research workers in universities in both the advanced and the developing countries and in regional and international organizations.

The course

Name:	Course in women's studies
Nature:	Integrated course to meet contemporary development needs
Length:	Nine months
Qualification:	Diploma in Women's Studies
Those who would benefit:	University graduates of both sexes
Organization:	The course is divided into three terms, two devoted to theoretical studies and one to fieldwork.
Assessment of participants:	Examination in the case of the two terms of theoretical studies, and in the case of the term of fieldwork submission of a dissertation dealing with some aspect of the subject of women.
Host institution:	The course would be added to the activities of one of the following: (a) schools of social service (b) departments of economic and social studies (c) further education institutes.

Syllabus of the course

1 Description of society in the Arab world and the position of women in that society.
2 The situation of women's education.
3 The women's movement in the Arab world.
4 Customs and traditions, and the role of the two sexes in them.
5 Laws and regulations governing the position of women in society.
6 Women's twofold responsibility.
7 Women in the world (examples).
8 The situation of women's studies and research on the subject.

Arabic sources

Muhammad al-Nūr ibn Dayfullāh, *Tabaqāt Wadd Dayfullāh* (family history), 1505, Khartoum.

'Abd al-Qādir, Sohā, *Waḍ' al-dirāsāt al-nisā'iyya fi-l-watan al-'arabī, 1960–1978* (*The Situation of Women's Studies in the Arab World, 1960–1978*). (Report by Egypt to Unesco.)

Dr al-'Abd, Ṣalāḥ, *'Ilm al-ijtimā' al-taṭbīqī wa-l-tanmiya fi-l-mujtama'al-'arabī* (*Applied Sociology and Development in Arab Society*), Dār al-ta'āwun, Cairo, 1972.

Arab League Committee on Women, *Reports* (sessions 1 to 9).

Arab States Centre for Basic Education (Arab Republic of Egypt), *Taqrīr warshat al-'amal 'an dawr wa-mushārakat al-mar'a fī tanmiyat al-mujtama'* (*Report of the Workshop on the Role and Participation of Women in the Development of Society*), Rabat, 1972.

Al-Sa'dāwī, Nawāl: all her books about women.

Ahmad Ibrahim, Fāṭima, *Tarīquna li-l-taharrur* (*Our Road to Emancipation*) (series of publications), *Sawt al-mar'a*, Khartoum, February 1982.

Kashif-Badri, Hagga, *al-Haraka al-nisā'īyya fi-l-sūdān* (*The Women's Movement in the Sudan*), University Publishing House, University of Khartoum, 1980.

Arab feminist magazines.

Foreign sources

Baffoun, Alya. 'La Recherche en science sociales sur la femme maghrébine', Report prepared for Unesco Committee of Experts, 1980.

Barbieri, Dr Teresita. 'La Recherche sur la femme en Amerique latine: bilan et perspectives', Unesco, SS–80/CONF.626/5.

Hacker, Helen Mayer. 'Women as a minority group, twenty years later' in *Who Discriminates against Women* (Florence Denimark ed.), Sage Contemporary Social Science Issues, 15, Sage Publications, Beverley Hills, California, 1974.

Women's Studies International Quarterly, Oxford University, Oxford.

Jean Lipman-Blumen and Ann R. Tickamyer, *Sex Roles in Transition, A Ten-Year Perspective*, reprinted from *Annual Review of Sociology*, Volume 1, 1975, New York.

Jean Roberts Chapman and Margaret Gates. *Women into Wives*, Sage Publications, Beverley Hills/London, 1976.

German Foundation of Developing Countries. Report of Regional Conference on Education, Vocational Training and Work Opportunities for Girls and Women in African Countries, Rabat, Morocco, 20–29 May 1971, Berlin, 1972.

Political and Economic Planning Paper: *Women in Top Jobs*, London, Allen and Unwin, 1971.

United Nations Office of Public Information. *Equal Rights for Women and Call for Action*, United Nations Declaration: Elimination of Discrimination against Women, 1967.

International Centre for Research on Women. *Keeping Women Out: A Structural Analysis of Women's Employment in Developing Countries*, Agency for International Development (AID), April 1980.

Unesco. *Unesco and International Women's Year, 1975*, Unesco Workshop, 1975.

Reidy, Karen. *African Women: A Select Bibliography*, African Studies Centre, 1974.

Dr El Abd, Salah. *Applied Sociology and Development in Arab Society*, Dar El-Ta'āwun Printing Press, Cairo, 1972.

6 The Conditions Required for Women to Conduct Research on Women in the Arab Region

FATMA OUSSEDIK

INTRODUCTION

The purpose of the present study is to put forward some material for reflection on the aims of a group of Arab women researchers. This step presupposes an identity of aims among Arab researchers, or of predetermined objectives corresponding to a similarity of working and living conditions in the group concerned. One of the characteristics of this group might be that of living in the region known as 'the Arab world'.

IS THERE SUCH A THING AS AN 'ARAB AREA'?

Inter-Arab integration

The 'Arab world' is a premise in the statements made by the Arab states. Is one succumbing to a 'mask effect' of ideological discourse if one questions the existence of this area, or does a precise physical area, the basis of an Arab ideology, really exist for the women of the Arab countries? To assert its existence, in present world circumstances, would imply an identity of conditions and a specific position of the Arab countries at the international level. Two facts must then be recognized:

1   in the first place, the political and economic structures of the Arab countries differ;
2   secondly, the Arab states will continue to assert in political forums that an Arab world exists, and to make more and more national and international statements on this point.

All the arguments put forward to prove the existence of this Arab world derive essentially from belonging to the Arab–Islamic culture.

However, to gain an overall view of the problem, the following fact must be borne in mind: although economic integration has not been achieved, it has been set as an objective by the Arab states, and this has led to the establishment of a number of institutions intended to assist in attaining it, such as the Arab League, the Arab Labour Organization and the Arab Iron and Steel Union.

Economic integration

At the economic level, the integrationist discourse is in line with the real interests of our national middle classes: the construction of a capitalist economy likely to enlarge their appointed place in the framework of international capitalism. The multinational corporations and the international middle classes have nothing to gain from allowing the formation of a united Arab front likely to modify the terms of trade. International capital prefers to incorporate these middle classes separately into the capitalist world market. These dominated middle classes have apparently tried to work out integrationist strategies in certain fields, as for example in that of iron and steel through the creation of the Arab Iron and Steel Union, whose membership is open to governments and private firms. According to its Constitution, the purpose of this union is to militate for inter-Arab integration in the field of iron and steel, but very few results have been obtained up to the present. For example, after three days of discussion during the Congress of the Union which was held at Algiers in 1972 on a common Arab strategy, no agreement was reached on any common project. Generally speaking, a study of the structure of trade in every one of the twenty-three countries which are members of the Arab League reveals the weakness of their trade relations.

Ideological integration and the status of women

At the ideological level, on the other hand, the integrationist discourse holds a prominent place. One of its functions is to express a distance *vis-à-vis* the world market. One of the places, the one we are dealing with, in which this ideological unity is founded is that of the discourse on women. One of the justifications for this may be found in the fact that our dominated middle classes at home do not succeed in playing their role in society of creating the new fabric required for economic development. In this context, in varying circumstances, women come up against the problem of employment. In this discourse, women are of such slight economic and political account in the Arab countries that they can only be concerned with religious ideology and morals. The elements which serve to perpetuate the oppression of women thus appear to be contained, on the one hand, in the arguments used to express the unity of the Arab world, which amount to an ideological area and, on the other hand, in specific economic practices which do not allow women to appear as economic agents or as citizens.

We shall consider two examples, whose economic and political conditions are very different: that of Algeria and that of the Gulf states.

Algeria

In Algeria, in 1977, 5. 9 per cent of the labour force was made up of women, which represents 3.5 per cent of the women of an age to work.

In spite of Article 39 of the Algerian Constitution, which stipulates that all citizens are equal in rights and duties and that any discrimination based on prejudice in respect of sex, race or religion is prohibited, it was considered that in a country with a high rate of unemployment, when a job was going it was preferable to give it to a man. In one of his speeches, the President of the People's Democratic Republic of Algeria clearly set out his policy line on employment in Algeria: 'There is the problem of unemployment; when a job is going, should it be given to a man or a woman? Should men stay at home while women go out to work? That is the problem' (Algiers, 8 March 1966).

The Gulf states

Here it is even less common for women to acquire the status of workers. To meet national needs, preference is given to importing labour from neighbouring countries and from South East Asia. The integration of women into the labour force would be tantamount to tampering with the harmony of family life, whose pattern follows a feudal and tribal vision and is perpetuated by the surge of development produced by the oil revenues. This situation is possible because family incomes are sufficient. No organized pressure is being exerted with a view to obtaining additional income from women's work. In this way, while oil revenues may be at the basis of a development of the material productive forces, they have not led to a development of human productive forces.

The problems involved

The initiation of reflection on the position of women in the Arab countries amounts to attempting to launch new dynamics at both the economic and the ideological levels. And this brings up the problem of the hegemony of one view of the world over the consciousness of the individual members of society, who, however, (1) do not recognize themselves in this view of the world, and (2) objectively do not share the same interests as those of the ruling classes, and have a different image of society.

The action taken to struggle against this situation and to do away with the mystification at both these levels is inseparable. In this respect Arab women researchers have a historic and social function to fulfil. They cannot elude it without implicitly approving the mystification, which is many-sided as far as they are concerned.

Without speaking on behalf of society as a whole, they could testify to their position as working intellectual women in Arab society. These women research workers in this century are the first Arab women to earn the status of intellectuals. They thus give the lie to the prevailing opinion which continues to treat them mainly as mothers or wives: 'political power, on account of the determining economic and cultural factors in dependent Arab-Muslim societies, has exploited sexuality as a strategic area in which to give concrete form to the type of society it has chosen' (F. Mernissi).

In their work of demystification, Arab women come up against sweeping statements in which reference is made to the national economy and to matters identified as such. These statements either constitute a justification of current practices or challenge the dominant model, while remaining within the area covered by the national economy as proposed by the authorities. These statements reject women out of hand, for none of their sectors of activity is recognized as being of economic value, apart from the sector of demography, and that in a guilt-making and manipulable context.

THOSE RESPONSIBLE FOR EXPRESSING VIEWS ON ARAB WOMEN

Western feminists

The statements made by feminists from the countries of the centre (Europe and North America) on the lot of women in the Arab world which deprive these women of the right to express themselves in the same way that the central authorities do will not make our societies change. On the contrary, such statements are picked up and used in the framework of the anti-imperialist struggle in its cultural and ideological form. And the claims of Arab women themselves are thus condemned even more for European centrism. In addition, works undertaken by foreign research workers are open to a great deal of criticism. We shall take the example of the book by Juliette Minces: *Les Femmes dans le monde arabe* ('Women in the Arab World').

This book may be analysed from two angles:

1   The first thing to criticize is precisely that European centrism which we find in the author. Although an attempt is ultimately made to consider the dichotomy 'tradition-modernity', the analysis as a whole rests on a scale starting from zero—tradition ('Islam' in the text). The Koranic teaching is considered in it as a mere cultural product. It is not scientifically explained as the teaching of a society about itself, hinged on its own economy and social structure. The author thus skips from the fourteenth to the twentieth century without noticing any variations in the utilization of this teaching, and therefore without explaining these variations. 'As regards the traditional societies to which Arab societies belong, they are not yet ready—and nor are the women—to take up an emancipated life which questions a century-old balance, based on a religion into the bargain . . .' (*Les Femmes dans le monde arabe*, p. 31).

2   This leads to inaccuracies inasmuch as the complex reality of the phenomenon studied is not taken into account: 'For while the former (emancipated, modernized by the West and privileged) can exercise all professional activities and lead a satisfying private life, for the vast majority of the others, their lack of the imagination which would allow them to consider other forms of relationships,

a different status, does nothing to lead them to do battle to change the conditions they live in' (p. 153). This passage is painful to read when one considers the suffering of the women. This suffering, rivalling in depth that caused by oppression and Arab women's lack of mastery over reality, is also systematically disregarded by the author.

In addition, Arab feminists are presented with no reference to the pain they endure in a cultural environment that crushes them, but only with reference to Europe. The author goes even further in saying that the women who have learnt how to write and to express themselves cannot testify to the position of women in their countries since 'the majority of them belong to modern middle class families'. How could anyone think of excluding middle class women from our societies when it seems that the oppression of women is partly due to the fact that the middle classes dominate? It is therefore impossible to define them in relation to the countries of Western Europe.

Arab women are the subject of oppression in their own societies, and have now become a subject of study for Western feminists. The statements made by these feminists on the misfortunes of the women of the Third World seem unfortunately to be tinged with colonial anthropology.

In addition, and above all, the only action which could have any effect on social dynamics is that of bearing witness to facts and refusing them on one's own behalf.

Algerian women researchers

In contrast to the Western feminists, with their second-hand impressions, Algerian women researchers are engaged in thinking about the problem from their own experience. Thinking it out from one's own experience means first of all, refraining from refusing to let the others speak, since consciousness precedes and accompanies the struggle; secondly, refraining from referring only to the view of themselves expressed by the authorities, for this includes a degree of mystifying consistency which would only allow us to respond to an underlying will for power, while human beings have to live through situations in their complexity.

Basing our thinking on people means understanding not only the way in which they live but also how they try to resist because alienation varies according to circumstances. There are social reasons for variations, and individuals can always find a solution.

We already have one opening: that of writing. What do we do with it as part of the whole called Arab women? We say the 'whole' to show the weight of ideology as a factor structuring the position in which we are placed. We form a special part of this whole, since we can express ourselves at university level in this field of ideology.

Which topics of reflection are suggested to us at present? In Algeria, women researchers work on the following main themes:

1   women and the rural world;
2   women and employment;
3   women and health;
4   the legal and political status of women;
5   statements on women—textbooks, mass media, literature.

Particular attention should be paid to the existence of the fifth topic, statements on women. Reflection on this point makes it possible precisely to identify breaches in the dominant view of the place of women in society. And this leads to the same procedure in respect of the other four topics. This gives a true militant dimension to the work of Algerian university women for, with this approach, every time a woman reflects on a given point she is trying to find a breaking point, to question a myth.

'It appeared necessary to us, at a time when the role and the status of women are constantly evoked at all levels of social discussion, that women themselves should make their voice heard by means of a scientific study of their real position' (Bulletin No. 3 of the Social Science Documentation Centre, on a meeting of Algerian women researchers). The preface to this publication deals with myth-hunting. It identifies three main themes in the discussion of society:

i   the liberation of women through vocational work;
ii   women as fully-fledged citizens; and
iii democracy.

The articles contained in this publication deal with the following subjects:

a   employment (Mrs Hakiki, Mrs Chaulet, Mrs Baghriche, Mrs Guerroudj);
b   health (Mrs Medjahed, Mrs Himri);
c   politics (Mrs Amrane, Mrs Saï);
d   general discussion on women (Mrs Talahite, Mrs Aïnad Tabet, Mrs Assia Djebbar);
e   the social position of women (Mrs Bentabet, Mrs Marouf, Mrs Salhi).

If we compare this with other studies on the Maghreb as a whole, such as that presented by Alya Baffoun, the same trends are to be noted.

The publications deal mainly with:

a   the legal status of women in the family (eight publications);
b   work (eight publications);
c   the family (eight publications);
d   planning (seven publications).

The analysis of the topics mentioned can only be meaningful if it is concerned with revealing the contradictions in the prevailing view of women in society, and reporting on specific situations of which women have first-hand experience.

Two particular topics will be analysed below as examples: employment and family planning in Algeria.

Employment

In accordance with the basic texts, women may accept paid work. In the Charte Nationale, p. 32, it is specified that 'on the basis of the principle of the equality of the sexes, socialism, which recognizes the essential place of women in the family as mothers, wives and citizens, encourages them, in the interests of society, to go to work'.

The Algerian woman should participate fully in the building up of socialism and in national development (Constitution, Article 81).

In improving the lot of women, activities should be undertaken aimed principally at transforming a negative type of mental and legal environment which may prejudice the exercise of their recognized rights as wives and mothers and their physical and moral security. (Charte Nationale, p. 71).

The qualities of wife and mother thus take first place. The right to work can only be recognized if it does not endanger them. This is brought out in the following quotation:

The intensive participation of the active sector of the population in the production process raises the problem of the employment of women. Women represent one half of the active population and constitute an appreciable reserve of the country's labour force; their immobilization can only be equated with a weakness in the economy. However, in integrating Algerian women into production circuits, account must be taken of the constraints inherent in the role of mothers and wives in the construction and consolidation of family life (. . .) The state should therefore encourage women to take jobs which correspond to their abilities and qualifications and, in this connection, set up an increasing number of training centres for women. (Charte Nationale, p. 144).

It is clear therefore that working women appear useful only as a reserve force which may be manipulated according to the economic needs of the country, the justification for this being the position held by women in the family as the guardians of values and traditions. The contradictions noted in the texts show the value of carrying out studies on two specific themes concerned with employment:

1   the mechanisms for the massive laying-off of women should constitute the main pole of research before the study of women's employment;
2   the structure of women's employment, that is to say the circumstances in which they go to work.

The preparation of such reflection from the standpoint of women themselves amounts to viewing the processes qualified as developmental with a critical eye.

This undertaking depends on the demystification of the social function in the prevailing view of women.

Family planning

At present, family planning occupies a considerable place in statements on women. It is usually considered in relation to the demographic aspect of development policies. In this connection, family planning and birth control are linked with the sorry state of the economies of the Third World countries, with many mouths to feed for whose presence women are held to be mainly responsible. For example, following the drought in Africa in recent years, national, regional and international authorities stressed the close link between reproduction and access to resources, and called on the medical services to solve the problem. This raises the following questions:

1   the women of the Maghreb countries and Egypt are actively discouraged from having more children at a time when the women of the Gulf states are urged to do the opposite;

2   these exhortations are made without reference to the actual material situations of women within the society as a whole. According to the traditions with which we are identified, the reproductive function alone is recognized as of value in women. In the circumstances, the policies with direct repercussions as regards their bodies lead women to be even further dispossessed. This prompts us to consider: (1) the ways of assuming motherhood, the desire to have children, and (2) the ways in which women resist policies concerning their bodies based on the dominant view and also on ideological feminine attitudes.

THE PRIORITY THEMES OF RESEARCH

It is always difficult to define priority themes for others. We shall therefore, on the basis of our view of research, try to throw light mainly on the theoretical breakthrough to be noted in the history of the organized oppression of women.

The important point here is to identify the breaches in the dominant view by expressing women's position. As a researcher, my view is that all the efforts to exclude women from the production sphere constituted attempts to reduce to the greatest extent possible the power they could wield over the elements involved in the reproduction of material goods.

One of the arguments employed is that of women's minimal output at work, which does not allow them to appear as economic agents. Through the examples of employment and family planning, we have endeavoured to show the link between the *de facto* prohibition to accede to the status of economic agent and the manipulation in respect of the body that family planning can constitute.

CONCLUSION

We have endeavoured to describe a position based on the identification of the weight of ideology on the position of Arab women, and this allows us to reiterate our conviction that women researchers, who are productive in the field of ideology itself, have a historic and social function to fulfil.

The grouping of women researchers would assist in determining common and differing factors in the specific positions of women in the Arab countries. Such a grouping would also make it possible to identify the mechanisms which contribute to making the position of Arab women one of the most difficult that exist, and one of those in respect of which women express themselves the least.

BIOGRAPHICAL NOTES

Baffoun, Alya. *La Recherche en sciences sociales sur la femme maghrébine* (*Research in social sciences on women in the Maghreb*), document prepared for Unesco, 1980.
Cahiers de documentation des sciences sociales (*Social Science Documentation Bulletins*), 1980, 3, Oran.
Mernissi, Fatima. Unpublished paper, University of Rabat, 1981.
Minces, J. *La Femme dans le monde arabe* (*Women in the Arab World*), 1980.
Rendel, *Report on Research and Educational Programmes for Women*, World Conference of the United Nations Decade for Women, Copenhagen, July 1980.

Basic texts:

Charte Nationale, Algiers, 1976.
Algerian Constitution, Algiers, 1976.

Statistical bulletins:

Algeria: *Recensement générale de la population et de l'habitat* (General Census of Population and Housing) (1966–1977)
Bahrain: *Statistical Bulletin,* 1979
United Arab Emirates: *Statistical Yearbook,* 1978
Iraq: *Statistical Yearbook,* 1978
Syria: *Statistical Yearbook,* 1970
Unesco: *Statistics,* 1972

7 Towards a Theoretical Framework for the Study of Women in the Arab World

AMAL RASSAM

All societies assign roles on the basis of gender; sex as a principle of social organization is found throughout the evolutionary spectrum of human societies that ranges from the hunting-gathering communities of the Küng of Africa to the industrial nations of the West. What does vary, however, is the social significance of gender and the status differential that accompanies the assigned social roles as well as the meaning that the resulting sexual asymmetry assumes within a specific cultural context. Within the Arab world with its patrilineal–patriarchal culture and Islamic ideology, sexual asymmetry assumes an extreme expression marked by the formal segregation of women, their veiling, and their relegation to the private sphere of the household. Islam, moreover, perhaps more so than any other religion, has developed a well-integrated view of women, their sexuality and their proper place in society. The Koran, *Hadith* and the various commentaries and treatises assign women a special status which is also translated into normative and legal prescriptions that detail their rights and obligations in their private roles of daughters, wives and mothers.

Understanding this extreme asymmetry and the general position of women in Arab-Islamic cultures is not, however, a problem *sui generis*. It is part of the general problem of understanding women in any society and as such it suffers from the same difficulties that characterize 'women's studies.'[1] Of these, the main one has to do with the persistent tendency to adopt a male-oriented view, one that treats 'women and women's issues' as being secondary if not peripheral to the understanding of society and culture. This male-biased view is itself based on the assumption that what is important and of central value in the study of a culture is limited to the norms and formal prescriptions, the rights and obligations which prevail among men who hold authority, control resources and act as power brokers. In sum, the formal domains of politics and economy. Women who have few rights and duties in the political sphere are thus assumed to be unimportant and marginal to the social system. From this perspective, studies that concentrate on women tend to remain so; in other words, they are rarely integrated into a wider perspective, one that views both men and women as being equally integral to the functioning of the system as a whole.

What is needed in general then is a new approach, one that would concentrate on the beliefs and activities of both men and women and on their interrelationships in any given cultural system. As A. Weiner has written, 'we need to understand the interrelationships between women and men, for it may be that these are the very interrelationships that form a cultural system. We need to compare the various ways in which women serve to limit male domains, for men, regardless of their separation from women in status, power, etc., are never free from women'.[2] This new shift in emphasis from treating women as marginal or at best as complementary to our understanding of the working of a social system to one that sees women and their activities as integral constituents of the system is all the more crucial when it comes to dealing with societies that practise extreme sexual segregation. For it is all too easy in this case to give in to the male-biased tendency to ignore or underevaluate women and their contribution to the working of the system as a whole.

How then is one to approach the study of women in the Arab world? To begin with, it is my contention that we are still far from being in a position to formulate any general theory that would interpret and explain women's status across time and place. The newness of the enterprise and the paucity of detailed and comparable data on Arab women preclude the emergence of such an encompassing theory that could explain the varying status found among Bedouin women, peasant women and the urban élite, for example. Moreover, the studies that do exist indicate the great extent and complexity of the issue in the context of a society with as long and rich a history as that of the Arab one. We are still at the stage of exploring the tip of the iceberg; much remains hidden. Nonetheless, given what we already know, and drawing upon comparable work from other cultures, I believe that we can begin to put together a general approach; one that could help us to interpret data as well as to guide future research. This approach, as I hope to make clear, is predicated on seeking the answers to a number of questions formulated in terms of such organizational concepts as 'patriarchy', 'relations of reproduction', and 'domestic labour'.

It is curious how the majority of us who study the condition of women in the Middle East generally tend to avoid the theoretical issues involved in such an undertaking. We rarely discuss the basic assumptions that inform our approach to the question of women's status, nor do we measure our findings against those from other culture areas. It is as if Moslem women represented a species apart, one subject to its own unique laws and imperatives. How many studies, for example, compare Syrian peasant women to their counterparts in Latin America? And how does the Egyptian woman doctor differ from the American one in terms of her relation to her husband and children? This tendency to treat Moslem women in a theoretical and contextual vacuum is clearly illustrated in the recent volume on *Women in the Moslem World*.[3]

In their valuable introduction, the editors, N. Keddie and L. Beck, discuss the major themes and issues around which the study of women in Islamic societies is usually organized. These include family structure and gender roles, the impact of capitalism and wage labour on household economy, the relationship between male dominance and Islam and the implications of women's participation in the wage labour market. They emphasize the great disparities that are found in women's status among nomads, peasants and city people and point out the significance of such variables as education, property and urbanization. More important perhaps, they caution against the too tempting tendency to see women's domination in the area as a simple reflex of Islamic ideology and correctly point out that 'the question is not why traditional Islamic culture has been more discriminatory toward women than other major cultures . . . the real question, which contains policy implications for population control, improved child rearing, educational development and economic change, is why Islamic society has been more conservative in its maintenance of old laws and traditions in this area than have other societies'.[4]

Nowhere, however, do they address themselves directly to an exposition and critique of the different theoretical frameworks that inform the various articles in their collection. Nor do they attempt to deal with the general question of how best to proceed with our inquiry into the organization of sexual asymmetry in Islamic societies.

Ethnographic studies of Middle Eastern societies usually refer to the existence of two separate and sharply differentiated social worlds; men are said to inhabit the public world of politics, religion and the market, while women are confined to the private sphere of the home. Implicit in this dichotomy of public/male, private/female is the assumption that power, viewed as belonging in the public-political domain, is a monopoly of the men and that women, being confined to the domestic sphere, are therefore powerless. As C. Nelson has argued, this misrepresentation of reality is largely the result of the fact that most ethnographers of the area have been North American or European males who as a result of their foreignness and maleness had little or no access to women and the household.[5] As one ethnographer put it, 'the segregation of women from men not closely related to them is one of the things that must at once meet the eye of any visitor to the towns and villages of the Trucial Coast; this segregation makes it difficult for a visitor to gain any precise knowledge of the women's position. Apart from its being difficult for a man to talk to women there, it is not even proper for him to ask very much about them, particularly to ask in any detail about specific cases . . . one can easily be misled, particularly in assessing the extent of male dominance'.[6]

Women anthropologists who focus closely on 'women's culture' have questioned the assumption that women, because they lack authority and visibility in the public domain, are actually without any power. They argue that 'men's power' and 'women's power' can be understood only in terms of the *reciprocity of influence* that prevails in interactive situations. This broad redefinition of social power as a particular kind of social relation is best formulated by Dennis Wrong, who wrote that,

the initial problem of defining social power is to recognize its special features as a particular kind of social relation, as reciprocity of influence. Reciprocity of influence—the defining criterion of social itself—is never entirely des-troyed in power relations except by physical violence . . . We cannot sever power relations from their roots in social interaction. One actor controls the other with respect to particular situations and spheres of conduct—or scopes—while the other actor is regularly dominant in other areas of situated conduct.[7]

This view of power as a reciprocity of influences has shifted the emphasis of research from social structure to social process; ethnographers who adopt this approach analyse cross-sexual power relationships in terms of 'the negotiated order'. They argue that men and women, as they interact, continually negotiate the rules that define and circumscribe the specific relationship and that power is therefore not limited to its formal aspects but must be viewed in terms of a dynamic and reciprocal process. What is important to understand then is how women influence men, and how they manage to obtain their own objectives.

Viewed from this new perspective, the segregation of men and women in the Middle East need not necessarily imply the restriction of women or their sub-ordination. 'What becomes relevant . . . is to recognize that despite the existence of segregated social worlds and the implication that there exists a differential distribution of social knowledge—the man's and the woman's—this know-ledge is structured in terms of relevances, and women's relevance structures intersect with those of men at many points.'[8] Thus men and women are seen to operate within different, but complementary, spheres which are equally important and necessary for the reproduction of the social order.

The recent work of women ethnographers on women in Moslem societies has been most valuable in correcting the all too rigid and formalistic conceptions of earlier scholars.[9] Rather than seeing the public/private dichotomy in terms of a simple and clear-cut ranked order with the 'public' superseding the 'private', or in terms of a separate and oppositional relationship between the two worlds of men and women, women researchers concentrate on the dialectical relation-ship between the two spheres and in so doing they reveal the contributions of both men and women to the social process. This more balanced view, which restores to women a certain measure of autonomy and an active role in society, is certainly a most important contribution and not to be underestimated. None-theless, I still feel that the original adoption of a public/private framework to interpret and explain male-female relations in Arab society is problematic if not altogether unsuitable. My misgivings have to do with the fact that I see it as being essentially descriptive and of limited use when one is attempting to explain the observed variations in women's status and historical change. To begin an inquiry into the subject by taking the public/private scheme as a 'given' is, in my opinion, to run the risk of distorting data by forcing them into one or the other of the two categories, and more important, it draws attention away from the central fact that Arab men and women live in one world, no matter how much it seems to be separated into two domains. The challenge is to understand the normative and structural imperatives that produce and reproduce this seeming dichotomy.

Scholars working within the Marxist framework do not conceptualize women's status in terms of the public/private dichotomy. Utilizing such concepts as 'patriarchy' and 'domestic division of labour', they seek to understand the genesis and perpetuation of women's universal subordination in terms of the social organization of labour in the household.[10]

Elaborating on Engels, Karen Sacks, for example, has argued that the genesis of the unequal power relations between men and women within the family is to be found in the sexual division of labour which prevailed in pre-capitalist patriarchal societies. Relations between men and women (which began as equal), underwent transformation as soon as production ceased to be confined to use value (i.e. the production of simple commodities for home consumption), and that patriarchal control obtained when men assumed ownership of the means of subsistence. Where production takes place exclusively within the household, a basis for unequal power relations between men and women exists under conditions where women's productive labour is confined to use value, while men produce for exchange and acquire property. The social significance of this unequal development is intensified, she adds, in systems where production for exchange assumes more and more importance at the expense of production for use value only. The result is that women's labour in such systems becomes appropriated by the men and women are seen as simply working for their husbands and families, rather than for the society. Capitalism further intensifies this division, as it displaces relations of exchange from household commodity production to the sale of labour on the market in exchange for wages.[11]

Not satisfied with this too narrow materialistic concept of patriarchy, a number of Marxist feminists have suggested widening the concept to include both 'relations of production' as well as 'relations of reproduction'.[12]

> The orthodox Marxist definition of patriarchy as a form of organization of labour in the household is inadequate, without, at the same time, locating how the sexual division of 'the social relations generated by the reproductive role of women' is structured in such a way that relations between the sexes are relations of domination and subordination.[13]

The concept of patriarchy, in other words, must take into account not only the control of women's labour, but also the control of her sexuality and fertility as well. To understand the specific form that patriarchy assumes in any given social formation, one must therefore anslyse the patterns of cross-sexual relations that prevail within the family as well as the household organization of labour and property ownership. The merit of this more inclusive notion of patriarchy is that it allows us to grant an autonomous significance to the ideological content of specific patriarchal systems and not simply to treat them as mere reflections of the division of labour and property.

The dual approach to the analysis of patriarchal systems in terms of the inter-action between the 'relations of reproduction' and the 'relations of production' promises to yield valuable insights into the problem of women's position and its historical dynamics. Ideally it should allow us to begin to chart 'the formation of the sexed subject in ideology through the operation of patriarchal family relations', while relating these to the larger social formation of which they are a part. I say ideally, because so far this sophisticated concept of patriarchy has not been worked out into any coherent analytical framework that allows us to collect, systematize and interpret data about women in a cross-cultural and historical perspective. None the less, notwithstanding its vagueness and abstraction at this time, the approach does provide a sound starting point for conceptualiz-ing the position of women within the dual framework of ideology and economy.

Drawing heavily and selectively on ideas and themes suggested by anthropo-logists who have worked within the public/private approach, as well as from the Marxist feminists, I shall attempt to formulate some ideas with regard to the issue of understanding women in Arab society. In other words, how does one go about finding the answer to the question of 'How does patriarchy operate in Arab-Islamic culture?'

As I said earlier, I do not feel that we have the necessary data which will allow us to construct a general theoretical framework. As will become clear, such data as we do have on male-female relations and women's status are still too meagre and limited to provide any generalizations; for example, we have little or no information on such important matters as the transformation of the Arab family during the last fifty years or on the history of women's participa-tion in factory work (such as took place in nineteenth century Egypt). Failing the formulation of an overall theoretical approach at this juncture, we can, nonetheless, begin to order our data and prepare our research agendas in terms of a number of questions and organizational concepts that, it is hoped, will yield the insights and knowledge which will permit us to undertake theoretical form-ulations. This work is all the more necessary today in view of the fact that Arab women, whether rightly or wrongly, are singled out as the targets of govern-ment plans and development projects.

I feel that women's status can only be understood in terms of the following three dimensions: the social organization of power, the ideological and institu-tional means of controlling women's sexuality, and the sexual division of labour in the society. From this perspective, the family/household becomes the logical focus for analysis, as it is the arena where these three areas intersect. Far from being simply the 'domain of women', the family/household in the Middle East is the basic socio-economic unit and the arena where the public/private dif-ferentiation dissolves. As such, the family/household may be considered as a system of structured cross-sexual relationships underwritten by a specific Arab-Islamic ideology. The problem then, as I see it, is not to probe into the origin of this complex, but rather to attempt to understand the specific mechanisms (both psychological and material) that allow it to function and to reproduce itself, as well as the nature of the forces that are causing it to change today. For example, it would be useful to conduct a series of in-depth studies (in different areas and among different sectors of the Arab world) to determine the specific conditions under which women leave the home to work in factories and offices. These studies would probe into the attitudes and reactions of the men and women involved in such a decision as well as the impact, if any, of this new role of the woman on her relations with the different members of her family. Only then can we begin to determine with any confidence the relationship, for example, between 'the cultural barriers of Islam' and the fact that Arab women are under-represented in the work force when compared with women in Latin America. My point is that unless we begin to conduct historical and comparative investigations into the structure and function of the Arab family/household, we will not be able to assess the significance of the observed variations in women's status, nor will we be able to evaluate the implications of the current transformation in sex roles.

With the family/household as our focus, we can begin to seek the answers to a number of questions; these questions are organized in terms of five major areas, each of which represents an important dimension in the understanding of 'women's position'. After listing these areas, I shall briefly discuss each in turn.

A. What is the prevalent ideology with regard to the nature of sexuality in the Arab world? What role does Islam play in this? Do men and women subscribe to the same view? How is this view articulated, disseminated and reproduced? Does it vary by class, or ethnicity? Does it vary among the peasants and the middle class?

B. How is gender identity constructed? How does one become 'male' and 'female' in Arab society? What rites and ceremonies celebrate 'maleness' and 'femaleness'? And what do these tell us about the social definitions of sexual categories? Do men and women subscribe to the same views of these categories? How are these categories realized in behaviour? What form does sexual antagonism take? How is it dealt with?

C. What are the normative patterns of interaction among members of the household? How are authority and power organized? What resources, both symbolic and material, are available to men and women as they go through their life cycles? And how do these interweave? What rights are exclusively female? And how do these relate to the male's formal and jural rights? What is the relation of women to property?

D. How is labour organized within the household? What rights and duties stem from this? Does this division vary among peasants and city-dwellers and how? Does the variation reflect the status of women? What are the implications of women's increasing participation in formal and informal sectors of the wage labour market? Does the economic independence of women lead to their social independence?

E. What is the role of the state in promoting and effecting changes in the area of women's status? What policies and programmes do the different Arab regimes follow with regard to women and development? What are the ideological, cultural and structural constraints that shape women's efforts to 'liberate' themselves? What forms do these efforts take among the different segments of society?

It is clear that these organizational questions range beyond the family/household to include the national political level of the state. This, I feel, cannot be avoided. Thus, for the most part we have to study women in the double context of the family and the state; for unless we begin to see women's lives as defined and shaped by ideological, political and economic forces, we will continue to fail to grasp the essence of their predicament and the nature of their situation.

A. THE IDEOLOGY OF SEX

The only comprehensive treatment of the subject of sexuality in medieval and modern Islamic thought is that done by the Tunisian sociologist Abdelwahab Bouhdiba in his book, *La Sexualité en Islam.*[14] Other works that treat the same issue, whether directly or indirectly, include those by Antoun, Dwyer, Mernissi, and Vieille.[15] All indicate the presence of a coherent and dominant ideological tradition that goes back to medieval formulations undertaken by leading Muslim jurists/scholars. As summarized (and simplified) by Fatima Mernissi in her book, *Beyond the Veil*, the classical Islamic concept of sex closely resembles the Freudian notion of the libido, or of raw instinct as a source of energy. Sexual instincts themselves have no connotation of goodness or evil apart from how they serve a specific social order. Female sexuality, however, is believed to be more 'natural' and more powerful than that of the male. As such, it is a matter of great social concern; for unless it is controlled, this powerful sexuality of the female is believed to be capable of causing *fitna*, or social chaos, and thus to threaten the social order. The control of this power, it is argued, requires greater powers of reasoning and strength of character than women possess. Men, believed to be superior to women morally, intellectually and physically, are 'naturally' vested with authority over women and are charged with their protection. The codes of female modesty, veiling and seclusion are thus all seen as solutions to the need to 'protect' society from the possible consequences of female sexuality.

Whether this view is true to 'the spirit of Islam' or whether it represents a 'corruption' of it is immaterial for our purposes. What is important is how this view, or any variant of it, is expounded in any specific community. How, for example, is this ideological complex 'used' to explain or justify such rules and practices as those of veiling and seclusion, and the 'cult of virginity'?

Since sexuality in the Middle East, as elsewhere, is the basic component of self-identity, it would be most valuable for us to know how Arab women view themselves and their sexuality in the light of this dominant ideology. Do they, for example, accept their received image and do they passively convey it to their daughters? Or do they have alternative constructs of their own? And if so, how do men and women negotiate their different views of each other?

From his work in a small Moroccan town, L. Rosen has argued that Moslem men conceive of their women in terms of a rigid overall 'natural' division that separates the two sexes:

> The nature of women is regarded as unalterably different from that of the men . . . and provided that women do not overlap the bounds of public decency and do not create unmanageable strains within the household, they are left to handle their own affairs.[16]

Women, on the other hand, do not conceive of their relations with men in terms of a natural and immutable opposition; rather they tend to focus on the social, as opposed to natural, relations between the sexes. Thus, 'they give the greatest emphasis to the ways in which men can be ignored, outflanked, or outwitted by the arrangements of various social pressures within the household and family'.[17] This more 'political' view of the men by the women is clearly demonstrated in such contexts as marriage arrangements, where the men and women come together to negotiate their different views and to arrive at mutually workable solutions. The fact that men and women take different views of particular events, concludes Rosen, leads to 'reality-bargaining' between them, which makes it possible for women to get their definition of the situation accepted, rather than necessarily acceding to the dominant male in the household.

B. THE SOCIAL CONSTRUCTION OF GENDER IDENTITY

The process through which individuals come to acquire their gender identities, i.e. are made 'male' and 'female', is another relatively neglected area of study. With the exception of H. Ammar's work on rural Egypt and H. Granqvist's on the peasants of Palestine in the mid-thirties, there is little detailed ethnography on socialization patterns, specially among the urban population.[18]

In his book, *Growing Up in an Egyptian Village* (published in the mid-fifties), Ammar describes in detail the differential socialization experiences of girls and boys among the peasants of upper Egypt. The pattern which emerges seems to be generally true for the rest of the region, at least among the peasant population.

According to Ammar, the differential treatment of boys and girls begins at birth; the birth of a boy is greeted with joy and public celebration, while that of the girls is ignored. Women with no male children are greatly pitied and may even be divorced by their husbands. In fact, the social recognition and inherent prestige of bearing sons is such that women themselves reinforce this value by the special treatment they accord their sons, who are greatly indulged at the expense of their sisters. Girls are assigned specific tasks and responsibilities from an early age and are often put at the beck and call of their brothers. At puberty, the girl is usually veiled and made to observe the rules of sexual modesty. In contrast, boys at this age are allowed maximum freedom of movement; relieved of domestic responsibility and physically mobile, they spend most of their time with their peer group. At around the age of thirteen or fourteen, the girls are married, at which time they leave their father's house for that of their father-in-law, where they begin their adult life cycle as they progressively fulfil the roles of 'bride', 'wife', 'mother', 'mother-in-law', and 'old woman'.

Without further elaborating this sketch, it is clear that the different developmental cycles of men and women begin very early in life and continue throughout, with that of the women being very closely tied to their sexual cycles. What we need to know more about are the psychological implications of this for the self-images of the male and female. How do women perceive the restrictions placed on them and their devaluation by the culture? And what, if any, implications do these perceptions have for women's ability to negotiate in the public domain? Are major changes taking place in the traditional patterns of socialization? Do these vary by class, and what are the implications of any changes?

C. SEX ROLES, POWER DIFFERENTIALS AND FAMILY RELATIONS

Sex role expectations and patterns of cross-sexual relations have at their base the differential access of men and women to the major sources of prestige and power in the society. To unravel the status of women, we must take into consideration the formal and informal sources of power that are available to women in the household. In a discussion of women and domestic power in Morocco, Rassam examines the fragmented and varying nature of the 'unassigned power' which women utilize as they progress through their roles of wife, mother and mother-in-law.[19] Following work in other patriarchal societies, she argues that the authority structure of the traditional patrilineal, patriarchal extended household, is such that it brings about conflict rather than co-operation among the co-resident group of women. This places serious limits on women's overall power (*vis-à-vis* the men) and reinforces their dependence on the male members of the household. A new wife, for example, occupies the lowest status and power position within her husband's household; her extreme youth ensures her helplessness and dependency. In fact, passivity and obedience are the ideal traits expected in a bride, whose position remains precarious until such time that she bears a son and validates her presence in the household.

Her mother-in-law, on the other hand, is both active and powerful. Her power derives from a number of different sources that include her role as the manager of the household, from her access to the father/patriarch, and from her close relationship to her adult son, a relationship that she closely guards from the wife whose own sources of power derive from her active sexuality and her procreative functions. Competing for the attention and loyalty of the husband/ son, the two women have contradictory demands; the wife tries to detach her husband from his natal family in order to establish her own, while the mother seeks to keep him integrated into hers. This structural conflict between the wife and her mother-in-law is often dealt with through witchcraft, or *shor*, which both women resort to in their efforts to alleviate tension and diffuse pent-up frustration. It would be interesting to find out how this specific pattern may be changing today as more and more young men leave home to set up their independent households, thus undermining the vitality of the extended one and undercutting the traditional power base of the mother-in-law.

Working within a similar framework, S. Morsy has investigated the relationship between familial power structure and the incidence of a specific form of folk illness among women in a village of lower Egypt.[20] Morsy explores the relation between sex roles and illness; more specifically she examines the way in which deviations from sex-role expectations are 'managed' through *uzr*, a form of spirit possession, and indicates the compensatory value of 'illness' to persons suffering social stress and role conflict:

> Power relations are intimately related to the onset of folk illness and to explanations of illness. Power relations within the family are by far the most significant precipitating factors associated with *uzr* . . . power differentials associated with forced marriage, the threat of divorce, and the domineering behaviour of affines (i.e. mother-in-law) were isolated as the ultimate cause of the affliction. Under conditions of stress the sick role offers a temporary modification of status.[21]

An era that still has to be investigated is that of the relation between the status of women and property. While it is well known that Islam grants women the right to own property and a share in their father's inheritance, few studies have examined the actual permutations in the relationship between property ownership and the position of women within the family. One of the few ethnographic studies to focus on this issue is V. Maher's study of *Women and Property in Morocco*.[22] By comparing the status of urban and rural women, Maher demonstrates a relationship between property, divorce rates and status of women. In the rural areas where the main property is in the form of land, women do not inherit their legal share; but they retain important rights and service obligations with their natal kin group, even after they marry and leave their village. These rights (to support and shelter, for example) reduce the economic and social dependence of these rural women on their husbands, and contribute to the high divorce rate that obtains in this group.

In the town, on the other hand, where property is in the form of movable capital, women are usually given their share of the inheritance. In receiving their shares, Maher argues, these women effectively sever their ties with their kin. This renders them more dependent on their husbands, a factor that contributes to the stability of the marriages among the propertied class. The irony, however, is that the economic and marital security of the townswoman is gained at the expense of her autonomy and freedom. Townswomen are secluded and are extremely subservient to their husbands. 'Women', concludes Maher, 'are caught in a dilemma, either psychological independence conditioned by patrilineal protection and control, poverty and heavy labour (i.e. the peasant women); or physical care at the price of social isolation, passivity and total subordination to male authority.'[23] If this is true, how can women escape this dilemma? Does their increasing participation in the wage labour market offer an outlet?

D. WOMEN, LABOUR AND THE WAGE MARKET

'Muslim countries consistently report the lowest female participation in economic activities outside of agriculture. In addition, there is evidence of a failure by the female work-force to respond to higher steps of economic development by a parallel increase in the number of women employed in non-agricultural activities.'[24] As Nadia Youssef points out, this failure is related to the traditionally established closed occupational opportunity structure that restricted women from employment sectors that presupposed close contact with men. Moreover, Muslim kin obligations ensured that divorced and widowed women be supported by their male relatives, a factor which eliminated their need to work for economic survival. But this seems to be changing now.

The increased monetization of the economy and the accelerated rate of urbanization in the region are already placing severe constraints on the family's ability to meet its traditional obligation to support its womenfolk. More and more women are forced to go outside the home to earn an income, a factor that will no doubt lead to a restructuring of relations within the household.

While a small number of women from middle class backgrounds manage to acquire the education and skills that allow them to join the professional ranks, the majority of women who join the labour force tend to concentrate in the urban informal sector, where they work as domestic servants, laundresses and petty traders. Egypt, so far, seems to be one of the few Arab countries to have developed a desegregated labour market; women are reported to be working side by side with men as skilled labourers in factories and even heavy industry (Youssef 1978).

The recent increase in migration to the oil-rich Gulf states must surely have a profound effect on the traditional division of labour and responsibility within the household. So far, there are few studies to indicate the impact of male emigration on such labour-exporting countries as Egypt, Algeria, Jordan and Yemen. One report from a rural area in Yemen indicates that the resultant labour shortage, as well as mechanization, have accentuated the division of labour in subsistence farming and significantly modified this division in off-farm rural employment.[25] With the young adult men away in Saudi Arabia, the heavy agricultural tasks such as ploughing and threshing are taken over by the older males, while women tend to the rest of agricultural chores. With the acquisition of farm machinery, the men are relieved from their work, but not the women, who continue with their tasks of planting, weeding and thinning. Off-farm employment, on the other hand, such as the construction of irrigation canals, has drawn Yemeni women into wage labour to replace the shortage of men. It seems, however, that these women who work side by side with the men transporting water and mud are paid half the wages of the men.

An area about which we know very little has to do with the women's contribution to the household economy, especially among the urban lower classes. In such countries as Morocco and Egypt, women-headed households seem to be on the increase. Whether this is simply a result of male emigration, or whether it signals a more profound and permanent transformation in the proletariat family structure has yet to be established. While it may be still too early to discern the combined impact of increasing industrialization, commercialization of agriculture, and urbanization on the social structure of the Middle East, there is no doubt that women will experience profound changes in their traditional roles and status. Youssef in fact locates 'the most crucial determinant for the continuing demise of the traditionally subordinate position of the Muslim woman in the economic constraints currently emerging . . . such constraints will increasingly challenge the control exercised by male members of the kinship group over their womenfolk and will lower the valuation of maternal related roles'.[26] This notwithstanding, the question remains: does the increased participation of women in the work-force necessarily result in their increased autonomy and 'emancipation'? What role, for example, does the state play in accelerating or retarding the social emancipation of women? And what implications does the present Islamic revival in the region have for the changing status of women?

E. WOMEN AND ROLE OF THE STATE

The primacy of the state in Middle Eastern society is such that it is important to take into consideration the regime's policies and actions with regard to the areas that bear directly or indirectly on the position of women. How otherwise can we make sense of the situation of women in various countries?

Most Arab leaders have expressed the need to mobilize women into the development process, but few have translated this objective into any concrete programmes that would radically alter the current status of women. No Arab regime, including the 'socialist' ones of Iraq and Algeria, has so far attempted to do what Atatürk did, namely to abrogate the Shari'a based Codes of Personal Status which tend to discriminate against women.[27]

In a brief but important article, Elizabeth White examines the relationship between women's educational achievement, participation in economic activities, and the enforcement of Islamic restrictions on women.[28] By restrictions, she means legal prescriptions and seclusion. After a comparative survey of several Islamic countries, White concludes that

> Although Islamic laws do not prohibit female education or participation in economically productive activities, these nations that are unwilling to reform those laws are also apparently unwilling to provide equal educational faculties for women or to encourage their entry into the labour force. The nations that have reformed the laws most inequitable and restrictive to women have higher female literacy, school enrolment, and reported female participation in economic activities.[29]

This observation refutes the notion of those who argue that legal reforms are really unimportant determinants of behaviour patterns, and puts a special burden on governments that have declared their commitment to have women participate fully in the social and economic development of their countries.

The ambivalence exhibited by Arab leaders with regard to the 'question of women' must be understood as part of a larger conundrum which consists in what is perceived as the contradictory demands of 'modernization' and those of 'cultural authenticity'. The problem is usually formulated in this way: how can one bring about basic socio-economic change while still maintaining a sense of pride in culture and a secure feeling of identity? In Arab–Islamic countries, much of this pride and sense of identity is bound up with Islam and the cultural heritage. Islamic values and notions of proper and improper behaviour inform the life-style of the majority of the population and significantly, they regulate the most intimate domain of personal and familial relations at whose core lies 'the question of women'. Hence the dilemma. Whether solutions to this and other cultural dilemmas are ultimately to be found at the national political level is outside the scope of this paper. My intention is simply to point out the complexity of women's status in the Arab world and to underscore the role of the state in any attempt at a proper evaluation of the problem.

CONCLUDING REMARKS

It is far too soon to develop an overall and coherent theoretical framework that could explain the status of Arab women in all its historical, regional and class varieties. At this stage we can do no more perhaps than to pose the problem and suggest a general approach to deal with it. This general approach, I have suggested, consists in investigating the family/household in terms of the five areas discussed above. The family/household, I have argued, is the arena where the ideological and economic forces intersect and where women's sexual and labour potential unfold. It is also the arena where the 'women's world' and the 'men's world' come together and out of which they differentiate. This differentiation into the 'public' and 'private' spheres, so notable in Arab society, is predicated on ideological as well as economic factors. Our task, by no means an easy one, is to discern how sexual ideologies and economic determinants (specifically those having to do with the deployment of household labour) interact in concrete situations to reinforce, contradict or to undermine one another. One way to approach this is to undertake historical studies of the family in comparative settings; to compare and contrast rural and urban families, for example, in Egypt during the last hundred years. Comparable work on the family in Europe is already beginning to yield valuable insights into the evolution in women's roles and family structure in the context of the capitalist transformation of society.

While the Arab experience need not mirror that of Europe in its details, there is little reason to doubt the similarity in overall trends. For example, everywhere in the Middle East, we see the erosion of the extended patriarchal family and the emergence of the individual, both male and female, as an independent actor on the social scene. The domination of the young by the old and of women by men is no longer taken for granted. Whether publicly debated or simply reflected in the practical arrangements and relationships within the household, sex roles are changing rapidly, much as they did in Europe. The emerging patterns, however, are still too fluid and too varied to allow any simple and valid generalizations. This, however, need not discourage us from beginning to work towards that goal.

NOTES

1. For an interesting and up-to-date evaluation of 'women's studies', see M. Z. Rosaldo, 'The uses and abuses of anthropology: reflections on feminism and cross-cultural understanding', in *Signs*, 5, 3 (1980): 389–418. Also Naomi Quinn, 'Anthropological studies on women's status', in *Annual Review of Anthropology* 6 (1977): 181–222. Rasoldo's article includes a good general bibliography on the subject.
2. Annette Weiner, 'Women's Wealth and Political Evolution in the Pacific', unpublished manuscript. See also Weiner's book, *Women of Value, Men of Renown*, University of Texas Press, 1976, for an articulate statement on the need to reconceptualize our thinking about women and their place in society.
3. Lois Beck and Nikki Keddie, eds., *Women in the Moslem World*, Cambridge: Harvard University Press, 1978.

4. Ibid., p. 27. The articles included in the volume, uneven as they are, represent a vast range of data and are a valuable source for the study of the status of Muslim women.

5. Cynthia Nelson, 'Public and private politics: women in the Middle Eastern world', in *Arab Society in Transition*, eds. S. Ibrahim and N. Hopkins, pp. 121–49

6. Quoted in Nelson's article, op. cit.: 133.

7. From an unpublished manuscript quoted in Nelson's article, op. cit.: 134.

8. Nelson, op. cit.: 134.

9. Among these are the following: Carla Makhlouf, *Changing Veils*, University of Texas Press, 1979; Vanessa Maher, *Women and Property in Morocco*, Cambridge University Press, 1974; Cynthia Nelson, 'Women and power in nomadic societies of the Middle East', in *The Desert and the Sown*, ed. C. Nelson, University of California, Berkeley, 1973.

10. The Marxist–feminist literature is too vast to attempt any listing here. I would single out two collections: *Capitalist Patriarchy and the Case for Socialist Feminism*, ed. Zillah Eisenstein, New York: Monthly Review Press, 1979; and *Feminism and Materialism: Women and Modes of Production*, eds. Annette Kuhn and Annmarie Wolpe, London, Routledge and Kegan Paul, 1978.

11. Karen Sacks, 'Engels revisited', in M.Rosaldo and L. Lamphere, eds. *Women, Culture and Society*, Stanford University Press, 1974.

12. For a discussion of this whole issue, see the collected papers in the volume, *Feminism and Materialism: Women and Modes of Production*.

13. Roisin McDonough and Rachel Harrison, 'Patriarchy and relations of production', p. 25 in Kuhn and Wolpe, *Feminism*, pp. 10–41.

14. Abdelwahab Bouhdiba, *La Sexualité en Islam*, Paris, PUF, 1975.

15. Richard Antoun, 'On the modesty of women in Arab Moslem villages: A study in the accommodation of tradition', in *American Anthropologist* 70, No. 4 (1968): 671–97; Fatima Mernissi, *Beyond the Veil: Male–Female Dynamics in a Modern Muslim Society*, Cambridge, 1975; Paul Vieille, 'Iranian women in family alliance and sexual politics', in Beck and Keddie, *Women*, pp. 451–73; Daisy Dwyer, *Images and Self-Images: Male and Female in Morocco*, New York, 1978; John Mason, 'Sex and symbol in the treatment of women: the wedding rite in a Libyan oasis community', in *American Ethnologist*, 2, No. 4 (1975): 649–61.

16. Larry Rosen, 'The negotiation of reality: male–female relations in Sefrou, Morocco', in Beck and Keddie, *Women*, pp. 561–85.

17. Ibid., p. 569.

18. Hamed Ammar, *Growing Up in an Egyptian Village*, London, 1954; Hilma Granqvist, *Marriage Conditions in a Palestinian Village*, Helsingfors, 1931.

19. Amal Rassam, 'Women and domestic power in Morocco', in *The International Journal of Middle Eastern Studies*, 12 (1980), pp. 171–80.

20. Soheir Morsy, 'Sex differences and folk illness in an Egyptian Village', in Beck and Keddie, *Women*, pp. 599–617.

21. Ibid., p. 611.

22. See also V. Maher, 'Women and social change in Morocco', in Beck and Keddie, *Women*, pp.. 100–24, 1978.

23. Ibid., p. 122.

24. Nadia Youssef, 'The status and fertility patterns of Moslem Women', in Beck and Keddie, *Women*, p. 91, 1978.

25. Mona Hammam, 'The continuum of economic activities in Middle Eastern social formations, family division of labour and migration', unpublished paper prepared for the Wenner-Gren Foundation for Anthropological Research, 1980. Hammam's paper contains a good discussion of the effects of migration on the traditional division of labour in the Arab world.
26. Youssef, 'The status and fertility patterns of Moslem wives', in Beck and Keddie, *Women*, p. 96, 1978.
27. For a discussion of the relationship between political ideology, legislation, and the status of women in Iraq, see Amal Rassam, 'Political ideology and cultural constraints: women and legislation in Iraq', paper prepared for a book on *The Politics of Law in the Middle East*, ed. Daisy Dwyer, (1981).
28. Elizabeth White, 'Legal reform as an indicator of women's status in Moslim nations', in Beck and Keddie, *Women*, pp. 52–69, 1978.
29. Ibid., p. 66.

SELECTED BIBLIOGRAPHY

Al-Qazzaz, A. *Women in the Middle East and North Africa: An Annotated Bibliography*, Modern Middle East Monographs, 2, Austin: University of Texas Center for Middle Eastern Studies, 1977.
Beck, L. and N. Keddie. *Women in the Muslim World*, Cambridge and London, Harvard University Press, 1978.
Fernea, E. and B. Bezirgan. *Middle Eastern Moslem Women Speak*, Austin and London, University of Texas Press, 1977.
Keddie, N. 'Problems in the study of Middle Eastern women', *International Journal of Middle Eastern Studies*, 10, No. 2, 1979.
Maher, V. *Women and Property in Morocco*, Cambridge University Press, 1974.
Van Dusen, R. 'The study of women in the Middle East: some thoughts', *Middle East Studies Association Bulletin*, 10, No. 2, 1976.
Youssef, N. *Women and Work in Developing Societies*, Berkeley, University of California Institute of International Studies, Population Monograph Series No. 15, 1974.

8 A Survey of Trends in Social Sciences Research on Women in the Arab Region, 1960-1980

SOHA ABDEL KADER

INTRODUCTION

This chapter presents a critical analysis of trends in social science research on the roles and status of women in the Arab region. It assesses research trends since 1960 in the fields of history, religion, sociology, anthropology, economics, political science and law, and analyses the particular themes dealt with by this research.

It is a well-known fact that the bulk of social science research on the Middle East has been undertaken by Western scholars, or by Arab scholars educated in Western institutions. This also applies to research on women in the Arab region. For this region, the bulk of the material reviewed is in English, and to some extent in French. However, there is growing interest in the development of endogenous social science research and methodology. There is evidence that governments, social science research institutions and national universities are making serious efforts to accumulate a body of knowledge in this area of research. Much of the data collected is as yet unanalysed and there is lack of co-operation and communication between the institutions within each country on the one hand and between the national institutions in the different countries on the other. Studies of the status and roles of women are of particular interest at the present time because of the overriding concern with socio-economic national development and the necessity of integrating women in its processes.

Defining the status of Arab women is no easy task. To what extent it is possible to speak of 'Arab women' as an entity is, of course, open to debate. As a cultural unit, the Arab world has been defined as 'complex and mosaic-like . . .', and 'intricately structured both vertically and horizontally', and it is said that the 'lack of communication has favoured the emergence of local differences beneath the overall but often rather thinly spread veneer of Islamic culture'. As such the Arab region has posed continual conundrums to researchers. So have its women.

HISTORY OF WOMEN IN THE ARAB REGION: THE 'GREAT WOMEN
OF THE ANCIENT MIDDLE EAST'

All accounts of the history of Arab women agree that:

(a) In pre-Islamic times women actively participated in all community activities
of the desert Arabs. There was free interaction between the sexes, and in fact
very few restrictions on marriage and divorce. Ilse Lichtenstadter, writing about
the period, says: 'Women, in that remote age, were an integral part of the
communal life; segregation and seclusion, which impoverished and narrowed the
life of Muslim women for centuries, were instituted much later.' (1967: p. 43.)

(b) Women in the early days of Islam in Arabia played an active role in the
social and political life of the community;

(c) the autobiographical sketches of 'Early Muslim Women' and the 'Great
Women in the Ancient Middle East' should serve as worthy examples for modern
women.

Ilse Seibert's *Women in the Ancient Near East* (1974) surveys women's life
in the Ancient Near East, especially in Asia Minor, the Syrian–Palestinian region
and what is now Iraq and the Islamic Republic of Iran. Drawing from ancient
documents and records, she provides a chronological table giving political-
historical periods with corresponding information on the status of women.

Joanna McKenna in *Great Women of the Ancient Middle East* (1975) provides a brief look at seventeen Middle Eastern women who have not only 'accomplished great feats' but who also represent a significant juncture in history.
The seventeen women include Hagar, the second wife of Abraham, Hatshepsut
and Nefertiti from Ancient Egypt, the Queen of Sheba from Yemen, Khadija,
wife of Muhammad, and Fatima, the sole surviving child of Muhammad.

Sabri discusses the exemplary virtues of 'Early Muslim Women'. Their faith,
courage, loyalty to their husbands, patience, knowledge and efforts to spread
Islam are illustrated by historical accounts of their activities and deeds (Sabri
1974).

Elizabeth Fernea and Bassima Bezirgan provide similar examples by pre-
senting translations of the literary works and writings of some of the early
Muslim women. Their book includes the works of such important historical
figures as Al-Khansa, poet of early Islam and Rabi'a, the mystic. Included also
is a biographical sketch of the life of 'Aisha, bint Abi Bakr, wife of the Prophet
Muhammad (Fernea and Bezirgan, 1977: pp. 3–76).

A number of studies in Arabic with a historical orientation also offer biographical sketches of famous Arab women and accounts of the lives of women
in ancient Arab civilization (Bahaim 1962; Nazir 1965; Hussein 1970). One
book by a Jordanian, Faiza Abdel Megeed, is almost an Arabic verion of *Muslim
Middle Eastern Women Speak* (Fernea and Bezirgan 1977). Appearing in 1968,

this book, *Women in Struggle*, includes biographical sketches and extracts of the works of such 'history makers' as Khadija, Fatima Al Zahra, Rabai El Adawiya and others. However, it also includes extracts from the works and lives of Western women such as Florence Nightingale and Helen Keller. The theme of the book is that the seclusion and confinement of Arab women in modern times has been an arbitrary measure that has deprived women of self-confidence. A look at the famous women in the Arab past nullifies the view that men alone were created for leadership in politics, war, and the building of civilizations. Women in the East, just like women in the West, have creatively contributed to the development of mankind. 'In my review of the lives of these immortal feminine characters', says the writer, 'I only offer an example for Arab women to follow' (Abdel Megeed 1968: p. 8).

ISLAM: THE DETERMINANT OF ARAB WOMEN'S STATUS?

Islam, as a creed and religion, and the Koran, the Prophet's sayings, and Islamic Shari'a as the source of personal statutes laws (laws governing marriage, divorce, inheritance, etc.) have been considered by many as important determinants of the status of Arab women.

Certainly, the debate over the position of women in Islam is a leitmotiv of Western literature on women in the Arab region. A review of this literature reveals that it is divided into two broad categories: studies which adopt a defensive posture, i.e., studies which maintain that Islam sustains rather than undermines women's rights; and studies which adopt a critical posture, i.e., studies that blame Islam for the low status of women and the inequality of the sexes prevalent in the Muslim world.

The Defensive Posture

The defenders of the position of women in Islam argue that while the Koran and the Prophet's original teachings may at the present time seem to subjugate women, an examination of the style of life prevalent during Muhammad's time indicates loose family ties, predominant polygamy, easy divorce and remarriage, and an obsession with sexual pleasures. Pre-Islamic institutions, particularly female infanticide and marriage by kidnapping, were highly unfavourable to women. In this respect, the Prophet's rulings were in fact directed towards improving the moral quality of life for both men and women. Islamic institutions, particularly of the 'Utopian Age of Islam', the seventh century, elevated the status of women by banning female infanticide, limiting the number of women a man could marry to four, imposing adequate provisions by the husband for his wife and children within marriage and even after divorce (Culver 1962; Badran 1971; Levy 1965; Yusef 1965; Charney 1971; Saleh 1977).

Further, women have been cruelly and mercilessly exploited by different religious and secular cultures during the course of history. By contrast, Islam, while it did not entirely remove the stigma of 'wickedness' and impurity which other religions had placed on women, in the eyes of Allah and in the Koran and Hadiths, all believers, men and women, are treated as equal (Nazat 1967). Polygamy, for instance, is considered particularly degrading to the status of Muslim women. However, all the prophets of the Old Testament (Abraham, David and Solomon) had more than one wife, and as such, Islam did not create this practice. In fact, it was advocated by the Koran as a limitation on prevailing customs, which allowed a man to marry more than four wives (Badawi 1972). In an interesting article on the topic, M. W. Gazder writes:

> It is an established fact that in France polygamy is practically recognized, with the only modification that the second wife is called a mistress and not a wife, and has not got the same status. This practice is also accepted particularly among the Latin races, of keeping a mistress. But what is the position of such a woman? She has no social standing and if she has a child, it inherits the stigma of her unreputable position! [Gazder 1973: p. 19.]

The contemporary 'low' status of Muslim women does not reflect the spirit of the Koran or Hadiths. Rather, it is the result of 'extra-Islamic conditions', misinterpretation of Koranic injunctions and abuses of Islamic Law. The influences of social custom and tradition and medieval times have, for instance, resulted in the acceptance of such social standards as the veiling and seclusion of women (Saleh 1972; Abdel Kader 1973; Espositio 1975).

It is thus in the true understanding and authentic interpretation of the spirit of the Koran and Hadiths that the salvation of women in Muslim countries lies. The future status of Muslim women lies with those who seek their freedom and emancipation within Islam, rather than with those who seek it without (Culver 1967). Preconceived notions about wrong interpretations of Islam have thus far prevented Western scholars and modern Arab intellectuals alike from studying it for solutions of the problems of modern Muslim society (Abdul-Rauf 1977; Fernea 1973; Abdel-Ati 1974).

Western stereotyped thinking also has prevented Western scholars from understanding the status of women in Islam. The role and status of Muslim women should not be judged by Western standards. A Middle Eastern Muslim woman's traditional role, like that of her Western counterpart, has been the bearing and raising of children, with her first responsibility to her family. The only difference is that Middle Eastern women have been shaped by a different culture, namely, Islamic culture. Today, Islamic religious rituals and practices are not obstacles to women's participation and self-fulfillment, but rather may offer them opportunities for socialization and public activities (Fernea 1972; Fernea 1973). In a study conducted on sex-role expectations among male and female students of both the Christian and Muslim faiths, no differences were depicted between the two groups as to role expectations for women (Dodd 1974).

It is even possible that in many ways Muslim women are endowed with certain attitudes and ways of living that may help them accommodate more successfully than Western women to conditions of change.

The position of women in the Middle East should not be blamed entirely on Islam, as it is directly related to the position of all people in the Middle East, male or female, adult or child, rich or poor. Their position is also a function of the socio-economic standards prevalent in countries of the region. As the standard of living rises, so too may that of the whole population including women (Abdel Kader 1973; Fernea 1973).

The Critical Posture

The critics of the status of women in Islam argue that in essence the Koran offers no real ethical codes or moral values regarding men-women relations. The enjoyment of physical pleasures, particularly for men, is accepted and provided for. Women, on the other hand, are primarily sexual objects to be protected from their own immoral qualities and to be hidden behind veils and curtains. Muslim marriage is based on the premise that social order can only be maintained if the woman's dangerous potential for chaos is restrained. Women are thus held as a prize piece of property, not as persons. A new sexual order and new legislation are needed to remove the limitations to women's potential (Bousquet 1966; Bullough 1973; Mernissi 1975; Anderson 1970).

According to such critics, ingrained patterns of Islamic culture and tradition are in many ways diametrically opposed to the Western way and inconsistent with the requirements of an industrial era. This is particularly so as the prevailing customs of the seclusion and veiling of women are considered as major obstacles, preventing women from participating in the vital process of socio-economic development in the Muslim world (Youssef 1972; 1971; 1974).

Arab Literature

The status of women in Islam is also a leitmotiv of Arabic literature on Arab women, but with a slightly different orientation. The majority of the literature in Arabic on Arab women deals with the position of women in personal statutes laws. These studies, specialized and intricate, are comparisons between the civil codes and the Islamic Shari'a, based on the Koran, and the Prophet's Hadiths. Most of them offer rationalization for the perpetuation of these laws rather than for their change (El Sebai 1966; Sha'ban 1965; Abdullah 1965; Khaleel 1964; El Berdissey 1965; El Tantani 1971; El Fakahany 1966; El Sebai 1973; Khatagy 1960; Abou Zahra 1960; Abdul Ati 1962; El Digwy 1972; El Husseiny 1969; El Hodany 1968). Some scholars concentrate on particular aspects of the law, such as divorce or polygamy (Shaker 1970; Meghaniya 1960; El Khouly 1962; El Sabouny 1962; Badran 1964; El Ghandour 1967; Ghazy 1970; Gouda 1969; El Attar 1972). One work is a comparative study of Islamic and American laws (Hassan 1966).

The authors of these works are lawyers or Islamic scholars and are mainly men, possibly because Muslim women are still excluded from holding leading and official religious positions.

Another set of studies covers the general topic of the position of women in Islam. Descriptive and defensive, they either analyse the position of women in Orthodox Islam (i.e., the Koran and Hadiths) or offer recommendations for the role of 'a Muslim Woman in a Muslim Society', again based on Orthodox Islam (El Giry 1975; Al Agad 1962; Abdel Bagy 1978; El Nawaury 1970; Mohammed 1963; El Ibrashy 1971; Derwaza 1968; El Wafy 1971). The Higher Council for Islamic Affairs, al Majlis al-A'la lil-Shuum al-Islamiyya, in Cairo issued a book in its series 'Studies in Islam': *Islam, the Liberator of Women* (Hussein 1968). The University of Al-Azhar also published a series of articles on the same topic in its periodical *Majallat al-Azhar* from October 1968 to May 1969.

Resolution of a Conflict: A Modern View

The position of Middle Eastern women has fluctuated historically, and consequently the two opposing points of view are justified. The belief that Muhammad bettered the pre-Islamic status of women or that Middle Eastern women are 'the serfs of the modern world' are both true and false. In fact, the truth obviously lies somewhere between the two contrasting points of view. The central paradox of Middle Eastern society may best be understood if one thinks of a straight line as representing that society. At one end stands the Koran, the codification of the word of God; at the other lie the forces of tribal and family custom (the word of Man). The understanding of the conflict between the Koran and local customs and traditions may resolve the issue.

As a recent book suggests, the resolution of this conflict and the combating of the stereotyped thinking of the past may lie in going to the 'primary sources' and in letting 'Muslim Middle Eastern Women Speak for Themselves' (Fernea and Bezirgan 1977).

LOCAL CUSTOM AND TRADITION: THE DETERMINANTS OF THE STATUS OF WOMEN WITHIN THE TRADITIONAL ARAB FAMILY

Of all the component features of Middle Eastern social organization, scholars seem to agree that the traditional Arab family is the most fundamental, the most important and the most resistant to change.

During the first part of this century and up to the 1960s Western sociologists and anthropologists accorded little attention in terms of empirical research to the traditional Arab family. Starting with the 1960s, a flood of sociological and anthropological studies on the Arab family made their appearance. In most of these studies, women and family are used synonymously, for a major concern was with the impact of the changing status of women in traditional Arab family organization and vice versa. The emerging movements for the 'emancipation' of Arab women were seen by many as powerful forces for revolutionary and radical change in the existing social order. At the same time, certain aspects of the traditional Arab family were seen to have a direct bearing on the lives of Arab women and so by and large determine their status. Sociologists and anthropologists have singled out the various features of the traditional Arab family as determinants of the status of women.

Private/Public Dichotomy: Female Seclusion and Veiling

Most researchers on the Middle East note the obvious social segregation between the sexes. Referred to as 'Men's World and Women's World' or 'The Public/ Private Dichotomy', it is another *leitmotiv* characterizing Western literature on male–female relations in the Middle East (Van Dusen 1976).

According to researchers, the highest value is placed upon the proper conduct of women before marriage and upon their marital fidelity (Hansen 1961; Goode 1963; Berger 1963; Antoun 1968; Patai 1969; Abu Zahra 1970; Dodd 1973; Mason 1975). Many explanations have been provided to explain these strong restrictions placed upon the behaviour of women. Some have found them a major contributing factor to the solidarity of the Arab family as 'a woman's status defines the status of all the men who are related to her in a determinate way' (Schneider 1971, p. 18). Others have found it only a rationalization for the subjection in which men hold women in the Middle East (Berger 1963).

Local tradition and custom in the Middle East separate men and women even more than the Koran might have intended, and the practices of veiling and seclusion help to maintain their two quite different societies. Veiling and seclusion did not exist in early Arabia. All historical accounts point to the fact that women in the early days of Islam in Arabia and the countries that came under the influence of the Arabs played an active role in the social and political life of the community. A study of the Koran and the Prophet's Hadiths shows that there is no particular injunction that indicates that women should be veiled or secluded from participation in public life. It was the Prophet Muhammad who first veiled his women in order to symbolize their special status as his wives. His purpose in veiling them was to distinguish them from other women of the community and to preserve their respect as being of special status. The spread of the practice of veiling and seclusion among the converts of Islam took the form of emulation of the Prophet and was more an urban than a rural phenomenon, because it was in the cities that the Arab influence was concentrated. Though at first a private and personal matter, which some people adhered to while others ignored, it became a widespread custom as the number of slaves and concubines increased (Nelson 1972). It was approximately one hundred and fifty years after the death of the Prophet that 'the system [of seclusion of women] was fully established . . . in which, among the richer classes, the women were shut off from the rest of the household under the charge of eunuchs' (Levy 1957).

Female seclusion and veiling have sometimes been used synonymously. However, though interrelated and mutually reinforcing, they signify two completely different things. Seclusion is the practice of confining women, after puberty, to their own company. Veiling, on the other hand, is the wearing of a head and face cover that conceals the hair and the lower part of the face. In essence, veiling is only symbolic of the seclusion of women. Today, there are no hard and fast rules as to the presence or absence of veiling in a certain region or among certain socio-economic groups. Generally it is more prevalent in urban centres and among the upper classes of urban and peasant societies (Patai 1969; Abdel Kader 1973).

The Traditional Arab Family

The traditional Middle Eastern family is extended. It is generally headed by an elderly man and consists of his wife (or wives), his unmarried daughters, his unmarried as well as married sons, and the wives and children of the latter (Patai 1969, pp. 84-9).

Because the traditional Arab family is patriarchal, patrilineal and patrilocal, daughters, when they marry, depart from their own extended families and become incorporated into the extended family of their husbands, although their own consanguinal families still remain responsible for their moral conduct. Some scholars maintain that this existing network of social relationships serves to protect and sustain women's rights (Rosenfeld 1960; Sweet 1967; Farsoun 1970; Lutfiyya 1970).

Cross-Cousin Marriage

Because it is practically non-existent outside the Middle East, the marriage of cousins is among the topics frequently dealt with by anthropologists and sociologists alike. The fact that marriage between children of two brothers is regarded as the ideal marriage preferred in practice to all other unions is reflected in everday linguistic usage, in numerous current proverbs and in stories. According to researchers, the custom has been confirmed and perpetuated by Muslim tradition and has remained alive to the present day, particularly in peasant and Bedouin societies (Khouri 1970; Barth 1970).

Endogamy

Beyond cross-cousin marriage, the Middle Eastern family is endogamous, meaning there is a preference for marriages contracted within a relatively narrow circle. In theory, Koranic Law permits a Muslim man to marry any woman and a Muslim woman to marry any man, provided they accept Islam. In practice, traditional customs have narrowed it down considerably, so that each social group tends to behave endogamously. Intermarriage among members of the three distinct social groups, Bedouins, peasants and townspeople, is discountenanced in theory and rare in practice. Within these social groups, marriage is again limited by socio-economic and kinship considerations.

Who Wants Change?

Today, the Arab family in its traditional form is most prevalent in Bedouin and peasant cultures that constitute approximately 65 per cent of the region. It is also prevalent with slight variations among the lower and lower middle classes of Arab cities and urban centres. It thus constitutes the traditional baseline from which all change must start.

Yet, who wants change? The heavy restrictions placed on women's activities, and their relegation, at least in the eyes of outside observers, to a position of inferiority, are not rejected by the women themselves. Studies indicate that women often constitute a stabilizing force, contributing to the perpetuation and continuity of tradition and custom. Because their rules are strictly delineated, their lives are sometimes easier, and their role performance is often more competent that that of men (Fuller 1961; Barclay 1964; Fernea 1965; Deng 1972; Beck 1975; Saunders 1975).

Further, close scrutiny of the lives of these women reveals that in essence they enjoy extensive power and that existing conditions allow them sufficient leeway to impose their wishes and desires, even if through devious and subtle means.

In an examination of the concepts of power, authority, status, and communication systems in nomadic and pastoral tribes, Dr. Cynthia Nelson (1974) states that ethnographers have been dominated by the concept of the public/ private dichotomy, a concept she challenges and rejects, at least in part. She further suggests that the prevalent social segregation is in reality beneficial to women. She writes:

> From the ethnographic literature, we know precious little about how women in these societies view their situation, whether they feel they have power or whether they wield it. [p. 553.]

Advocating a redefinition of power to encompass how men and women are involved in 'negotiating their social order', she suggests that ethnographers should raise a different set of ethnographic questions, which have been hitherto neglected. Such questions include:

> What are the normative constructs that facilitate, limit and govern 'negotiations'? What are the sanctions open to women? In what ways can and do women set up alternatives for men by their own actions? How do women influence men? Who controls whom about what? How is control exercised? How do women control men? Other women? How conscious are women of their capacity to influence? [p. 554.]

In other words, questions that examine the role and position of women in Middle Eastern society from the standpoint of the women themselves. In partial answer, Dr. Nelson cites references to ethnographic studies that indicate that women can and do exercise a greater degree of power in spheres of social life than has heretofore been appreciated (Peters 1966; Mohsen 1967; Cunnison 1966; Leinhardt 1972; Aswad 1967; Schneider 1971). These ethnographic studies indicate that women exercise influence in three major social spheres: (a) mediation; (b) sorcery; (c) the religious or supernatural spheres.

Her view is supported, in our opinion, by the fact that in spite of the abundance of literature on the urban upper class women's demands for emancipation, very few studies reveal that either rural, Bedouin, or urban lower and lower middle class women ask for or desire any change.

THE 'EMANCIPATION' OF ARAB WOMEN

The basic features of the traditional Arab family have been consistent with the demands of an agricultural way of life. Technological development, spread of mass communications, and improvement of transportation facilities have brought about fundamental changes in Arab society, which have in turn affected the family. However, to Western researchers in the 1960s, the rising status of Arab women and their emergence into the world of affairs seemed to be one of the most powerful forces for change, not only in the Arab family but in Arab society generally. Consequently a large number of studies dealing with the 'emancipation' of Arab women and the changing patterns of the traditional Arab family made their appearance.

Causes of 'Emancipation'

According to these studies two major factors have been influential in bringing about a change in the status of Arab women. One is evolutionary and attributed to the spread of 'modernization', usually taken to mean the spread of Western culture and the concomitant spread of movements for the 'emancipation' of women. The second is revolutionary and imposed as, after decolonization, governments of the newly independent countries came to view the integration of women in the national economy as essential to socio-economic development.

Indices of 'Emancipation'

Increased enrolment of women in all levels of education, their increased participation in work outside the home, their acquisition of the right to vote, and the demands of the militants among them for change in legislation (especially the Personal Statutes and Labour Code) were considered empirical indices of increased 'emancipation'. Consequently, many of these studies are statistical and historical.

Magnitude of 'Emancipation'

Most studies agree that the changes in the status of Arab women were not uniform across social classes or in rural and urban areas. 'Emancipation'— at least in terms of increased education and participation in the labour force —was a demand emanating mostly from the upper and middle classes of urban areas.

The urban population of the Arab world represents only thirty-two per cent of the total, and 'emancipated' Arab women represent only a small proportion of this sector.

In 1962 Morrow Berger wrote:

Only on the well-insulated university campuses of the Arab World can one regularly see respectable unmarried young men and women talking freely with one another with the implied consent of their absent elders. Although the relations between men and women in the Arab World are changing every day, they are still governed, especially in less sophisticated social classes and places, by old and strict codes of meeting, mating and, the creation of families. [Berger 1962, pp. 117-18.]

Consequences of 'Emancipation'

'Emancipation' is incongruent with the persistent features of the traditional Arab family predominant almost everywhere in the Arab region. As such, it is a persistent source of conflict. Yet the foregoing sections have indicated that the majority of women in the Bedouin and peasant societies and in the urban lower and lower middle classes of the Arab region seem basically satisfied with the existing social order. Unaware of the alternatives, none of them questions or is militant against 'overt' male dominance. In spite of the strictness of the moral sex code, they are well-adjusted and find implicit and covert ways for self-fulfillment and the realization of their ends.

It is the educated, urban middle class women who most ardently seek change, and it is they who suffer the most. It is also the Arab urban family that has undergone changes in relationships between men and women.

Although, by virtue of education, Middle Eastern college students are un-representative of Middle Eastern young people in general, they are the area's most articulate group. Consequently, most of the studies conducted in the 1960s were conducted among college students (Najarian 1959; Muhyi 1919; Melikian 1960; Daghestani 1970; El-Din Ali 1966).

Results of these research studies reveal that it is these young educated urban women who bear the burden of change and the concomitant complexities of the psychological problem of adjustment to a society in a state of transition. Without historical precedent they were often at a loss to deal with the new conditions in which they found themselves. At times of crisis and decision the prevailing traditions catch them unawares, sometimes submerging them and paralysing their movement forward.

According to Sayegh, 'born in a middle class family, in a capital city like Beirut, Cairo, or Tunis, an Arab girl's life today is only intangibly different from an American girl's' (Sayegh 1968). The intangibles are, however, sometimes harder to fight than the obvious injustices that exist in the law and local custom and tradition. The over-protectiveness of parents is still a factor, as well as the feeling of being constantly watched, talked about, or spied on. 'The "newness" makes Arab women nervous, like débutante skaters, and the doors open in childhood mysteriously close at maturity' (Sayegh 1968).

When the customary ways of doing things break down or are no longer adequate, social disorganization takes place and is reflected in various forms of social pathology. However, Dr. Ibrahim Abdulla Muhyi concludes that the emancipated young women 'are not neurotic. They are reacting in a healthy way to a world that is in a state of change' (Muhyi 1959, p. 57).

Among the male and female college students, there is awareness of the inequality between the sexes in terms of rights, but male students show a strong reluctance to give up their supremacy.

Men are still reluctant to give women equal freedom in their choice of vocation or of friends, but less strict than their fathers, whereas women subjects demand equal rights. [Melikian 1960, p. 25.]

Generalizing from such studies, scholars conclude that even if, in principle, Middle Eastern men accept the equality of the sexes, in practice they resist it.

There is resistance among men to the more obvious concomitants of equal status for women, such as freedom to move in public, adoption of European dress and manners and employment outside the home. [Berger 1962, p. 149.]

Men seem to embrace the basic processes leading to emancipation, that is, education and industrialization, not out of conviction of the equality of the sexes but as a result of the strong desire for 'national strength'.

As to the 'changing patterns' of the traditional Arab family, researchers of the 1960s detected two types of families existing side by side among urban upper and middle classes: a liberal type of family and a more traditional type. The former is characterized by a certain adoption of Western ideals, the latter still immune to Western influence.

In a recent book, *Arab Society in Transition*, Saad Ibrahim and Nicholas Hopkins indicate that the contemporary urban family is reluctantly, but steadily, moving in the direction of egalitarianism. It is not totally traditional as it was between the ninth and nineteenth centuries, but it is not totally modern in the Western sense either. The contemporary urban Arab family is an Arab version of the nuclear family and it is in a state of transformation and change in structure, functions, and values (Ibrahim and Hopkins 1977).

Arabic Literature on the Emancipation of Arab Women

The most well-known book in Arabic literature on the emancipation of Muslim women is the book by Qasim Amin, *The Emancipation of Women*, first published in Egypt in 1899. Still popular and widely read, it has been repeatedly reprinted. However, a number of books dealing with the same topic have since made their appearance (Badwan 1970; Ali 1973; El Zobaidy 1973; Tibi 1968).

Amin was educated in the West and, like many other men of his class, enjoyed a higher educational level than the majority of the population. He thus came to change his attitudes towards women and to demand a more active role for wives, sisters, mothers, and daughters than prevailing traditions allowed. A similar note is echoed in modern writings. In the introduction to a Lebanese study, *Women in the Twentieth Century* (Al Sabiq 1978), Michael Noima, a well-known Lebanese literary figure writes:

> Woman in the twentieth century is almost a new being who, if witnessed by the eyes of past centuries, may be unrecognizable and unaccepted. This new being has changed the nature of mankind and demonstrated to it that it cannot fly with one wing, the man, but must fly with two equally functional wings: man and woman. [Al Sabiq 1978, p. i.]

The book describes the various social, political, philosophical, scientific and industrial revolutions in the West and how women emerged there working in different fields side by side with men, 'even in space' (Al Sabiq 1978). Obviously, the implication is that Arab women should take Western women as an example.

Maybe the only equivalent in modern Arabic literature to Qasim Amin's books is the work of Dr Nawal El Sadawy. A gynaecologist by education and of some years' practice, Dr Sadawy in recent years has concentrated her research efforts on the subject of sexuality in the Arab world. She published four books in sequence: *Women and Sex (1)*, in 1972, *Women and Sex (2)*, *Woman is the Origin*, in 1974, *Man and Sex* in 1976 and *The Hidden Face of Eve* in 1977.

Her first book *Woman and Sex*, designated as 'the first frank and scientific look at the sexual problems of women in Arab society', was received to some extent with the same degree of disapprobation and hostility that was accorded the works of Amin. The *Hidden Face of Eve* reviews the history of Arab women from pre-Islamic times to present, and discusses the image of Arab women in literature.

Dr Sadawy's works may be seen as the very first attempt in Arabic literature on women to synthesize the literature of the 'liberation movement' in the Western world with the literature on the status and conditions of Arab women. She refers extensively and in detail to the works of Freud, Karen Horney, Kinsey, Masters and Johnson and others who have studied female sexuality and psychology, but she also draws extensively from the works of Juliette Mitchell, Germaine Greer and Simone de Beauvoir. Eclectic in her approach, she uses English, French, German and Arabic literature on medicine, psychology, history, biology and economics (numerous references are made to Marx's works).

However, in our opinion, the explosive nature of her works lies mostly in the first chapters of her first book *Women and Sex*, where she discusses the issue of virginity and the almost irrational fear and anxiety families experience until their daughters are delivered intact to their husbands. She gives accounts of some of the cases she encountered while practising her profession as a gynaecologist. Commenting on the contradictions inherent in the virginity cult, she deplores the fact that parents, perhaps because of extreme social pressure, are primarily concerned about preserving the virginity of their daughters at almost any cost and to the exclusion of perhaps more important attributes of personal integrity such as truthfulness, honesty, diligence, mental development, etc. According to her, integrity is considered a masculine attribute. Referring to her own experience she writes:

> Very often, the epithet 'male' followed me whenever I excelled in my studies or work. If I kept my word and fulfilled my promise, they said 'man'; if I walked fast in flat shoes, they said, 'man'; if I practised sports and built up my muscles, they said, 'man'. [Sadawy 1972, p. 14.]

Dr Sadawy is also a novelist, and through her works one gets a glimpse of the situation of women in contemporary society, their dilemmas and their relationships. Cynthia Nelson describes her as 'one of the most fascinating figures writing about the feelings and conditions of women in contemporary Egypt . . . who has earned the reputation over the past ten years as *the* radical feminist in Egypt today' and as 'the Germaine Greer of Egypt' (Nelson 1978).

However, there are Arab writers who totally refute the theory of 'equality of the sexes'. In his book *Women: This Mystery*, Abbas Mahmoud Al Aqqad (one of the most famous scholars in the Arab world) reviews the status of women in history and argues that feminists and the militants for equal rights are in reality destroying every chance for prestige (*karama*) for women. Men and women are inherently different, and by driving women to play men's roles, feminists are depriving them of every chance for supremacy, particularly in the home and in domestic life, where they rightly belong.

Throughout history, during the Greek, Roman, Chinese, and Indian cultures, women who engaged in public affairs (such as rich widows who opened their homes to poets, writers and painters) were 'fair play for irony and fun-making'. It is only as keepers of their homes and as mothers of their children that women were respected and venerated. When women in Eastern or Western ancient cultures were allowed to hold positions of leadership and acted as queens or priestesses, it was only because of the absence of male inheritors. In such positions women were expected to behave like men, not like women (Al Aqqad 1970, pp. 17-24).

Aqqad believed modern society to be in a state of disequilibrium and the demands for equal rights to be only a manifestation of the deviations and abnormalities of this state of disequilibrium. It is for a return to the normal and natural ordinance of giving women supremacy within homes and in domestic spheres that feminists should fight, if they should fight at all.

One author, Al Magdoub, goes so far as to claim that emancipation of women leads to a higher crime rate. In the introduction to a book entitled *Women and Crime* he writes:

> The twentieth century has been characterized by the acquisition by woman of a number of rights that she never enjoyed before, the right to education, the right to work, the right to vote and to take on political leading roles, and other rights . . . In light of these changes in the status of women, there has been increased concern with studies of the impact of this change on women themselves, their relationships with men and the family and other areas . . . At the same time the problem of crime has not received similar attention . . . although it is a well-known fact and a logical deduction that the rate of crime is directly related to the advent of women into public life and the crimes she commits increase as her responsibilities increase . . .
>
> The criminal behaviour of women should be seriously studied, particularly because of its impact on security and peace and particularly because women as mothers have a tremendous influence on their children and are solely responsible for their socialization . . . [Al Magdoub 1977, pp. 3-5.]

The author then proceeds to provide data to support his hypothesis that the number of crimes committed by women increases as their participation in public life increases. The implications of a study such as this for the question of female emancipation are of course open to debate, but the study is a scientific one that draws on data compiled by Western and Middle Eastern scholars alike. Though the study analyses the rate and types of crime as related to age, marital status, literacy, employment and rural-urban residence of women, it does not refer particularly to Arab women, or even to any particular country in the Arab region, but to women generally.

WOMEN'S POLITICAL AND LEGAL STATUS

Political Status

Very little research has been done on the political roles of women in the Arab region.[1] Beraet Ungor, in an article on 'Women in the Middle East and North Africa and universal suffrage', published in the *Annals of the American Academy of Political and Social Science*, No. 378 (1968), expressed the view that the 'emancipation of women and equalization of their political rights have been successful only in part in the countries in the Middle East . . . The condition of women depends on the behavior of men . . .' (Ungor 1968, p. 72).

She further points out that the participation of women in political activities is viewed as a function of their status as a whole, and that while governments encourage and stimulate co-operation, and while most women in the Arab region enjoy the right to vote, public opinion is reticent.

Though the militants among women are interested in politics and to some degree in the labour unions, they have not organized themselves, and thus women do not constitute an electoral force which can open the way to positions of leadership. Though some women work in the women's divisions of political parties, they tend to be followers, not leaders, and are elected only to the extent that they are chosen by men within the parties.

Ungor suggests that the political training of women should begin in school. Women should be instructed in civic and political matters and given a taste for public affairs and public administration. Women's organizations and associations which display meritorious activity in cultural and philanthropic areas ought to become more interested in the civic education of women (Ungor 1968, pp. 72–81).

Several studies have focused on the role of Arab women in nationalist and national liberation movements. Extensive historical data and examples prove that the political mobilization of women and nationalist movements are strongly associated. As the struggle for nationalistic goals intensified, demands for equality of women and programmes to meet those demands emerged within the movements. Separate women's organizations with separate infra-structure keep the 'woman question' on the political agenda in the pre- and post-independence periods (Fluehr-Lobban 1975).

A more recent trend in sociological and anthropological research is to consider political roles in the wider context of 'power relations'. Within this conceptual framework it is pointed out that women enjoy a great deal of power, particularly in mediation, where they use subtle manipulation to reach their ends (Nelson 1972).

Legal Status

Islam itself does not discriminate between men and women as far as contractual obligations are concerned, and there is no opposition to women participating in public affairs. That is why development in political rights in the Arab countries has taken place more rapidly than the evolution in personal and family rights.

The efforts of feminists and progressive thinkers in the Arab world have been most frustrated in the area of personal statutes law. A number of studies have tackled the problem of the status of women in these laws. These studies are descriptive, and compare personal statutes laws to Islamic Shari'a (Abdul-Rauf 1972; Anderson 1970; Badawi 1972; El Sayed 1968).

The status of Arab women in the labour codes has been studied by institutions. The most important contribution in this respect is a book issued by the Arab League, which is a compilation of all legislation and declarations relating to the status of Arab women in the laws.

PARTICIPATION OF ARAB WOMEN IN NATIONAL DEVELOPMENT

The picture portrayed by official statistics of Arab women's participation in production is that they are relatively inactive, their labour force participation rates being recorded as among the lowest in the world. Middle Eastern countries report the lowest female participation rate in economic activities outside agriculture, as they are almost absent from the occupational and industrial sectors of employment. Their participation in the agricultural sector, though not the lowest in the world, is still small.

The very bleak picture presented by statistical data of the low participation rate of Arab women in economic activities is contested on a number of counts. Many explanations have been given for this discrepancy in the large body of literature on the general topic of 'Women and development' that has made its appearance in recent years. Understandably such literature deals mainly with 'non-Western', 'traditional' or 'low-income' countries; in other words, the developing countries of the Third World, of which the Arab region is a part.

This body of literature came into being partly as a result of the growing concern on the part of local, revolutionary governments and international development agencies to integrate women in national strategies for economic development. Promoting women's participation in development was viewed notably as a means to:

1   Increase per capita income over time through an increased investment in human resources;

2   Limit fertility, the struggle for development being defined as a race between

capital accumulation and population growth, as working women tend to have fewer children;

3   Improve their status, sense of selfhood and independence.

What gave this research on women and development its impetus was the failure of both local and international programmes to accomplish more than piecemeal success. It was felt that more research was needed to point out possible problem areas and indicate ways in which more realistic development programmes can recognize and support women's contribution to the economic sector.

From the emerging body of literature a number of new truths came to light. One of these was the realization that Arab women, like women in other traditional societies, are doing more than statistics show. Nikki Keddie and Lois Beck, in the introduction to *Women in the Muslim World*, are of the opinion that statistical data do not present a true image of the participation of Arab women in economic activities. The cause for this lies in 'the tendency of Western industrial societies to regard as work only what is directly paid, and to adopt this definition in censuses throughout the world'. They and others rightly argue that such a distinction makes no sense, however widely it is used, in precapitalist societies and in many parts of Third World societies today. Zdenek Vavra, in a monograph on 'Demographic aspects of manpower in Arab countries', points out that it is very difficult to define the main features of female economic activity in the Arab region using statistics alone. In addition to the fact that the female labour force participation rate differs so much from country to country, it is the female labour force participation estimates that suffer the most from the variations in concepts and methods of enumeration used. Present techniques obliterate the economic and social participation of women in both the intra-familial and extra-familial dimensions of life.

Certain recent studies attempt to enumerate the ways in which Arab women actively contribute to the economy and the many productive roles they play that are obviously overlooked by the present system of enumeration. Setting aside housework, childbearing, and childrearing, which, as Lois Beck and Nikki Keddie note, 'the current fashions do not consider as work', there are workers in traditional occupations, such as hired fieldworkers, weavers, and craftspeople, midwives and curers, domestic servants and others who do work that goes unremunerated (women work long hours and receive little or nothing in wages) and hence is unaccounted for in the census data.

In essence, what this argument says is that all women work, often from early childhood, but this simple fact is often ignored. In a mimeographed paper on 'Nomadism, mobility and the status of women', Elise Boulding argues that there is less gender-based role differentiation among nomads than among settled people. Nomadic women live in a more participatory society than settled women; their skills and decision-making and adaptive abilities are considered essential and are highly respected by men. In contrast, settled women live in a more structured and confining environment. The roles of women in societies 'on the move' should serve as examples for the increased participation of women in all levels of society (Boulding 1974).

Aziza Hussein and others argue that rural women, who constitute 60 per cent of the Arab female population, are the backbone of agricultural production. Not only do they look after the agricultural household, but they also do a great deal of intensive cultivation in the field, in addition to dairy farming, animal husbandry, and the like (Hussein 1979).

In a recent, unpublished review of the literature on the role of women in development, Roxann Van Dusen states that though literature is abundant in terms of published books, articles, reports, unpublished reports, conference papers and correspondence, yet little is known about the problems of developing areas and even less about the problems of women in these areas: 'The state of knowledge about Near Eastern women and their role in these societies is abysmal' (Roxann Van Dusen).

Reviewing the literature, she sets forward four hypotheses: (1) that the literature on women in development is not policy-oriented; (2) that the obstacles to reaching women are almost insurmountable; (3) that little is known about Near Eastern women; and (4) that available literature gives the impression that women in the Near East don't work and don't want to work.

Near Eastern women, she says, are not a homogeneous group and not concentrated geographically or by social class. There is a surfeit of information on traditional customs and taboos, so that for every possible project activity, it is easy to point out reasons why it might not work. At the same time, vital information, both statistical and descriptive, on existing social conditions and the distribution of those conditions within the society of each country is lacking.

We know that the recent social trends in the Near East have altered traditional social relationships and that social and economic differences within countries of the area are far greater than differences between countries, but there is very little information (longitudinal or subnational) to back up intuition. In short, we know that Middle Eastern society is changing, but we really know very little about how it is changing, or in which direction.

CONCLUSIONS AND RECOMMENDATIONS

What does the foregoing tell us about women in the Arab region?

1   From history we learn that women in pre-Islamic times and during the early centuries of Islam were active in public life and responsible members of the community. Their current seclusion is an imposed, arbitrary measure, the result of 'extra-Islamic' conditions and other historical developments.

2   From studies of a religious orientation we learn that there is an on-going controversy between the defenders and the critics of the status of women in Islam. Yet Islam is here to stay, and the 'salvation' of women lies in the return to 'primary sources' and the true understanding of the spirit of the Koran and Hadiths.

3   From sociological, anthropological and ethnographic studies we learn that custom and tradition are more responsible than Islam for the sexual segregation and the public/private dichotomy that is prevalent in Middle Eastern society.

4   From these same studies we learn that 'emancipation' of women, usually taken to mean Westernization and manifest in increased education and increased participation in the labour force, is basically an urban phenomenon prevalent among the upper classes. The lifestyle and status of the majority of women in rural, nomadic and urban lower classes remain predominantly unchanged.

5   From economic studies we learn that as yet there is no agreement on the manner in which women should be integrated into national development.

6   From political studies we learn precious little, save that women tend to be followers and not leaders and that politics remains an exclusively male domain.

7   From legal studies we learn that women are discriminated against in personal statutes laws and that efforts to overcome this have hitherto failed.

What does this tell us about the status of research on women in the Arab region?

1   Researchers dealing with the topic in the Arab world have tended to treat women as one cohesive whole, homogeneous in all needs and resources. Individual differences, social and economic differences, rural–urban differences, and regional, ethnic, religious and other differences are usually ignored.

2   In studying women in the Arab region, researchers often use imported models and imported methodology which undermine the understanding of indigenous cultures and hence of the conditions of women. These models and methodology ignore the structural and dynamic aspects of the societies in question. Their results can be best defined as measures of 'modernity' or more particularly as measures of 'similarity/dissimilarity' with Western culture.

3   There is as yet no consensus about empirical indicators of women's status. The most frequently used indicators are labour force participation and enrolment at the different educational levels. Theoretical definitions of status attempt to measure 'prestige, power and esteem'. Empirical indicators are not comprehensive, and statistical data are often biased. Theoretical definitions invariably involve value judgements.

4   The wider spectrum of multi-disciplinary and multi-regional studies being

currently undertaken can only answer questions that transcend cultural boundaries as well as rural–urban differences. They are only useful for a general understanding of the situation of women. In this respect Western scholars and Arab scholars alike seem to be attempting to place all women on a continuum with, say, the least emancipated at one end and the most emancipated at the other. Is there then a universal ideal that all women must seek to attain? Is there an agreement as to the best and most ideal status for women?

5   Partly as a result of these biases, and in spite of the large number of people who have spent and continue to spend considerable time and effort studying women in the Arab region, we in fact know very little about the situation and needs of women in the Arab region.

6   While we have much to draw upon in studying the roles of women in the region, there is also much unexplored terrain. There is an unevenness in available information, with a surfeit and repetition in some areas and a dearth of data in others.

7   The bulk of the literature centres on the eternally controversial issue of whether Islam has raised or lowered the status of women. There is little concern with how Islam in reality and in everyday life affects the lives of women. Further, there seems to be an over-emphasis by Western scholars on the 'eccentricities' of the values, norms and belief systems of Islam.

Following an ethnographic and anthropological approach, researchers have found the semi-isolated villages of the region ideal for conducting studies comparable with those conducted on the American Indians, African tribes or the Pacific Islanders. While the elucidation of such unusual practices as veiling and cross-cousin marriage may possibly be interesting, it leaves vitally important areas of research virtually unexplored. Many of the above-mentioned studies have become standard and classic references that are used for generalization about the lives of the people living in the whole region, regardless of socio-economic, historical, political or social change.

8   Though the 1970s witnessed a shift from ethnological and anthropological studies to studies on women in education, women in the labour force, problems of working women etc., such studies are already falling into the same errors and exhibit the same shortcomings as village studies. Instead of studying women in rural areas and generalizing from them to women in all strata of life, scholars study urban upper class women and generalize from them to women in the whole Arab region. Both Western scholars and Middle Eastern scholars— the former limited by an inadequate knowledge of Arabic and problems of gaining acceptance, and the latter coming from urban upper classes—find research on the situation of urban upper class women more feasible.

9   The area of women and development seems to be a promising field that is

likely to produce some comprehensive and up-to-date data on women in the Arab region. Studies in this area are conducted and financed by international institutions, which allow extensive and detailed research. Such studies are often undertaken as preliminary steps to the implementation of some development project which requires an assessment of the existing conditions, rather than justification for the preservation or the change of the status quo. One shortcoming of such studies is that they also tend to seek generalizations, as the Arab region is considered only one part of the developing world. Their aim is to produce a body of theory applicable to developing countries in Latin America, Africa and Asia as well as in the Arab region. Further, there is as yet no agreement as to how best to integrate women into national development.

10   Last, but by no means least, there has been a negligence and ignorance of the subjects under study, namely, the women themselves. Most researchers speak *for* women but none or very few ask women to speak for themselves. Instead of arguing whether Islam is beneficial or detrimental to women's roles, it might be best to study what aspects of religion women practise, and what aspects of it they think is of importance to their lives. Militant feminists in the Arab World, after a long struggle, succeeded in gaining the right to vote for women. To their disappointment very few women go to the polls or run for election. Feminists at present are struggling to change the status of women in personal statutes laws, yet to what extent are the majority of women in the region aware of or resentful of the legal discrimination against them? Even if the laws change, there are deeply embedded cultural values that prevent women from using their rights. It is the majority of the women in the region who must come to realize the sources and causes of the problems they face, if indeed they are aware that they face problems. Maybe they can shed light on other areas, other difficulties and possible solutions for them.

Recommendations

What the status of research on women in the Middle East amounts to is that we have some knowledge about some aspects of women's lives in some parts of the Middle East and for some strata. What is needed is to evolve a theoretical framework within which information can be accumulated, the unevenness of the data assessed and the gaps filled. We suggest the following:

1   Interdisciplinary, comprehensive research should be designed to provide data and information on the various countries of the region as well as on the social classes within these countries.

2   If it is absolutely necessary to treat the Arab region as one culture, then more efforts must be made to collect comparable data. The ideal situation is to design identical studies that can be conducted simultaneously in two or more

countries of the region. On the other hand, in order to study what distinguishes the countries of the region, a premium should be put on joint projects and co-operation on the individual level.

3   To avoid repetition and duplication, more efforts must be made to improve communication on the individual and institutional level. It is generally agreed that there is a wealth of unexploited data in the region. A large number of censuses and nationally representative surveys have been making their appearance. In addition there are school records, government records, and marriage and divorce civil registers that can be studied and synthesized. Social scientists must work in closer co-operation with national planning bodies. The Ministries of Health, Labour, Education, Economic Affairs and Social Affairs have been undertaking a great deal in terms of the collection of raw data. Much of this data is still unexamined and unanalysed.

4   To study women within individual countries, indices of social strata must be developed. Age, rural/urban residence and education have been suggested as differentiating factors. Ethnic, sectarian and even religious differences should be examined, as there are many minority groups in the Arab region.

5   Efforts should also be made to develop research tools and a research methodology suitable to the different countries of the region. In this respect the question of the feasibility of research conducted by women should be examined. There is evidence that the literature of the Middle East on women produced by women offers considerably different images of the society from the images offered by the literature produced by male researchers. This is not to suggest that all research on women should be done *by* women, but that the best methods of reaching women should be used.

6   What is needed is studies to assess the reality of women living in the region and to look at problems of real concern to them. 'Economic independence', 'sexual equality', 'power, prestige and esteem', 'emancipation' and 'self-realization' are not particularly relevant, as they are culturally defined and can only be viewed holistically within the context of the society under study. There should be more probing to understand how women in the region view their situation and what they feel are problem areas where change is needed, if any.

7   The Organization for the Promotion of Social Sciences in the Middle East (OPSSME), later replaced by the Association of Social Sciences in the Arab region (ASSARTI), is an example of the kind of association that should be developed in the region. By arranging annual and periodical meetings, publishing a newsletter, and preparing a Directory of Social Scientists in the Middle East, it has offered channels of communication for the social scientists of the region. It has also paved the way for the development of indigenous social science research and methodology. By welcoming non-Middle Eastern scholars

as honorary members, it has ensured that local and national social scientists are not deprived of the knowledge and experience of their Western counterparts.

NOTES

1. A recent publication, *Femmes et politique autour de la Méditerranée* (ed. Christiane Souriau) examines the political roles of women in Syria, Lebanon and Egypt. The publication, which is a collection of essays, was prepared by the Centre d'études féminines de l'Université de Provence (CEFUP).

SELECT BIBLIOGRAPHY

I. Arabic references

Periodicals

Al-Hammar, A. 'Education and Human Resources in the Arabian Gulf: A Qualitative Perspective', *Journal of Gulf and Arabian Peninsula Studies*, Vol. I, No. 3, July 1975, pp. 111-24.

Al-Tsa, M. 'The First Regional Conference for Women in the Arab Gulf', *Journal of Gulf and Arabian Peninsula Studies*, Vol. 1, No. 3, July 1975, pp. 225-30.

Badawi, G. A. 'Status of Women in Islam', *Al-Ittihad*, Vol. 8, No. 2, September 1971, pp. 7-15.

Badawi, G. A. 'Polygamy in Islam', *Al-Ittihad*, Vol. 9, No. 1, January 1972, pp. 19-23.

Barazangi, N. H. 'The Position of Women in the Contemporary Muslim World', *Al-Ittihad*, Vol. 13, April 1976, pp. 18-26.

Farrag, F. A. 'Women, Man, Society', *Al-Talia*, 11th year, No. 24, 1975.

Hamed, N. 'Muslim Women: Role and Responsibility', *Al-Ittihad*, Vol. 11, Spring 1974, pp. 13-14.

Hubaysh, H. 'The Role of Women in Arab Armies', *Al-Jundi Al-Lubnani*, Vol. 36, No. 1, 1972, pp. 20-5.

Hussein, A. 'The Woman's International Year', *Education of Masses*, Vol. 3, 1975, pp. 133-50.

Jameelah, M. 'The Feminist Movement Versus the Muslim Woman', *Al-Ittihad*, Vol. 11, Fall 1973, pp. 13-16.

Mohanna, A. I. 'Woman's Position in Islam', *Majallat Al-Azhar* (Cairo), October 1968, pp. 11-13, December 1968, pp. 9-12, January 1969, pp. 5-7, February 1969, pp. 5-13, April 1969, pp. 6-9, May 1969, pp. 9-12.

Oweiss, S. 'On the Eve of the International Woman's Year', *Afaq Arabiya* (Baghdad), No. 4, December 1975, pp. 84-9.

Rushdi, I. 'The Role of Home Economics in the Development of Women', *Education of the Masses*, Vol. 4, 1975, pp. 124-7.

Saber, M. el D. 'The Woman's Education and Training in Relation to Social Development', *Education of the Masses*, Vol. 3, 1975, pp. 30-8.

Salman, A. M. M. 'Polygamy and the Status of Women in Islamic Society', *Majallat al-Azhar* (Cairo), Vol. 38, No. 1, 1961, pp. 17-24.

Shaalan, M. 'Women and Revolution', *Al-Talia*, Eleventh Year, No. 24, 1975.

Siddiqui, Z. 'Islamic Personality and Social System. Part 3: Family Life and Personal Relations', *Al-Ittihad*, Vol. 12, No. 2, Winter 1975, pp. 14–18.
Tibi, B. 'The Problem of the Emancipation of Women in The Modern Arab Society', *Al-Taliah*, Vol. 4, No. 11, 1968, pp. 68–79.
Wagih, I. 'The Young Girl Today: Between the Home and the School', *El Idha El Libiyya*, Vol. 4, No. 18, 1964, pp. 22–3.

Books and bibliography

Abdel-Atti, M. H. *General Principles of Personal Statutes Legislation*, Cairo, Maktabit El Qahira El Haditha, 1962.
Abdel Baqi, Z. *Women Between Religion and Society*, 1978.
Abdel Hag, El S. M. *Women and the Problem of Urbanization*, Cairo, 1978.
Abdel Megeed, F. *Women: Their Struggle in the Different Fields*, Cairo, Ministry of Culture, Al Mouassasa El Missriya El Amma lil Taaleef wal Nashr, 1967.
Abu-Zeid, H. *Paving the Road Before Working Women*, Cairo, Ministry of Social Affairs, 1964.
Abu Zahra, M. *Personal Statutes*, Cairo, Dar El Fikr El Arabi, 1960.
Ahmed, T. A. *Woman: Her Struggle and Her Work*, Cairo, Dar El Gamaheer, 1964.
Al-Aqqad, A. M. *Woman in the Koran*, Cairo, Dar El Hilal, 1962.
Al-Aqqad, A. M. *Woman: That Mystery*, Beirut, Dar El Kitab Al Araby, 1970.
Al-Charif, M. B. *Al Islam Wal Ousra*, Cairo, 1972.
Ali, M. A. *The Subjugation of Women*, Cairo, El Dar El Qawmiya Lil Tibaa Wal Nashr, 1973.
Al Magdoub, A. A. *Women and Crime*, Cairo, Dar El Nahda El Arabiya, 1977.
Al Sabiq, G. *Women in the Twentieth Century*, Beirut, 1978.
Amin, K. *The Emancipation of Women*, Cairo, Dar El Ma'aref, 1970.
Badran, B. A. *Marriage and Divorce Laws in Islam: An Analytical Comparative Study*, Alexandria, Dar El Ma'aref, 1964.
Baihaim, M. G. *Woman in Arab Civilization and Arabs in the History of Women*, Beirut, Dar El Nashr Lil Gamieen, 1962.
Dirwaza, M. A. *Woman in the Koran and Prophet's Hadiths*, Beirut, Al Maktaba Al Assriya, 1968.
El Abani, M. N. El D. *Veiling of Moslem Women in the Koran and Sunna*, Cairo, Dar El Gihad, 1978.
El Attar, A. N. T. *Polygamy from Religious, Social and Legal Perspectives*, Cairo, Magma El Bohoth Al Islamiya Al Azhar, 1972.
El Berdissi, M. Z. *Personal Statutes*, Cairo, Matbait Dar El Taalif, 1965.
El-Bindary, A. W. *The Working Wife and Marital Rights*, Cairo, Al Matbaa Al Alamiya, 1969.
El Digwy, M. *Personal Statutes for Moslem Egyptians and a Comparison to Arab Legislation*, Cairo, The High Council for Islamic Affairs, 1972.
El Fakahany, H. *Personal Statutes Laws*, Cairo, Dar El Ma'had El Gadid Lil Tibaa, 1964.
El Ghandour, A. *Divorce in Islamic Sharia and Law: A Comparative Study*, Cairo, Dar el Maaref, 1967.
El Giry, A. M. M. *The Islamic Perception of Women*, 1975.
El Hashmy, A. *Woman in Pre-Islamic Poetry*, Cairo, Matbaet El Maaref, 1960.
El-Hodary, A. *Personal Statutes*, Cairo, Maktabit Kuliat El Azhar, 1968.
El-Husseini, M. M. S. *Personal Statutes*, Cairo, Matbaet Dar El Ta'alif, 1969.
El-Ibrashi, M. A. *The Status of Women in Islam*, Cairo, Dar El Shaab, 1971.

El Khamash, S. *Arab Woman and the Traditional Backward Society*, Beirut, Dar El Haqiqa, 1973.

El Khashab, H. T. and El Shibing, M. *The Mother and Her Role in Life*, Cairo, Mouassassit Al Matbouaat Al Haditha, 1960.

El Khouly, El. B. *Islamic Procedures for Marriage and Divorce*, Cairo, High Council for Islamic Affairs, 1962.

El Nawawy, A. *Moslem Woman in Moslem Society*, Cairo, Matbait El Saada, 1970.

El Sabouny, A. R. *The Extent of Freedom of a Wife to Divorce in Islamic Sharia*, Damascus, University of Damascus, 1962.

El Sadawy, N. *Woman and Sex*, Beirut, Al Mouassassa Al Arabia Lil Dirassat Wal Nashr, 1972.

El Sadawy, N. *Woman and Sex—Woman is the Origin*, Beirut, Al Mouassassa Al Arabia Lil Dirassat Wal Nashr, 1974.

El Sadawy, N. *Man and Sex*, Beirut, Al Mouassassa Al Arabia Lil Dirassat Wal Nashr, 1976.

El Sadawy, N. *The Naked Face of Arab Women*, Beirut, Al Mouassassa Al Arabia Lil Dirassat Wal Nashr, 1977.

El Shafi, K. *The Development of Women*, Dar El Kitab El Araby. n. d.

El Sibai, M. *An Explanation of Personal Statutes Laws*, Damascus, Matabi Dar El Fikr, 1963.

El Sibai, M. *Woman Between Islamic Sharia and Law*, Alleppo, Al Maktaba Al Arabia, 1966.

El Tantawi, M. *Personal Statutes in Islamic Sharia*, Cairo, Dar El Nahda El Arabia, 1971.

El Zobdy, S. *The World of Women*, Cairo, Allam Al Kottob, 1973.

Fuad, N. A. *Women in the Poetry of El Bohtori*, Cairo, Dar El Maaref, 1962.

Ghazy, M. G. *Divorce*, Cairo, Matbait Al Madani, 1970.

Gouda, A. S. *Polygamy*, Cairo, The Higher Council for Islamic Affairs, 1969.

Haffar al Kuzbari, S. *Nisa Mutafawiqat* (Femmes Supérieures), Beirut, 1961.

Hussein, A. *Islam: The Liberator of Women*, Cairo, The Higher Council for Islamic Affairs, 1968 in Studies in Islam, Series, Vol. 88, 8th year, October 1968.

Hussein, A. I. *Important Women in Islamic History*, Cairo, Maktabit El Nahda El Missriya, 1970.

Ibrahim, Z. *The Psychology of Women*, Cairo, Maktabit Misr, n. d.

Immara, M. *Islam and Women in the Opinion of Mohamed Abdou*, Cairo, Al Qahira Lil Thaqafa Al Arabiya, 1975.

Khafaqi, A. R. *Judicial Personal Statutes*, Cairo, Maktabit El Nahda El Massriya, 1960.

Madkour, M. S. *Family Laws in Islam*, First Part, 1969.

Meghaniya, M. G. *Marriage and Divorce in the Five Sects of Islam*, Beirut, Dar Al Ilm Lil Malaeen, 1960.

Mohamed, A. H. I. *Women in Islam*, Cairo, El Dar El Qawmiya Lil Tibaa Wal Nashr, 1963.

Omar, Abdullah. *Islamic Precepts and their Impact on Personal Statutes*, Cairo, Dar El Maaref, 1965.

Qutb, M. 'Islam and Women' in *Islam, The Misunderstood Religion*, Kuwait, Ministry of Awqaf and Islamic Affairs, 1967, pp. 173–243.

Qutub, I. *Present and Future Trends in Research in Relation to Family*, Cairo, 1963.

Radwan, H. *Women Between The Past and The Present*, Beirut, Matabit El Ollum, 1970.
Ramzi, H. *Bibliography of Published Arabic Books on Women 1972-1973*, National Center for Sociological and Criminological Research, 1973.
Shaaban, Z. El D. *Sharia Laws of the Personal Statutes: Year 1959*, 1960.
Shaaban, Z. El D. *The Islamic Precepts of Personal Statutes*, Cairo, Matbait Dar El Taalif, 1965.
Shaker, A. M. *Divorce System in Islam*, Cairo, Maktabit El Nagah, 1970.
Shaker, A. M. *The Crisis of Sex in Arab Novels*, Beirut, Dar Al Afaq Al Gadida, 1978.
Wafi, A. A. W. *Woman in Islam*, Cairo, Maktabit Al Gharb, 1971.

Special Reports

Anonymous. 'Arab Women and National Development', *Proceedings of Seminar Organized by UNICEF, Arab League and ASFEC*, 4 Volumes, Cairo, September 1972.
Anonymous. *Agreements, Declarations, Documents and Recommendations Related to the Status of Women*, Social Development Department, Arab League, International Woman's Year, 1975.
Anonymous. *Report on Measures and Activities Undertaken by the Arab Women's Commission During the International Woman's Year, 1975*, Social Development Department, Arab League, 1976.
Anonymous. *Statistical Abstracts for Arab Countries, 1970-1975*, Arab League, 1977.
Anonymous. 'The Status of Women in the Islamic Family', *Proceedings of the Seminar held December 2-22, 1975. The International Islamic Center for Population Studies and Research Al-Azhar University*, Cairo, 1977.

II. English, French, German and Italian references

Articles in periodicals

Abdul-Ati, H. 'Modern Problems, Classical Solutions: An Islamic Perspective on the Family', *Journal of Comparative Family Studies*, Vol. 5, No. 2, Autumn 1974, pp. 34-54.
Abu-Lughod, J. 'Egyptian Marriage Advertisements: Microcosm of a Changing Society', *Marriage and Family Living*, Vol. 23, May 1961, pp. 127-36.
Abu-Zahra, N. 'On the Modesty of Arab Muslim Villagers: A Reply', *American Anthropologist*, Vol. 72, No. 5, October 1970, pp. 1079-87.
Afza, N. 'Women in Islam', *Muslim News*, Vol. 6, No. 8, February 1978, pp. 30-3.
Al Hamadani, M. and Abu-Laban, B. 'Game Involvement and Sex Role Socialization in Arab Children', *International Journal of Comparative Sociology*, Vol. 12, 1971, pp. 182-91.
Al-Talib, N. 'Status of Women in Islam', *Islamic Literature*, Vol. 15, No. 6, 1969, pp. 57-64.
Anderson, J. N. D. 'Recent Reforms in Family Law in the Arab World', *Zeitschrift für Vergleichende Rechtwissen*, Stuttgart, Vol. 65, 1963, pp. 1-77.
Anderson, J. N. D. 'Reforms in the Law of Divorce in the Muslim World', *Studia Islamica*, Vol. 31, 1970, pp. 41-52.
Anderson, J. N. D. 'The Role of Personal Statutes in Social Development in

Islamic Countries', *Comparative Studies in Society and History*, The Hague/ Ann Arbor, Vol. 13, No. 1, 1971, pp. 16-31.

Anderson, J. N. D. 'Modern Trends in Islam: Legal Reform and Modernization in the Middle East', *International and Comparative Law Quarterly*, London, Vol. 20, No. 1, 1971, pp. 1-21.

Anonymous. 'La femme et la législation des pays arabes à la lumière des accords internationaux', *Travaux et jours*, No. 2, 1974, pp. 71-6.

Anonymous. 'Femmes. Elles s'en mêlent', *Jeune Afrique*, No. 660, 1973, p. 52.

Ansari, G. 'Status of Women in Different Societies: A Comparative Survey', *Review of Ethnology*, Vienna, Vol. 3, No. 18, 1972, pp. 137-42.

Ansari, G. 'On the Modesty of Women in Arab Muslim Villages: A Study in the Accommodation of Traditions', *American Anthropologist*, Vol. 70, No. 1, 1968, pp. 671-97.

Awad, B. A. 'The Status of Women in Islam', *Islamic Quarterly*, Vol. 8, 1974, p. 17.

Ayad, M. 'L'évolution du droit civil sous le régime socialiste arabe', *Egypte Contemporaine*, Cairo, Vol. 55, No. 317, July 1964, pp. 5-17.

Badr El Din, A. 'The Arab Working Woman as Seen in Our University Girls', *Arab Observer*, Cairo, July 12, 1965, pp. 42-3.

Boutaleb, M. 'Journée Internationale de la Femme: approfondir les bases de l'émancipation', *Révolution Africaine*, No. 576, 1975, pp. 42-4.

Boutarfa, S. D. 'Le voile', *Revue de l'Institut des Belles Lettres Arabes*, Vol. 26, 1963, pp. 297-321.

Chamberlain, J. H. 'The Family in Islam', *Numen*, Amsterdam/Leiden, Vol. 5, 1968, pp. 119-41.

Charles, N. 'Women in the Arab World', *Middle East Sketch*, Vol. 1, March 1975, pp. 28-30, April, pp. 27-8.

Charnay, J. P. 'Condition féminine et rapports sociaux dans l'Islam contemporain', *Cahiers de l'Orient Contemporain*, Paris, Vol. 27, October 1969, pp. 4-6; December 1969, pp. 4-7.

Charnay, J. P. 'La musulmane dans la ville moderne', *Politique Etrangère*, Paris, Vol. 34, No. 2, 1971, pp. 141-5.

Chehata, C. 'L'évolution moderne du droit de la famille en pays d'Islam', *Revue des Etudes Islamiques*, Paris, Vol. 37, No. 1, 1969, pp. 103-14.

Chemali, M. and Fadlallah, I. 'Témoinage d'étudiantes et d'étudiants', *Conférences du Cénacle*, Vol. 17, No. 5-6, 1963, pp. 53-64.

Dajani, N. H. 'Liberal and Traditional Attitudes of Arab University Students', *Middle East Forum*, Vol. 36, No. 1, January 1960, pp. 33-7.

Daurat, B. 'The Limit of Polygamy in Islam', *Journal of Islamic and Comparative Law*, Vol. 3, 1969, pp. 21-6.

Davies, E. 'Lifting the Veil', *Middle East Inter*, February 1975, pp. 28-9.

Debeche, D. 'La femme et la condition juridique en pays d'Islam', *Dialogues*, Paris, Vol. 7, January 1964, pp. 20-35.

Dicaprio, J. M. 'The Family in Islam', *Islamic Culture*, Vol. 12, No. 10, 1966, pp. 37-48.

Dodd, P. D. 'Concerning the Effect of Religious Affiliation on Woman's Role in Middle Eastern Society', *Journal of Comparative Family Studies*, Vol. 5, No. 2, Autumn 1974, pp. 117-29.

Dodd, P. G. 'Family Honor and the Forces of Change in Arab Society', *International Journal of Middle East Studies*, Vol. 4, No. 1, 1973, pp. 40-54.

Eekelaar, J. M. 'The Dissolution of Originally Polygamous Marriages', *International and Comparative Law Quarterly*, London, Vol. 15, 1966, pp. 1181-9.

El-Din Ali, B. 'Planning for Development of the Arab Family', *Arab Journal*, Vol. 3, No. 4, 1966, pp. 33-7.

El-Sayed, D. H. 'The Institution of Marriage in Islam', *Journal of Islamic Studies*, Vol. 1, No. 1, July 1968, pp. 45-88.

Elwan, S. 'The Status of Arab Women', *Women Speaking*, January-March 1975.

El-Zayyat, L. 'Une femme engagée', *Eléments*, No. 8-9, 1971, pp. 43-6.

Espositio, J. L. 'Women's Rights in Islam', *Journal of Islamic Studies*, Vol. 14, No. 2, Summer 1975, pp. 99-114.

Farrag, O. L. 'Arab Women and National Development', *Les Carnets de L'Enfance*, Vol. 23, 1973, pp. 87-97.

Faruqi, L. L. 'Women's Rights and the Muslim Women', *Islam and the Modern Age*, Vol. 3, 1972, pp. 76-99.

Fernea, E. and Joseph, S. 'A Brief Commentary and Report on the Round Table and Panels on Women's Roles Held at the 1975 Middle East Studies Association Meetings', *Middle East Studies Association Bulletin*, Vol. 10, No. 2, May 1976, pp. 20-3.

Feroze, M. R. 'The Reform of Family Laws in the Muslim World', *Journal of Islamic Studies*, Vol. 1, 1962, pp. 107-30.

Gazder, M. W. 'Women in Islam and Christianity', *Muslim News International*, Vol. 12, 1973, pp. 18-21.

Gibb, H. A. R. 'Women and the Law', in *Colloque sur la Sociologie Musulmane, Correspondence d'Orient Actes*, Bruxelles, September 1961, pp. 233-48.

Graziani, J. 'The Momentum of the Feminist Movement in the Arab World', *Middle East Review*, Vol. 7, No. 2, 1974, pp. 26-33.

Hashim, A. 'Muslim View of the Family and the Place of Women in Islamic Society', *The Islamic Review*, April 1962, pp. 20-2.

Hilal, J. M. 'Father's Brother's Daughter Marriage in Arab Communities: A Problem for Sociological Explanation', *Middle East Forum*, Vol. 46, No. 4, 1970, pp. 73-84.

Hilal, J. M. 'The Management of Male Dominance in Traditional Arab Culture: A Tentative Model', *Civilisation*, Bruxelles, Vol. 21, No. 2, 1971, pp. 85-95.

Hinchcliffe, D. 'Polygamy in Traditional and Contemporary Islamic Law', *Islam and the Modern Age*, New Delhi, Vol. 1, 1970, pp. 13-38.

Idris, H. R. 'Le mariage en occident musulman', *Studia Islamica*, New York/Paris, Vol. 32, 1970, pp. 157-67.

Karm, H. 'The Family as a Developing Social Group in Islam', *Asian Affairs*, Vol. 62, 1975, pp. 61-8.

Kassees, A. S. 'Cross-Cultural Comparative Familism of a Christian Arab People', *Journal of Marriage and the Family*, Vol. 34, 1972, pp. 538-44.

Keyser, J. 'The Middle Eastern Case: Is there a Marriage Rule?', *Ethnology*, Vol. 13, No. 3, 1974, pp. 293-309.

Latham, J. D. 'Ibn Abd-Al-Ra'uf on the Law of Marriage: A Matter of Interpretation', *The Islamic Quarterly*, Vol. 25, No. 1, January-March 1971, pp. 3-16.

Levey, M. and Souryal, S. S. 'Galen's on the Scribe of Women and the Surets of Men from the Unique Arabic Text', *Studies in Islam*, Vol. 9, No. 1, January 1972, pp. 1-37.

Linant, B. Y. 'La répudiation dans l'Islam d'aujourd'hui', *Revue Internationale de Droit Comparé*, Paris, Vol. 14, No. 3, 1962, pp. 521-48.

Lodi, Z. 'Study of the Status of the Married Woman in the Roman Law, English Common Law, Church Law and Islamic Law', *Islamic Review and Arab Affairs*, Vol. 58, No. 10-11, 1970, pp. 26-9.

Maleka, C. 'Islam and the Emancipation of Women', *The Islamic Review*, November–December 1965, pp. 34-69.

McCullaugh, W. H. 'Social Organization and the Life Cycle in an Arab Village', *Harvard Journal of Asiatic Study*, Vol. 27, 1967, pp. 103-67.

Melconian, M. 'Arab Women: In Hot Pursuit of a Feminist-Oriented Economy', *Arab Economist*, Vol. 7, August 1975, pp. 18-26.

Melikian, L. 'The Dethronement of the Father', *Middle East Forum*, Vol. 36, No. 1, 1960, pp. 23-6.

Mohamed, A. Z. 'Certains aspects des relations conjugales, leur particularité en droit musulman', *Egypte Contemporaine*, Cairo, Vol. 58, No. 327, 1967, pp. 79-124.

Muhyi, I. A. 'Women in the Arab Middle East', *Journal of Social Issues*, Vol. 15, No. 3, 1959, pp. 45-57.

Najarian, P. 'Adjustment in the Family and Pattern of Family Living', *Journal of Social Issues*, New York, Vol. 15, No. 3, pp. 28-44.

Najarian, P. 'Changing Patterns of Arab Family Life', *Middle East Forum*, Vol. 36, No. 1, January 1960, pp. 11-17.

Nasiri, M. 'A View of Family Planning in Islamic Legislation', *Islamic Review and Arab Affairs*, London, No. 3, 1969, pp. 11-18.

Nazat, A. 'Women in Islam', *Islamic Literature*, Vol. 13, 1969, pp. 5-24.

Nejjari, F. 'Dans quelle mesure existe-t-il une égalité entre hommes et femmes en Islam?', *La Pensée*, Rabat, Vol. 1, No. 1, 1962, pp. 35-40.

Nelson, C. 'Public and Private Politics: Women in the Middle Eastern World', *American Ethnologist*, Vol. 1, No. 3, August 1974.

Pruvost, L. 'Promotion de la femme et législation', *Revue de L'Institut des Belles Lettres Arabes*, Vol. 31, 1968, pp. 347-55.

Qadri, M. B. A. 'Polygamy', *Islamic Thought*, Vol. 14, 1970, pp. 1-17.

Rosenfeld, H. 'On the Determinants of the Status of Arab Village Women', *Man*, Vol. 60, 1960, pp. 66-70.

Rosenfeld, H. 'Change, Barriers to Change and Contradictions in the Arab Village Family', *American Anthropologist*, Vol. 70, No. 4, 1968, pp. 732-52.

Roumani, D. 'Personnalité de la femme en Islam', *Pensée Chi'ite*, Paris, No. 1-3, 1966, pp. 27-36, pp. 21-30, pp. 31-6.

Saab, E. 'Statut et conditions de la femme orientale', *Action Proche Orient*, Vol. 22, May 1964, pp. 46-8.

Saleh, S. 'Women in Islam: Their Status in Religious and Traditional Culture', *International Journal of Sociology of the Family*, Vol. 2, March 1972, pp. 35-42.

Saleh, S. 'Women in Islam: Their Role in Religious and Traditional Culture', *International Journal of Sociology of the Family*, Vol. 2, September 1972, pp. 193-201.

Samaan, N. J. 'La femme arabe au seuil de la liberté', *Croissance des Jeunes Nations*, Vol. 23, June–July 1963, pp. 29-31.

Sayegh, R. 'The Changing Life of Arab Women', *Middle East*, Vol. 8, No. 6, 1968, pp. 19-23.

Schneider, J. 'Of Vigilance and Virgins: Honor, Shame and Access to Resources in Mediterranean Societies', *Ethnology*, Vol. 10, No. 1, 1971, pp. 1-24.

Serjeant, R. B. 'Recent Marriage Legislation from Al-Mukalla with Notes on

Marriage Customs', *Bulletin of the School of Oriental and African Studies*, University of London, Vol. 25, 1962, pp. 472-98.

Shaltout, M. 'The Position of Women in Islam', *Man*, Vol. 32, No. 7, 1960.

Sultan, F. 'Status of Women in Iqbal's Thought', *Islamic Literature*, Vol. 17, No. 1, 1971, pp. 49-54.

Tillion, G. 'La condition des femmes entre le passé et l'avenir', *Carnets de L'Enfance*, Paris, No. 8, June 1968, pp. 72-9.

Tomeh, A. 'The Impact of Reference Groups on the Educational and Occupational Aspirations of Women College Students', *Journal of Marriage and the Family*, Vol. 30, No. 1, 1968, pp. 102-10.

Tomeh, A. 'Birth Order and Kinship Affiliation', *Journal of Marriage and the Family*, Vol. 31, February 1969, pp. 19-26.

Tomeh, A. 'Cross Cultural Differences in the Structure of Moral Values: A Factorial Analysis', *International Journal of Comparative Sociology*, Vol. 11, No. 1, March 1970, pp. 18-33.

Tomeh, A. 'Birth Order and Friendship Associations', *Journal of Marriage and the Family*, Vol. 32, August 1970, pp. 360-9.

Tomeh, A. 'Patterns of Moral Behavior in Two Social Structures', *Sociology and Social Research*, Vol. 55, No. 2, January 1971, pp. 149-60.

Tomeh, A. 'Birth Order and Familial Influences in the Middle East', *Journal of Comparative Family Studies*, Vol. 2, Spring 1971, pp. 88-106.

Tomeh, A. 'Birth Order Club Membership and Mass Media Exposure', *Journal of Marriage and the Family*, February 1976, pp. 151-64.

Ungor, B. 'Women in the Middle East and North Africa and Universal Suffrage', *Annals of the American Academy of Political and Social Science*, No. 375, 1968, pp. 72-81.

Youssef, N. H. 'Social Structure and the Female Labor Force: The Case of Women Workers in Muslim Middle Eastern Countries', *Demography*, Vol. 8, November 1971, pp. 427-40.

Youssef, N. H. 'Differential Labor Force Participation of Women in Latin American and Middle Eastern Countries: The Influence of Family Characteristics', *Social Forces*, Vol. 51, December 1972, pp. 135-53.

Youssef, N. H. 'Cultural Ideals, Feminine Behavior and Kinship Control', *Comparative Studies in Society and History*, Vol. 15, No. 3, 1973, pp. 326-47.

Zeghari, M. 'Evolution des structures familiales dans les pays en voie de transformation sociale, économique, politique et institutionnelle', *Familles dans le Monde*, Paris, Vol. 15, September–December 1962, pp. 132-49.

Zikria, N. A. 'The Status of Women in Islam', *Journal of the Islamic Medical Association*, Vol. 7, No. 1, February 1976, pp. 19-21.

Books and bibliographies

Abdul-Rauf, M. *Marriage in Islam*, New York, Exposition Press, 1972.

Allman, J., Ben Ashour, C. and Stone, T. *A Bibliography of Social Science Research on the Family in the Arab States*, Paris, Unesco, Population Coordination and Research Unit, Department of Social Sciences, September 1974.

Al-Qazzaz, A. *Women in the Arab World: An Annotated Bibliography No. 2*, California State University, Sacramento, Association of Arab American University Graduates, Inc., Detroit, Michigan, August 1975.

Al-Qazzaz, A. *Women in the Middle East and North Africa: An Annotated*

Bibliography, Middle East Monographs No. 2, Center for Middle Eastern Studies, University of Texas at Austin, 1977.

Al-Sabani, A. *The Family in Islamic Society*, Beirut, Beirut Press, 1968.

Ammar, H. 'The Aims and Methods of Socialization in Silwa', in *From Child to Adult: Studies in the Anthropology of Education* (J. Middleton, ed.), New York, Natural History Press, pp. 226–49.

Anderson, J. N. D. 'The Eclipse of the Patriarchal Family in Contemporary Islamic Law', in *Family Law in Asia and Africa* (J. N. D. Anderson, ed.), London, Allen and Unwin, 1968, pp. 221-34.

Anderson, J. N. D. 'The Islamic Law of Marriage and Divorce', in *Readings in Arab Middle Eastern Societies and Cultures* (A. M. Lutfiyya and C. W. Churchill, eds.), The Hague, Mouton/New York, Humanities Press, 1970, pp. 492-504.

Antoun, R. *Arab Village*, Social Science Series, No. 29, Bloomington, Indiana University Press, 1972.

Beck, D. F. 'The Changing Moslem Family in the Middle East', in *Readings in Arab Middle Eastern Societies and Cultures* (A. M. Lutfiyya and C. W. Churchill, eds.), The Hague, Mouton/New York, Humanities Press, 1970, pp. 567-77.

Beck, L. G. and Keddie, N. (eds.), *Muslim Women*, Cambridge, Massachusetts, Harvard University Press, 1976.

Berger, M. 'Men, Women and Families', in *The Arab World Today*, New York, Doubleday, 1964, pp. 117-53.

Berque, J. 'Women's Intercession', in *The Arabs: Their History and Future*, New York, Praeger, 1964, pp. 172-89.

Bousquet, G. H. *L'Ethique sexuelle de l'Islam*, Paris, Maison neuve et Larose, 1966.

Bullough, V. L. 'Sex is Not Enough: Women in Islam', in *The Subordinate Sex: A History of Attitudes towards Women*, Urbana, Illinois, University of Illinois Press, 1973, pp. 134-52.

Charnay, J. P. 'Social Relationships and the Conditions of Women', in *Islamic Culture and Socio-economic Change*, Leiden, The Netherlands, E. T. Brill, 1971.

Coulson, N. J. *Succession in the Muslim Family*, Cambridge, England, Cambridge University Press, 1971.

Culver, E. T. 'Women in Islam', in *Women in the World of Religion*, New York, Doubleday, 1967, pp. 270-81.

Daghestani, K. 'The Evolution of the Moslem Family in the Middle Eastern Countries', in *Readings in Arab Middle Eastern Societies and Cultures* (A. M. Lutfiyya and C. W. Churchill, eds.), The Hague, Mouton, 1970.

Drewes, C. W. J. 'The Beginning of the Emancipation of Women in the Arab World', in *Nederlands Arabishe Kring*, 1955-1965, Leiden, Brill, 1966, pp. 47-66.

El-Daghestani, K. 'The Evolution of the Moslem Family in the Middle Eastern Countries', in *Readings in the Arab Middle Eastern Societies and Cultures* (A. M. Lutfiyya and C. W. Churchill, eds.), The Hague, Mouton/New York, Humanities Press, 1970, pp. 554-66.

Fernea, E. and Bezirgan, B. *Middle Eastern Muslim Women Speak*, Austin and London, University of Texas Press, 1977.

Fernea, R. and Fernea, E. W. 'Variation in Religious Observance among Islamic Women', in *Scholars, Saints and Sufis* (N. B. Keddie, ed.), Berkeley, University of California Press, 1972, pp. 385-401.

Fuller, A. H. 'The World of Kin', in *Readings in Arab Middle Eastern Societies and Cultures* (A. M. Lutfiyya and C. W. Churchill, eds.), The Hague, Mouton, 1970, pp. 526-34.
Gaudefray, D. M. 'The Family', in *Muslim Institutions*, New York, Barnes and Noble, 1968, pp. 127-38.
Giele, J. Z. and Smock, A. C. (eds.), 'Women and Society', in *International and Comparative Perspective*, New York, Wiley, Interscience, forthcoming.
Goode, W. J. 'Changing Family Patterns in Arabic Islam', in *World Revolution and Family Patterns*, New York, The Free Press, 1963, pp. 87-163.
Gulick, J. *An Annotated Bibliography of Sources Concerned with Women in the Modern Muslim Middle East*, Princeton Near East Paper No. 17, Princeton, New Jersey, Princeton University Press, 1974.
Hamady, S. *Temperament and Character of the Arabs*, New York, Twayne Publishing Company, 1960.
Hammond, D. and Jablow, A. *Women: Their Economic Role in Traditional Societies*, A Cummings Module in Anthropology, No. 35, Merilo Park, California, Cummings Publishing Company, 1973.
Ibrahim, A. M. 'Women in the Arab Middle East', in *The Modern Middle East* (R. Nolte, ed.), New York, Author Press, 1963.
Ibrahim, S. E. and Hopkins, N. 'Family and Sex Roles in Transition', in *Arab Society in Transition*, Cairo, The American University in Cairo Press, 1977, pp. 81-173.
King, J. S. *Women and Work: Sex Differences and Society*, Great Britain Department of Employment, Manpower Paper No. 10, London, Her Majesty's Stationary Office, 1974.
Laffin, J. 'As Arab Men See Women', in *The Arab Mind Considered: A Need for Understanding*, New York, Taglinger, 1975, pp. 98-105.
Lerner, D. *The Passing of Traditional Society: Modernizing the Middle East*, New York, Free Press, 1958.
Levy, R. 'The Status of Women in Islam', in *The Social Structure of Islam*, New York, Cambridge University Press, 1965, pp. 91-134.
Lichtenstadter, I. *Islam and the Modern Age*, New York, Bookman Associates, 1958.
Maccoby, E. E. and Nagy, J. C. *The Psychology of Sex Differences*, Stanford, California, Stanford University Press, 1974.
Masry, Y. (Al). *Le Drame sexuel de la femme dans l'orient arabe*, Paris, Laffont, 1962.
Mattiasson, C. J. (ed.), *Many Sisters: Women in Cross-Cultural Perspectives*, New York, The Free Press, 1974.
McKenna, J. F. *Great Women of the Ancient Middle East*, Cleveland, Greater Cleveland Association of Arab Americans, 1975.
Mednick, M. S., Tangri, S. S. and Hoffman, L. W. (eds.), *Women and Achievement: Social and Motivational Analyses*, New York, John Wiley, 1975.
Nelson, C. 'Women and Power in Nomadic Societies of the Middle East', in *The Desert and the Sown: Nomads in the Greater Society* (C. Nelson, ed.), Berkeley, University of California Institute of International Studies, 1973, pp. 43-59.
Patai, R. 'The Family', in *Golden River to Golden Road: Society, Culture and Change in the Middle East*, Philadelphia, University of Pennsylvania, 1969, pp. 84-114.
Patai, R. *The Arab Mind*, New York, Charles Scribner's Sons, 1973.

172   *Soha Abdel Kader*

Peristiany, J. G. *Honour and Shame*, Chicago, Chicago University Press, 1966.
Peristiany, J. G. *Mediterranean Family Structures*, 1976.
Protho, E. T. and Lutfy, N. D. 'Modesty and the Role of Women', in *Changing Family Patterns in the Arab East*, Beirut, American University of Beirut Press, 1974, pp. 117-70.
Rauf, M. A. *Marriage in Islam*, New York, Exposition Press, 1972.
Rosenfeld, H. 'The Contradictions between Property, Kinship and Power as Reflected in the Marriage System of an Arab Village', in *Contributions to Mediterranean Sociology* (J. Peristiany, ed.), The Hague, Mouton, 1968.
Seibert, I. *Women in the Ancient Near East*, New York, Abner Schram, 1974.
Somekh, S. *The Changing Rhythm: A Study of Najib Mahfuz's Novels*, Leiden, Brill, 1973.
Tomiche, N. 'La femme en Islam', in *Histoire mondiale de la femme* (P. Grimal, ed.), Paris, Nouvelle Librairie de France, 1967, 4 vols.
Tomiche, N. 'The Situation of Egyptian Women in the First Half of the 19th Century', in *Beginnings of Modernization in the Middle East* (W. Polk *et al.*, eds.), Chicago, The University of Chicago Press, 1968, pp. 171-84.
Van Nieuwenhuijize, C. A. *Social Stratification and the Middle East*, Leiden, Brill, 1965.
'Women in the Middle East—The Continuing Struggle', *Anthology of Articles by the Middle Eastern Study Collective*, Women's Center School, P.O.B. 134, West Newton, Massachusetts 0.2156.
Youssef, N. H. *Women and Work in Developing Countries*, Berkeley, University of California, Population Monograph Series, No. 15, 1974.
Youssef, N. H. 'Women in Development: Urban Life and Labour', in *Women and World Development* (I. Tinker, ed.), New York, Overseas Development Council, 1976, pp. 70-7.
Yusuf, H. S. 'In Defense of the Veil', in *The Contemporary Middle East* (B. Rivlin and J. S. Szyliowicz, eds.), New York, Random House, 1965, pp. 335-59.
Yehia, M. A. and Rihani, M. 'A Bibliography of Recent Research on Family and Women in the Arab States', *Paper Presented to the Institute for Women's Studies in the Arab World*, Beirut University College, 1976.

Conference and unpublished papers

Ahmed, W. 'Constraints and Requirements to Increase Women's Participation In Integrated Rural Development', *Paper Presented at the Seminar on the Role of Women in Integrated Rural Development with Emphasis on Population Problems, Sponsored by United Nations Food and Agriculture Organization*, Cairo, 1974.
Al-Qazzaz, A. 'Current Status of Research on Women in the Arab World', unpublished paper presented at the 8th Annual Convention of the Association of Arab American University Graduates, Chicago, 17 October 1975.
Arnaldez, R. 'Le Coran et l'émancipation de la femme', in *La Femme à la recherche d'elle-même*, Seminaire de la pensée marxiste, Paris/Lyon, La Palatine, 1965.
Auerbach, E. S. 'Are Women in a Male Dominated Society Oppressed?', *A Paper Presented at the American Anthropological Association, 72nd Annual Meeting*, New Orleans, 28 November-2 December 1973.
Badran, H. 'Women, Population and Integrated Rural Development', A Paper Presented at the Seminar on the Role of Women in Integrated Rural Development

with Emphasis on Population Problems, Sponsored by United Nations Food and Agriculture Organization, Cairo, 26 October–3 November 1974.

Badran, H. 'Deliberations of the International Women's Year Conference and Its Relationship to the Arab Region', *A Paper Presented at a Seminar on the Status of Women in the Islamic Family, International Islamic Center for Population Studies and Research*, Cairo, 1975.

Bateson, M. C. and Thompson, C. A. 'Women's Part in Interpersonal Quarreling and Third Person Mediation', *Paper Prepared for the 1974 Middle East Studies Associations Annual Meeting*, Boston, 1974.

Beck, L. G. 'Honor, Shame and Self-Identity among Pastoral Nomadic Qashqa'i', *Paper Prepared for the 1973 Middle East Studies Associations Annual Meeting*, Milwaukee, 1973.

Beck, L. G. 'Political Roles of Women in Pastoral Societies', *Paper Prepared for the 1975 Middle East Studies Association Annual Meeting*, Louisville, 1975.

Boserup, E. 'Employment of Women in Developing Countries', *Proceedings of the International Population Conference*, Vol. 1, Liège, International Union for Scientific Study of Population, 1973.

Boserup, E. Women and Their Role in Peasant Societies, London, University of London, Center of International and Area Studies, 1974 (mimeo).

Boulding, E. 'Nomadism, Mobility and the Status of Women', paper prepared for the Eighth Congress of Sociology, Toronto, 1974 (mimeo).

Bujra, A. 'The Relationship Between the Sexes Amongst the Bedouin in a Town', *A Paper Presented at the Mediterranean Social Science Council Conference*, Athens, 1966.

Charnay, J. P., 'Stratification économique et dimensions culturelles dans les pays arabes', *A Paper Presented at the International Political Science Association 9th World Congress*, Montreal, 1973.

Davis, S. S. 'Analytical Problems in the Anthropological Study of Women', *Paper Prepared for the 1975 Middle East Studies Association Annual Meeting*, Louisville, 1975.

Dixon, R. B. 'The Roles of Rural Women: Female Seclusion, Economic Production and Reproductive Choice', *A Paper Presented at the Conference on Population Policy from a Socio-Economic Perspective*, sponsored by Resources for the Future, Washington, D.C., 1975.

Dodd, P. C. 'Concerning the Effect of Religious Affiliation on Woman's Role in Middle Eastern Arab Society', *A Paper Presented at the Eighth World Congress of Sociology, Session on Sex-Roles and Society*, Toronto, 1974.

El–Hamamsy, L. S. 'Population Planning and Belief Systems in Peasant Society', *A Paper Presented at the Conference on Technological Change and Population Growth, Social Research Center, California Institute of Technology*, 6–8 May 1970.

El-Khayat, G. 'A Study on the Evolutionary, Medical, and Psychological Aspects of Female Employment in a Third World Country', *Delivered at the Mexico Women in Development Seminar*, 1975.

El-Sanabary, N. 'The Education of Women in the Arab States: Achievements and Problems, 1950–1970', unpublished paper presented at the Symposium on Near Eastern Women Through the Ages, University of California at Berkeley, March 1975.

El-Shamy, H. M. 'The Dichotomous Structure of Emotions in the Arab Family', unpublished paper presented to the 11th Annual Meeting of the Middle East Studies Association, New York City, November 1977.

Fahmy, N. and Ramzi, N. 'Woman's Role in Social Development', *A Paper Presented at the Afro-Arab Parliamentary Congress*, Cairo, May 1974.

Farag-Badawi, N. 'Hakim and Shaw: On Woman', unpublished paper presented at the 11th Annual Meeting of the Middle East Studies Association, New York City, November 1977.

Fernea, E. W. 'Women in the Middle East', unpublished paper delivered at the Middle East Symposium, California State University, Sacramento, April 1973.

Fernea, E. W. 'The Dynamics of Change in the Status of Middle Eastern Women', *A Paper Presented at the Symposium of Near Eastern Women Through the Ages*, Berkeley, 1975.

Fernea, E. W. and Bezirgan, B. 'Women's World, Female Festivals', *Paper Prepared for the 1975 Middle East Studies Association Annual Meeting*, Louisville, 1975.

Fluehr-Lobban, C. 'Women and National Liberation in the Arab World', unpublished paper presented at the 8th Annual Convention of the Association of Arab American University Graduates, Chicago, October 1975.

Haddad, Y. 'The Image of Women in Contemporary Muslim Literature', *A Paper Presented at a Workshop on the Status and Role of Women in Contemporary Muslim Societies, Center for the Study of World Religions, Harvard University*, 19 April 1975.

Haddad, W. and Aboutalib, S. 'Le Statut légal de la femme musulmane dans plusieurs pays du Moyen-Orient', United Nations Economic and Social Office, Beirut, 1972 (mimeo).

Keddie, N. 'Problems in the Research on Women in the Middle East: Confessions of a Co-Editor', unpublished paper presented at the 9th Annual Meeting of the Middle East Studies Association, Louisville, November 1975.

Nelson, C. 'Seclusion and Emancipation: Changing Roles of Man and Woman in the Middle East', unpublished paper, American University of Cairo, Cairo, 1972.

Nelson, C. 'Between Social Worlds: The Case of Nomadic Women', *Working Paper Prepared for Nomad Symposium: The Desert and the Sown: A New Conceptualization*, Cairo, 1972.

Othman, I. 'Family Adjustment to Social Change', *Unesco Workshop on Family Adjustment to Social Change in the Middle East and North Africa*, Beirut, 1-5 July 1974.

Peters, E. 'Consequences of the Segregation of the Sexes among the Arabs', unpublished paper delivered at the Mediterranean Social Science Council Conference, Athens, 1966.

Saber, I. 'Research Studies of the Status of a Ramallah Arab Woman', unpublished paper submitted for a Special Seminar in Field Studies, Wayne State University, Winter 1970.

Shafie, E. and Bassyouni, A. 'The Role of Women in Economic and Political Development', in *Proceedings of the Afro-Arab Inter-Parliamentary Women's Conference*, Cairo, May 1974.

Simmons, E. B. 'Cultural Assumptions and Women's Roles in Development', Liberian Institute of Public Administration, Monrovia; n.d. (mimeo).

Totten, W. M. 'The Extended Family in Islam: Its Background and Some Modern Developments', unpublished paper, American University of Beirut, 1972.

Van Dusen, R. A. 'Integrating Women into National Economics: Programming Considerations with Special Reference to the Near East', unpublished paper submitted to the Agency for International Development, Washington, July 1977.

Youssef, N. H. 'Women's Status and Fertility in Muslim Countries of the Middle East and Asia', unpublished paper presented at the Annual Meeting of the American Psychological Association, New Orleans, 1974(a).

Youssef, N. H. 'Women and Agricultural Production in Muslim Societies', unpublished paper presented at the Seminar, 'Prospects for Growth in Rural Societies: With or without Active Participation of Women', Princeton, New Jersey, 1974(b).

Youssef, N. H. 'Fertility and Labor Force Patterns among Women in Islamic Society', *A Paper Presented at the Symposium of Near Eastern Women Through the Ages*, Berkeley, 1975.

Zerbe, E. A. 'The Inadequate Portrayal of the Social Problems of Women by Maghreb and Mashrek Novelists', *Anthropology and Literature Conference*, Urbana, Illinois, 1974.

Zerbe, E. A. 'New Feminist Consciousness among Arab Women Novelists', *Regional Women's Conference*, Bloomington, Indiana, 1975.

Zerbe, E. A. 'Role of Women in Arabic Literature', *Presented for the Arab American University Graduates Conference in Chicago*, October 1975.